Divers Voyages Touching the Discovery of America and the Islands Adjacent

Collected and Published by Richard Hakluyt

EDITED BY JOHN WINTER JONES

CAMBRIDGE UNIVERSITY PRESS

Cambridge, New York, Melbourne, Madrid, Cape Town, Singapore,
São Paolo, Delhi, Dubai, Tokyo

Published in the United States of America by Cambridge University Press, New York

www.cambridge.org
Information on this title: www.cambridge.org/9781108008044

© in this compilation Cambridge University Press 2010

This edition first published 1850
This digitally printed version 2010

ISBN 978-1-108-00804-4 Paperback

This book reproduces the text of the original edition. The content and language reflect the beliefs, practices and terminology of their time, and have not been updated.

Cambridge University Press wishes to make clear that the book, unless originally published by Cambridge, is not being republished by, in association or collaboration with, or with the endorsement or approval of, the original publisher or its successors in title.

CAMBRIDGE LIBRARY COLLECTION
Books of enduring scholarly value

Travel and Exploration

The history of travel writing dates back to the Bible, Caesar, the Vikings and the Crusaders, and its many themes include war, trade, science and recreation. Explorers from Columbus to Cook charted lands not previously visited by Western travellers, and were followed by merchants, missionaries, and colonists, who wrote accounts of their experiences. The development of steam power in the nineteenth century provided opportunities for increasing numbers of 'ordinary' people to travel further, more economically, and more safely, and resulted in great enthusiasm for travel writing among the reading public. Works included in this series range from first-hand descriptions of previously unrecorded places, to literary accounts of the strange habits of foreigners, to examples of the burgeoning numbers of guidebooks produced to satisfy the needs of a new kind of traveller - the tourist.

Divers Voyages Touching the Discovery of America and the Islands Adjacent

The publications of the Hakluyt Society (founded in 1846) made available edited (and sometimes translated) early accounts of exploration. The first series, which ran from 1847 to 1899, consists of 100 books containing published or previously unpublished works by authors from Christopher Columbus to Sir Francis Drake, and covering voyages to the New World, to China and Japan, to Russia and to Africa and India. Volume 7 (1849) is an edition of accounts of exploration in the New World and in the Caribbean islands originally published by Richard Hakluyt in 1582. Hakluyt himself was a priest who acted as chaplain to Sir Robert Cecil, the Secretary of State to Elizabeth I and James I. He was a self-taught geographer and an enthusiastic supporter of colonial ventures in the New World, believing that England should not be left behind France and Spain in the rush to claim new territories.

Cambridge University Press has long been a pioneer in the reissuing of out-of-print titles from its own backlist, producing digital reprints of books that are still sought after by scholars and students but could not be reprinted economically using traditional technology. The Cambridge Library Collection extends this activity to a wider range of books which are still of importance to researchers and professionals, either for the source material they contain, or as landmarks in the history of their academic discipline.

Drawing from the world-renowned collections in the Cambridge University Library, and guided by the advice of experts in each subject area, Cambridge University Press is using state-of-the-art scanning machines in its own Printing House to capture the content of each book selected for inclusion. The files are processed to give a consistently clear, crisp image, and the books finished to the high quality standard for which the Press is recognised around the world. The latest print-on-demand technology ensures that the books will remain available indefinitely, and that orders for single or multiple copies can quickly be supplied.

The Cambridge Library Collection will bring back to life books of enduring scholarly value (including out-of-copyright works originally issued by other publishers) across a wide range of disciplines in the humanities and social sciences and in science and technology.

WORKS ISSUED BY

The Hakluyt Society.

DIVERS VOYAGES TOUCHING THE
DISCOVERY OF
AMERICA,
ETC.

M.DCCC.L.

DIVERS VOYAGES

TOUCHING THE DISCOVERY

OF

AMERICA

AND THE ISLANDS ADJACENT.

COLLECTED AND PUBLISHED
BY RICHARD HAKLUYT.

PREBENDARY OF BRISTOL,
IN THE YEAR 1582.

EDITED,
With Notes and an Introduction,
BY
JOHN WINTER JONES,
OF THE BRITISH MUSEUM.

LONDON:
PRINTED FOR THE HAKLUYT SOCIETY.

M.DCCC.L.

THE HAKLUYT SOCIETY.

Council.

SIR RODERICK IMPEY MURCHISON, G.C.St.S., F.R.S., Corr. Mem. Inst. Fr., Hon. Mem. Imp. Acad. Sc. St. Petersburg, &c., &c., PRESIDENT.

VICE-ADMIRAL SIR CHARLES MALCOLM, KNT. } VICE-PRESIDENTS.
THE EARL OF ELLESMERE.

REAR-ADMIRAL SIR FRANCIS BEAUFORT, K.C.B.
CHARLES T. BEKE, ESQ., Phil. D., F.S.A.
CAPTAIN C. R. DRINKWATER BETHUNE, R.N., C.B.
THE LORD ALFRED S. CHURCHILL.
WILLIAM DESBOROUGH COOLEY, ESQ.
BOLTON CORNEY, ESQ., M.R.S.L.
THE RIGHT REV. LORD BISHOP OF ST. DAVID'S.
SIR HENRY ELLIS, K.H., F.R.S.
JOHN FORSTER, ESQ.
R. W. GREY, ESQ., M.P.
THOMAS HODGKIN, ESQ., M.D.
JOHN HOLMES, ESQ.
JOHN WINTER JONES, ESQ.
P. LEVESQUE, ESQ.
THE VERY REV. THE DEAN OF ST. PAUL'S.
THOMAS RUNDALL, ESQ.
THE RIGHT HON. THE LORD ADVOCATE OF SCOTLAND.
THE HON. HENRY E. J. STANLEY.

R. H. MAJOR, ESQ., F.R.G.S., HONORARY SECRETARY.

INTRODUCTION.

THE "Divers Voyages touching the Discoverie of America", was the first publication of the active-minded and public-spirited clergyman from whose name the Hakluyt Society has derived its designation. To many members the question will naturally suggest itself, why, having thought the *name* worthy adoption, the *work* should have been so long postponed. The following is the explanation of this circumstance. When the Hakluyt Society was instituted, the first work proposed for publication was the "Divers Voyages"; but it having been ascertained that the late intelligent American bookseller, Mr. Rich, had contemplated publishing a fac-simile reprint, and that he had had cut a fount of black-letter type for that purpose, application was made to him, in order to ascertain whether he still proposed carrying that design into effect. Mr. Rich, in reply, stated that he was willing to leave the work in the hands of the Society, provided the Council would print it as he himself had proposed to do, and would purchase the type he had had cast for it. As it was not deemed advisable to adopt this proposition, and as a separate publication by the Society would have interfered prejudicially with Mr. Rich's prior right, it was considered proper to forego what would certainly have been the most appropriate leader of their series, and to adopt some other work. When, however, after the lapse of three years, the subject was again mentioned to Mr. Rich, he stated that he had abandoned his intention of publishing the book; and the Society, being now unfettered, lost no time in placing it in course of preparation.

Before making any remarks upon the work itself, it will be proper to say something of the compiler; than whom few, perhaps, have better deserved an honourable place in the memory of their countrymen, and none have commanded more general respect with those who have taken the trouble to make themselves acquainted with his far-seeing and patriotic views, and the untiring perseverance with which he sought to make his views effective. It is hardly necessary to refer here to the solitary exception to this feeling of admiration for the labours of an honest, upright man, which is presented in the person of Mr. Biddle, in his *Memoirs of Sebastian Cabot*. Mr. Tytler, in his *Historical View of the Progress of Discovery on the more Northern Coasts of America*, has sufficiently exposed the animus of Mr. Biddle's strictures.

The ancestors of Hakluyt were established at a very early period in the county of Hereford. The family seat was at Yatton; and they must have ranked amongst the principal landowners of the county. In the list of sheriffs, given by Duncumb in his *History of Herefordshire*, we find that Walter de Hackluit filled that office in the first, second, third, and fourth years of Edward II; Hugh Hackluit, in the tenth and eleventh years of the same reign; Edward Hackluit, in the thirty-first, thirty-second, and thirty-third years of Edward III; Leonard Hackluit, knt., in the second year of Hen. IV; and a Ralph Hackluit in the seventeenth year of Edw. IV, and again in the twenty-third of Hen. VII, and tenth of Hen. VIII. The list of members for the county, contained in the same work, presents us with Walter de Hackluite, in the sixth year of Ed. II; Edmund Hakelute, in the first year of Ed. III; Edmund Fitz-Edmund Hackluit, in the twenty-eighth of Ed. III; Edward Hackluit, in the thirty-first of Ed. III; and Leonard Hakkluyt, in the ninth, eleventh, and seventeenth years of Rich. II. We also learn, from the General Introduction to the same work, that Walter Hakelut was knighted, with several others, in the thirty-fourth year of Ed. I; and in a return of the principal inhabitants of Herefordshire, made to royal commissioners in the twelfth year of Henry VI, we find, in the list of knights, Walter Hackluit, and in that of the gentlemen, William Hackluit, Hugh Hackluit, and Egidius Hackluit. One Thomas Hakeluyt was chancellor of the diocese of Hereford in the year 1349. It appears also, from the two following documents, that Thomas Hakeluytt, probably the head of the family, was in the wardship of Henry VIII, and Edward VI. Vizt.:

1. " An indenture, made the 8th day of August, anno 28 Hen. VIII, between William Beuyle, gentleman, Roger Acton, gentillman, twoo of the cousins and heyres of John

Suggewas, deceased, Philip Baskerwile, Esq., and Elizabeth, his wife, late wife of James May, one other of the cousins and heyres of the said John Suggewas, and Richard Watkyn, gentilman, the king's com̄ittee of the body and lands of Thomas Hakeluytt, sonne and heyre of John Hakeluytt, Esq., deceased, one other of the cousins and heyres of the said John Suggewas, on the one partie, and John White, on the other partye, etc., for a messuage in Grafton in com. Heref. Datum A°. 21, H. 8."—*Visitation of Huntingdonshire*, p. 45, published by the Camden Society.

2. " Extract from a Court Roll held at Kyngstaple, in the county of Hereford, 26 April, 1 Ed. VI, containing a memorandum that Thomas Havarde, Esq., the king's feodary, had granted to Thomas Mynde all the purpartie of Thomas Hakeluyt, gent., the king's warde, and one of the lords of Kingstaple, of the copice of Cary Woodde and lands in Castelldichefelde, Vaughans Welle, and Moche Cavene, to hold during the minority of the same Hakeluyt, paying yearly the sum of three shillings and eight pence." [Additional Charters and Rolls, No. 1351, Brit. Mus.]

The subject of this memoir was born about the year 1553, in or near London as it has been conjectured, but upon what authority does not appear, unless it be the circumstance of his having been educated at Westminster school, in which he informs us he was one of the queen's scholars. He was elected to Christ Church College, Oxford, in the year 1570, being then seventeen years of age. He took his degree of Bachelor of Arts on the 19th of February 1574, and that of Master of Arts on the 27th of June 1577. The love of cosmography, and maritime discovery, for which he became so justly distinguished at a later period of his life, had been implanted in him while he was yet a scholar at Westminster. The following is the graphic account of his introduction to this fascinating pursuit, given by himself in the dedication to Sir Francis Walsingham, prefixed to the first edition of his *General Collection of Voyages and Travels*.

" I do remember that being a youth, and one of her Majestie's scholars at Westminster, that fruitful nurserie, it was my happe to visit the chamber of M. Richard Hakluyt, my cosin, a gentleman of the Middle Temple,[1] well knowen unto you, at a time when I found lying open upon his boord certeine bookes of cosmographie with an universall mappe: he seeing me somewhat curious in the view thereof, began to instruct my ignorance by shewing me the division of the earth into three parts after the olde account, and then according to the latter and better distribution into more. He pointed with his wand to all the known seas, gulfs, bayes, straights, capes, rivers, empires, kingdoms, dukedoms, and territories of ech part; with declaration also of their special commodities and particular wants which by the benefit of traffike and intercourse of merchants are plentifully supplied. From the mappe he brought me to the Bible, and turning to the 107th Psalme, directed mee to the 23rd and 24th verses, where I read that they which go downe to the sea in ships and occupy by the great waters, they see the works of the Lord and his woonders in the deepe, etc., which words of the Prophet, together with my cousins discourse (things of high and rare delight to my yong nature) tooke in me so deepe an impression, that I constantly

---

[1] Wood, in his *Athenæ Oxonienses*, vol. ii, p. 186, edit. Bliss, falls into a confusion between the cousins, and states that our author studied law in the Temple. The mistake is natural, inasmuch as Richard Hakluyt of Yatton was himself distinguished for his geographical knowledge, and frequently applied to for advice by merchants and others.

resolved if ever I were preferred to the university, where better time and more convenient place might be ministred for these studies, would, by God's assistance, prosecute that knowledge and kinde of literature, the doores whereof (after a sort) were so happily opened before me."

He did not forget this resolution when the opportunity for carrying it into effect arrived. He proceeds, in the same dedication :—" According to which my resolution, when not long after I was removed to Christ Church in Oxford, my exercises of duety first performed, I fell to my intended course, and by degrees read over whatsoever printed or written discoveries and voyages I found extant either in the Greeke, Latine, Italian, Spanish, Portugall, French or English languages; and in my publike lectures was the first that produced and shewed both the olde and imperfectly composed and the new lately reformed mappes, globes, spheares and other instruments of this art for demonstration in the common schooles, to the singular pleasure and generall contentment of my auditory." It is much to be regretted that Hakluyt does not say specifically where these lectures were delivered. Oldys, in his memoir of Hakluyt, printed in the *Biographia Britannica*, expresses himself in such a manner as to lead to the supposition that they were read at Oxford, but the silence of Anthony a Wood on the subject at least throws much doubt upon the correctness of such an inference. It may not be out of place here to mention a curious error into which Oldys has fallen respecting this same lectureship.

Speaking of the publication of the present work he

says, quoting from notes he tells us he had made many years before, "It appears, in the epistle dedicatorie, that his lecture of navigation, before mentioned, was so well approved of by the renowned Sir F. Drake, that he made some proposals to continue, and establish it in Oxford, upon the prospect, which Mr. Hakluyt soon after had, of some engagement abroad." It is difficult to imagine, as the reader will be able to judge for himself by turning to page 16, that the man who wrote this sentence could possibly have seen the epistle dedicatorie in question. The proposal for *founding* a lectureship, not *continuing* one, came from Hakluyt himself, in consequence of what he had heard of the good results of such establishments in Spain, and of what he knew of the fatal consequences resulting from the too general ignorance of our own seamen: and the place was not Oxford, where, for the purpose he had in view, it would be totally useless, but London, or about Ratcliffe; in the very centre, in fact, of the localities most frequented by mariners of all grades. It had no reference whatever to Hakluyt's lectureship, whether at Oxford or elsewhere; of which, although his own statement is specific that he did, at some time before 1589, deliver lectures on cosmography, he leaves us to form our own conclusions as to the probable period and locality. There is, no doubt, however, as to the reality and earnestness of Hakluyt's exertions in this direction. He returns to the subject in the dedication of the first volume of the second edition of his Collection, where he urges on the Lord Admiral Howard the importance of establishing such a lectureship in London.¹ The honour due to the suggestion was not the less that the suggestion itself was allowed to pass unheeded by those with whom it rested to give this boon of nautical instruction to our seamen. Let us hope that this now national reproach is about to be effectually removed.²

¹ See also Hakewill's *Apology*, 3rd edit. 1635, fol. p. 310, where Hakluyt's suggestion is particularly noticed.

² In a paper addressed to Lord Mahon, president of the Society of Antiquaries, and printed in vol. xxxviii of the *Archæologia*, p. 283, Mr. Payne Collier publishes for the first time two highly interesting letters from Hakluyt to Sir F. Walsingham. The first letter is for the most part upon the subject mentioned in the text. As Mr. Collier does not say where the original is to be found, we print it as it appears in the *Archæologia*.

" Right Honorable,

" The famouse disputations in al partes of the mathematikes, which at this present are held in Paris, for the gayning of the lecture which was erected by the worthy scholer Petrus Ramus, to the great increase of those excellent sciences, put me in mynd to sollicite your honour agayne and agayne for the erection of that lecture of the arte of navigation, whereof I have had some speach with your honour, Sir Francis Drake, and Alderman Barnes and other. And that you might meet with al inconveniences, which might frustate the expected profit, which is hoped for by the erection of the same, I send your honour here the testament of Petrus Ramus, newly put out agayne in printe, and sent unto mee by monsur Bergeren, Ramus his executor; whereby you may see, first the exceeding zeale that man had to benefit his countrey, in bestowing 500 livers, which (as your honour knoweth) is fiftie pound sterling, upon establishing of that lecture, bequeathing not halfe so much to al the kindred and friends he had. Secondly, you may note, that he, being one of the most famouse clerkes of Europe, thought those sciences, next after divinitie, to be most necessarie for the common welth, in that he erected a newe lecture of the same, whereas there was one before erected, and endued with fiftie

It is very probable that some proposals had been made to Hakluyt to accompany Sir Humphry Gilbert in his last and fatal voyage to Newfoundland, in the year

pound stipend, by the kinges of France. Thirdly, that most provident order, which the good man by his will hath taken, is most requisite to be put in execution in England; which is, that everie three yeares there shalbe publicke disputation, signified to al men by publicke writing, wherein it shalbe free for any man, for three monethes space, to dispute agaynst the reader for the tyme being; who, yf he be found negligent, or yf any one of the competitours be found more worthy by the opinion of certayne indifferent men of lerninge, chosen out of the purpose to be judges, that then the unworthie shall give place to the more sufficient; who, so being placed, is bound in three yeares space to read through the course of the mathematikes.

"Yf, by your honour's instigation, her Majestie might be enduced to erecte such a lecture in Oxford, and the like for the arte of navigation might by some other meanes be established at London, allowing to each of them fiftie poundes yearly, with the same conditions, in my simple judgment it would be the best hundred poundes bestowed these five hundred yeares in England. For it is not unknowne to your wisdome, how necessarie for service of warres arithmeticke and geometrie are, and for our new discoveries and longe voyages by sea, the arte of navigation is, which is compounded of many partes of the aforesayd sciences.

"Understandinge heartofore of your honour's great abundance of busines, and your dangerouse sicknes, I thought it not meet to trouble your honour with such thinges as I had carefully sought out here in France, concerning the furtherance of the westerne discoveries, but chose rather to imparte the same with Mr. Carlile, which thing also I did. But, being lately advertised of your recovery (for which I humblie thanke almightie God), I was bold to signifie unto your honour my dealing with Horatio Palavicini, to become an adventurer in those westerne voyages, and, among other talke, alleadged your good disposition to the same; which he hearing of, replyed very cheerfully, that yf he were moved thereto by the least word from your honour, he would put in his hundred pound adventure or more. If Mr. Carlile be gone, yet it might come in

1583 ;[1] but no particulars are to be found recorded.
The circumstance that Hakluyt contemplated taking
part in the expedition is alluded to in a letter ad-

good tyme to serve Mr. Frobisher's turne, yf your wisdome shall
like well of yt, seeing he setteth not forth, as I understand, until
the beginning of May.

" I understand that the papistes give out secretly in the towne,
that there shall shortly come forth a confutation of the defence of
the execution of justice in England, which was set forth in English
and French in London. When yt cometh forth, I trust to have it
with the first.

" There is good hope that the minister, and those that were
taken lately with him in Paris, by the abbot of St. Geneveva, shall
very shortly be set at libertie; for the King secretly seemeth to
favour them; and they have very discreetly aunswered for themselves, that they were not at any communion or sermon, but that
they met together to consult whether to go out of Paris to some
place lawful by the edict. A frind of myne told mee he heard a
frier inveigh very exceeding bitterly agaynst them in a sermon
before a great congregation of people.

" Wee have heard by divers letters from Geneva that, besides
the earthquake, which was there about the end of Februarie, which
untyled many houses, and overthrewe many chymneis in the towne,
there is besides a whole village, in the contrey of Vallaye, swallowed
up, being foure dayes journey of Geneva.

" Those that favour the Spanish here in the towne have spred al
abroad, these two or three dayes, that Monsur is dead, which is
nothing so.

" Thus leving other matters and advertisementes of importance
to them unto whom they apperteyne, with remembraunce of the
continuance of my humble dutie to your honour, and your worthy
and vertuouse sonne in lawe, I leve you to the merciful protection
of the Almightie. Paris, the first of April, 1584.

" Don Antonio, his captaynes, and his fleet, are not yet departed
from Paris, but look every day to depart.

" Your honour's most humble

" RICHARD HAKLUYT."

[1] The second letter from Hakluyt to Sir F. Walsingham, pub-

dressed to him by Stephanus Parmenius, of Buda (one of those engaged in the expedition), on their arrival at the port of St. John. His words are

lished by Mr. Collier in the paper before quoted from (ante p. viii), refers to a "motion heartofore made" to him by Sir F. Walsingham whether he could be contented to accompany an expedition to America, in which he expresses his willingness to go and to employ all his observations, readings and conference whatsoever for that object. It does not appear that he contemplated any pecuniary adventure in the undertaking, as he refers his "entertaynment in this voyage" to Walsingham. The voyage here contemplated was most probably that of Sir Francis Drake to the West Indies and Carthagena in South America, the English fleet leaving England in the month of September 1585. It is certain, however, that Hakluyt did not accompany it. The letter, as given by Mr. Collier, is as follows:—

"Right Honourable,

"I understand from your servant Curtis your good acceptation of my hastie letter, your special favour and good will towardes mee, as also your expectation of my diligent inquirie of such thinges as may yeld any light unto our westerne discoverie. For the two former I yeld you most humble thankes; and for the later, I nether have nor will omitte any possible diligence, expecting intelligences thereof from Roan, Diepe, and St. Malo very shortly.

"In Paris I have seen in one man's house, called Perosse, the value of five thousand crownes worth of furres, as sables, bevers, otters, and other sortes, which he bought in August laste of the men of St. Malo; and the yeare before, he told mee he bestowed four thousand crownes with them in the like commoditie. He gave me further to understand that he saw great quantitie of buffe hides, which they brought home, and sent into the lowe countreys to sell. All which commodities, with diverse other of noe lesse value, are brought out of the most northerly partes of those countreys, whereunto our voyage of inhabiting is intended.

"And now, because I knowe that this present enterprise is like soone to waxe colde, and fall to the ground, unlesse in this second voyage all diligence in searching everie hope of gayne be used; and calling to mynd that your honor made a motion heartofore unto me,

"Non statueram ad te scribere, cùm in mentem veniret promissum literarum tuarum. *Putebas te superiore jam Junio nos subsecuturum.* Itaque de meo statu whether I cold be contented to goe myselfe in the action, these are to put your honor out of doubte, that for myne owne parte, I am most willing to goe now in the same this present setting forth, and in the service of God and my countrey to employ al my simple observations, readinges, and conference whatsoever. For obtaining leave of my L. Ambassador heere to departe, I doubt not but to find meanes of myselfe, seeing he may have inough to supply my roome.

"For leave of my colledg, and entertaynment in this voyage, I will wholly referre yt unto your honor, who wish me so well as you will not see my poore estate impared. Because the tyme is exceeding shorte, I wold desire your honor's present aunswere; uppon sight whereof, with winges of Pegasus, I wold fly in England.

"I have talked twise with Don Antonio of Portugal, and with five or sixe of his best captaynes and pilots, one of whom was born in Easte India. They al wish al prosperitie to Her Majestie and yourselfe, and say that, if the Queene of England wold joyne with their master, whose strength by sea they commend unto the skyes, they know how the King of Spayne, our mortal enemy, might easily be met withal, and she much enriched. The number of Portingalls which hange uppon the poore King are aboute an hundred or sixe score: diverse of them are lately come out of the Easte India, overlande by Tripoly in Siria. They have a voyage in hand, with five or sixe sayle of ships, which are in preparing at Newe Haven for the coste of Guinea, and the castle of Mina, wherein most parte of the Portingalls aforesayd are to be employed, being joyned in company with the French. They set forward, as I heare, within this moneth.

"One Sinior Andreas, borne in Savoy, is nowe, I heare, in Paris, which hath bin lately in the Island of Japan, with whom, by meanes of Doctor Pena, I shall have conference within a day or two. Diverse other intelligences, tending toward the furtherance of our western planting and discoverie, I looke for from sondry places very shortly. In the meane season, with remembrance of my humble dutie to your honor, and to your worthy and honorable ex doctore Humfredo certiorem te fieri jusseram. Verum sic tibi non esset satisfactum, etc."—*Hakluyt*, vol. iii, p. 161. Whatever may have been his intention in this respect, it may be presumed that his plans were changed, in consequence of his having been appointed chaplain to Sir Edward Stafford, ambassador from Queen Elizabeth to the court of France. At this period, also, he is said to have held a professorship of divinity, but we are not told where ; it could hardly have been at Oxford, for if so it would not have been omitted in the *Athenæ Oxonienses*. In the month of May 1585, during his residence at Paris with the British embassy, the reversion of the next prebendal stall that should become vacant was secured to him by the queen's mandate ; and in the same, or the following year, he, by virtue of this grant, took possession of the first stall in the cathedral of Bristol, which at that time became vacant by the death of Dr. John Gough. Notwithstanding this preferment he did not, as he informs us himself, give up his post of chaplain

sonne-in-lawe, I cease for the present, and beseech the Almightie to hold you bothe in his safe garde.

"It was told me by Perosse, of whom I spake before, and by Andrew Thevet, the Kinges cosmographer, that Duke Joyeuze, Admiral of France, and the Cardinal of Burbon and their frindes, have had a meaning to send out certayne ships to inhabite some place of the north part of America, and to carry thither many friers and other religiouse persons; but I thinke they be not in haste to doe yt. Paris, from my Lord Ambassadour's house, the vijth of Januarie, 1584.

"Your honor's most humble to command,

"RICHARD HAKLUYT, Preacher."

to the British embassy at Paris until the year 1588, when he returned to England with Lady Sheffield, sister to his early patron the Lord Admiral Howard, after a residence in France of five years. Elizabeth had granted to Sir Walter Raleigh letters patent, dated the 25th of March 1584, authorising him, in the usual terms, to discover, search, and find out such remote heathen and barbarous lands, countries, and territories not actually possessed by any Christian prince, nor inhabited by Christian people, as to him, his heirs, etc., should seem good. This patent Raleigh, in the latter part of this year 1588, assigned to Hakluyt, and several other gentlemen and merchants, as a corporation of counsellors, assistants, and adventurers, for the purpose of carrying out the object of the patent. On the 20th of April 1590, he was instituted to the rectory of Wetteringsett cum Blochford, in the county of Suffolk. The next event we find recorded in the life of Hakluyt, apart from his literary labours, is that of his marriage, which is supposed to have taken place in or about the year 1594. About the year 1605, he succeeded Dr. Richard Webster as a prebendary of Westminster.

Hakluyt, by his writings, and by his personal exertions with several persons of influence, was the chief promoter of a petition, addressed to King James in the year 1606, praying that he would grant patents for the colonization of Virginia. A charter was in consequence granted, bearing date April 10, 1606, by which two companies were formed, subsequently known as the London Company, and the Plymouth

Company. The tract of country lying between the thirty-fourth and forty-fifth degrees of latitude was to be divided into nearly equal portions, one of which was to be enjoyed by each of the said companies. The first settlement was effected by the London, or South Virginian Company; the chief adventurers in which, as patentees, were Sir Thomas Gates, Sir George Somers, Richard Hakluyt, and Edward Maria Wingfield.

Notwithstanding the extraordinary interest our author took in maritime discovery, and his extensive intercourse with seafaring men of all grades, it does not appear that he was ever tempted to quit his native country, with the exception of his sojourn in France. Contenting himself with the peaceful task of collecting and recording the accounts of other men's doings, it is not surprising that his life should afford so little of incident to be recorded. He died on the 23rd of November 1616, and was buried in St. Peter's Church, in Westminster Abbey, on the 26th of the same month. He left one son, who inherited from his father a fair estate, which, it is said, he had not the prudence to keep, and an illustrious name, which he knew not how to value.

Hakluyt had three brothers; one older, and two younger than himself. Of the eldest, Thomas, we are only told that he was elected from Westminster school to Trinity College, Cambridge, in 1567. The next, Oliver, was educated at the same college, and afterwards practised, with distinction, as a physician. The youngest, Edmund, held the post, for four years, of tutor to the Lord William Howard, the eldest son of the earl of Nottingham.

Having given this hasty sketch of the life of our author, we now proceed to the discussion of those labours, by which his name has become inseparably connected with the history of maritime discovery and enterprise. It has been already stated, that he had been chosen to lecture on cosmography and navigation; but his views extended much farther than instructing his countrymen in these branches of knowledge. He saw clearly the course in which lay the advantage and glory of his country; he saw that maritime traffic, and the acquisition of territory by colonization, were the means by which England was to improve the moral condition of her people, and maintain her position as a great naval power. Anxious to promote these objects, he cultivated the acquaintance of all who could give him information, and sought the protection of men who, appreciating his views, could assist him in carrying them into effect. No labour, no expense deterred him. In the account of the " English Voyage to Newfoundland in 1536", given by him in his *General Collection*, p. 517-519; vol. iii, p. 129-131; he says, "One Master Hore, of London, a man of goodly stature, and of great courage, and given to the studie of cosmography, encouraged divers gentlemen, and others, being assisted by the king's favour and good countenance, to accompany him in this voyage of discovery", and that " his persuasions tooke such effect, that within short space many gentlemen of the innes of court, and of the chancerie, and divers others of good worship, desirous to see the strange things of the world, very willingly entered into action with him." This was a very disastrous voyage; remarkable for the intense sufferings of the crew, and the very curious incident of their obtaining partial relief for their hunger by taking from an osprey's nest the fish the parent bird brought in great abundance to its young. Hakluyt was so anxious to obtain correct particulars of this voyage, that he rode two hundred miles, in order to obtain the facts from the lips of one Thomas Butts, then the only survivor of the adventurers in the said voyage. He was incessantly employed in the examination, collection, transcript, and translation of accounts of voyages and travels, charters, letters, and documents bearing in any way upon his subject, and in correspondence with men eager to impart information, obtain advice and assistance, or to encourage him in his laudable and patriotic efforts. The celebrated Abram Ortelius, and Gerard Mercator, were among those who exchanged with him friendly communications upon the subjects of common interest between them. Sir Francis Walsingham, Sir Robert Cecil, the Lord High-Admiral Howard, Sir Philip Sydney, and Sir Francis Drake, were among those who supported him in his labours by their commendations, and encouraged him to proceed. On the 11th of March 1583, Sir F. Walsingham writes to Hakluyt, thanking him for the exertions he had made to assist in "the discovery of the western parts yet unknown", and wishing him to continue "his travaile in these, and like matters."—

Hakluyt Collection, vol. iii, p. 181. And by a letter of the same date, addressed to the Mayor of Bristol, Sir Francis Walsingham recommends the Bristol adventurers to confer with the bearers of his letter, R. Hakluit and Thomas Steventon, on the subject of some ships these Bristol merchants were about to fit out for the purpose of accompanying Sir Humphry Gilbert in his ill-fated expedition before referred to. *Ib.*

The first work which issued from our author's pen was the collection now republished; and it is not improbable that it may have been this work to which Sir F. Walsingham more particularly alluded in his letter of the 11th March 1582, when he spoke of Hakluyt's exertions to assist in the discovery of the western parts yet unknown. It would be impossible to explain Hakluyt's views, or the object towards which his exertions were directed, more clearly than he has himself done in the epistle dedicatory to Sir Philip Sydney, prefixed to this work. The glory of England; the advantages of colonization, as a means of employing the idle, of rendering the laws less sanguinary, by diminishing the necessity for capital punishment, and of enlarging the commerce of the country; the extension of the knowledge of navigation, particularly amongst our merchant seamen; and the conversion of the savage, and consequent promotion of the worship and glory of God, are all brought forward in their turn. We shall have much to say, in the course of this Introduction, upon the various pieces of which this collection is composed; but we postpone our remarks for the present, in

INTRODUCTION. xix

order to dispose of the other works which either emanated from our author, or were produced at his suggestion. These will be taken in the order of their production, as nearly as we have been able to ascertain it.

He did not neglect his favourite pursuit during his residence in France; but made diligent inquiries for information, not only among cosmographers and others, but also in the libraries, both public and private. During his researches he discovered a manuscript account of Florida, a country which had been visited, and to a certain extent explored, by Ribault in 1562, and by Laudonniere in the following years. Perceiving the interest and importance of this work, he engaged, at his own expense, Martin Basanier to publish the book at Paris, in French, in the year 1586.[1] It is dedicated to Sir Walter Raleigh; and the editor takes occasion to bestow high praises upon Sir Walter, for the enterprise he displayed in his then late discovery of Virginia. This work does not contain Ribault's own account of his voyage. The attention this book excited in France, encouraged Hakluyt to present it to his countrymen in an English dress, and it was published in London, in the year 1587, with the following title:

"A notable historie containing foure voyages made by certayne French captaynes unto Florida; wherein the great riches and fruitefulnes of the countrey, with the maners of the people, hitherto concealed, are brought to light; written,

[1] See Dedication to vol. ii. of the 2nd edition of his general collection.

all saving the last, by Monsieur Laudonniere, who remained there himselfe as the French king's lieuetenant a yere and a quarter; newly translated out of French into English by R. H. London: imprinted by Thomas Dawson, 1587. 4to."

Hakluyt has prefixed to his translation a dedicatory epistle to Sir Walter Raleigh, encouraging him to prosecute the colonization of Virginia, by pointing out the advantages, and probable resources of the district.

In the year 1587 he also published, at Paris, a revised edition of Peter Martyr Anghiera's work, *De orbe novo*. This edition appeared with the following title:

"De orbe novo Petri Martyris Anglerii Mediolanensis Protonotarii et Caroli quinti Senatoris Decades octo, diligenti temporum observatione et utilissimis annotationibus illustratæ, suoque nitori restitutæ, labore et industria Richardi Hakluyti Oxoniensis Angli, etc. Parisiis, 1587." 8°.

Amongst other improvements in this edition, mentioned in the Latin dedication to Sir Walter Raleigh, prefixed to the work, he observes: "Cartam geographicam præcipua operis loca continentem ut perpendicularem appendicem adjunxi, memor illius quod vere dicitur 'Geographiam esse historiæ oculum'." The map here referred to is one of the world, and is dedicated to Hakluyt in the following words: "Doctiss. et ornatiss. Rich. Hakluyto F.G.S. Cui potius quam tibi orbem hunc novum dicassem? cum tu assiduis eruditisque libris tuis ipsum eundem in dies illustriorem reddas. Eum igitur uti tua humanitate dignum est accipe, teque nos vicissim amabimus. Paris. Cal. Maij. 1587." This map is of very rare occurrence. There is prefixed a dedication, in Latin, to Sir Walter Raleigh, occupying nine pages Many years afterwards, Michael Lok, whose name is intimately connected with the maritime history of this period, translated Anghiera's work into English at the recommendation of Hakluyt. The title is as follows:

" The historie of the West Indies, containing the Actes and Adventures of the Spaniards which have conquered and peopled those countries, inriched with varietie of pleasant relation of the manners, ceremonies, lawes, governments, and warres of the Indians. Published in Latin by Mr. Hakluyt, and translated into English by M. Lok. Gent. London. Printed for Andrew Webb."

This publication preceded by a very short time the permanent colonization of Virginia, the first English settlement in America; and it is but just to presume, that the public and private efforts of our author must have had a most important influence in directing attention towards these establishments, from which such mighty results subsequently followed. We shall have to refer to his exertions in this respect on more than one occasion.

It has been stated, in the early part of this narrative, that Hakluyt was one of those to whom, in the year 1588, Sir Walter Ralegh assigned his patent for the prosecution of discoveries in heathen lands. Whether this circumstance directed his attention more particularly towards the maritime exertions of the English, or whether, as he himself states,[1] he was roused by the reproach of want of enterprise, brought

---

[1] Dedication to the first edition of his general collection.

against his countrymen by foreigners, certain it is that about this time he bent all his efforts towards the arrangement of materials for a work which should show that the English had not been idle, or unsuccessful. This project, and its author, are thus referred to by Philip Jones, in the dedication to Sir Francis Drake, prefixed to his *Certain briefe and speciall Instructions for Gentlemen, &c., employed in services abroad.* London: 1589. 4to.

" I confesse that although my propension was alwaies to endevor somthing for the inlargement of your name and honor, having so well deserved of this commonwealth and of every particular thereof, yet I was motioned to remember yourselfe in the impression of this Index by my very good and learned friend Mr. Richard Hackluyt, a man of incredible devotion towarde yourselfe and of speciall carefulnesse for the good of our nation; as the world injoying the benefit of some of his travels can give testimonie, and is possible to give better if that rare and excellent worke which he now plyeth once come to publike view. In the mean time I record his diligence," etc.

The result of these labours appeared toward the end of the year 1589, in the publication of a folio volume, with the following title:—

" The principall navigations, voiages and discoveries of the English nation made by sea or over land to the most remote and farthest distant quarters of the earth at any time within the compasse of these 1500 yeeres: devided into three severall parts according to the positions of the regions wherunto they were directed. The first conteining the personall travels of the English into Judæa, Syria, Arabia, the river Euphrates, Babylon, Balsara, the Persian Gulfe, Ormuz,

INTRODUCTION. xxiii

Chaul, Goa, India, and many islands adjoyning to the south parts of Asia: together with the like unto Egypt, the chiefest ports and places of Africa within and without the streight of Gibraltar, and about the famous promontorie of Buona Esperanza. The second, comprehending the worthy discoveries of the English towards the north and north-east by sea, as of Lapland, Scrikfinia, Corelia, the Baie of S. Nicholas, the Isles of Colgoieve, Vaigats, and Nova Zembla toward the great river Ob, with the mightie empire of Russia, the Caspian sea, Georgia, Armenia, Media, Persia, Boghar in Bactria, and divers kingdoms of Tartaria. The third and last, including the English valiant attempts in searching almost all the corners of the vaste and new world of America from 73 degrees of northerly latitude southward to Meta Incognita, Newfoundland, the maine of Virginia, the point of Florida, the baie of Mexico, all the inland of Nova Hispania, the coast of Terra Firma, Brasill, the river of Plate to the streight of Magellan and through it, and from it in the South Sea to Chili, Peru, Xalisco, the gulfe of California, Nova Albion upon the backside of Canada further than ever any Christian hitherto hath pierced. Whereunto is added the last most renowned English navigation round about the whole globe of the earth. By Richard Hakluyt, master of artes and student some time of Christchurch in Oxford. Imprinted at London by George Bishop and Ralph Newberie, 1589." Fol.

The dedication to Sir Francis Walsingham, prefixed to this edition, contains some interesting particulars relating to the life of the author; and of which Oldys, in his memoir of him in the *Biographia Britannica*, has made good use. In the address to the reader, Hakluyt explains the character of his work in the following concise terms.

" I meddle in this work with the navigations onely of our

owne nation. And albeit I alleage in a few places (as the matter and occasion required) some strangers as witnesses of the things done, yet are they none but such as either faythfully remember or sufficiently confirme the travels of our owne people, of whom (to speake trueth) I have received more light in some respects than all our owne historians could affoord me in this case, Bale, Foxe, and Eden onely excepted."

His anxiety to communicate the best information he possessed, is shown in the account of " The Ambassage of Sir Hierome Bowes, to the emperour of Moscovie, 1583", printed at page 491 of the first edition of his General Collection, in some copies of which this narrative will be found to have been reprinted, with the title altered, as follows:

" A briefe discourse of the voyage of Sir Jerome Bowes, knight, her majesties ambassadour to the emperour of Muscovia, in the yeere 1582: and printed this second time according to the true copie I received of a gentleman that went in the same voyage for the correction of the errours in the former impression."

Having now given a definite form to his work, he went on with increased energy. "The honour and benefit of this commonwealth", he says, "hath made all difficulties seem easy, all pains and industry pleasant, all expenses of light value and moment to me." In 1598 he published the first volume of a second edition of his Collection, and two other volumes followed in the two succeeding years. The first volume is dedicated to the Lord Charles Howard, Earl of Nottingham; and it may be mentioned (*par parenthèse*) as a curious fact that, neither in this dedication, nor in any part of the introductory matter, does he make the slightest allusion to the first edition. The second and third volumes are dedicated to Sir Robert Cecil, the principal secretary of state, " whose earnest desires to do him [Hakluyt] good, lately broke out into most bountiful and acceptable effects." The titles of the several volumes of this edition are as follows:

" The principal navigations, voiages, traffiques and discoveries of the English nation made by sea or over land to the remote and farthest distant quarters of the earth at any time within the compasse of these 1500 yeeres: devided into three severall volumes according to the positions of the regions whereunto they were directed. This first volume containing the woorthy discoveries, etc. of the English toward the north and north-east by sea, as of Lapland, Scrikfinia, Corelia, the baie of S. Nicholas, the isles of Colgoieve, Vaigatz, and Nova Zembla toward the great river Ob, with the mighty empire of Russia, the Caspian sea, Georgia, Armenia, Media, Persia, Boghar in Bactria, and divers kingdoms of Tartaria. Together with many notable monuments and testimonies of the antient forren trades and of the warrelike and other shipping of this realme of England in former ages. Whereunto is annexed also a briefe commentarie of the true state of Island and of the Northern seas and lands situate that way. And lastly the memorable defeate of the Spanish huge Armada, anno 1588, and the famous victorie atchieved at the citie of Cadiz, 1596, are described. By Richard Hakluyt, *etc.* Imprinted at London, by George Bishop, Ralph Newberie, and Robert Barker, 1598." Fol.

In the dedication to the volume, Hakluyt addresses the Lord-Admiral strongly on the subject of the

e

establishment of a lectureship, on navigation, in the city of London.[1]

" The second volume of the principal navigations, voyages, traffiques, and discoveries of the English nation made by sea or over land to the south and south-east parts of the world at any time within the compasse of these 1600 yeres: divided into two severall parts. Whereof the first containeth the personall travels, etc., of the English through and within the streight of Gibraltar to Alger, Tunis, and Tripolis in Barbary, to Alexandria and Cairo in Ægypt, to the isles of Sicilia, Zante, Candia, Rhodus, Cyprus and Chio, to the citie of Constantinople, to divers parts of Asia Minor, to Syria and Armenia, to Jerusalem and other places in Judæa; as also to Arabia downe the river of Euphrates to Babylon and Balsara, and so through the Persian gulph to Ormuz, Chaul, Goa, and to many islands adjoyning upon the south parts of Asia; and likewise from Goa to Cambaia and to all the dominions of Zelabdim Echebar, the great Mogor, to the mighty river of Ganges, to Bengala, Aracan, Bacola, and Chonderi, to Pegu, to Jamahai in the kingdome of Siam, and almost to the very frontiers of China. The second comprehendeth the voyages, trafficks, etc., of the English nation made without the streight of Gibraltar to the islands of the Açores, of Porto Santo, Madera, and the Canaries, to the kingdomes of Barbary, to the isles of Capo Verde, to the rivers of Senega, Gambra, Madrabumba, and Sierra Leona, to the coast of Guinea and Benin, to the isles of S. Thomé and Santa Helena, to the parts about the cape of Buona Esperanza, to Quitangone

[1] In some copies of the first volume of the second edition, the voyage to Cadiz in 1596 is altogether suppressed or reprinted. Where this is the case, the title-page is found to bear date 1599, and that part of it which refers to the expedition to Cadiz is omitted; other alterations of a minor character being also introduced into it.

neere Mozambique, to the isles of Comoro and Zanzibar, to the citie of Goa beyond cape Comori, to the isles of Nicubar, Gomes Polo, and Pulo Pinaom, to the maine land of Malacca and to the kingdome of Junsalaon. By Richard Hackluyt, *etc.* Imprinted at London by George Bishop, Ralph Newbery, and Robert Barker, anno 1599."

" The third and last volume of the voyages, navigations, traffiques and discoveries of the English nation, and in some few places where they have not been, of strangers, performed within and before the time of these hundred yeeres to all parts of the Newfound world of America or the West Indies, from 73 degrees of northerly to 57 of southerly latitude: as namely to Engronland, Meta Incognita, Estotiland, Tierra de Labrador, Newfoundland, up the Grand bay, the gulfe of S. Laurence, and the river of Canada, to Hochelaga and Saguenay, along the coast of Arambec to the shores and maines of Virginia and Florida, and on the west or backside of them both to the rich and pleasant countries of Nueva Biscaya, Cibola, Tiguex, Cicuic, Quivira, to the 15 provinces of the kingdome of New Mexico, to the bottome of the gulfe of California, and up the river of Buena Guia: and likewise to all the yles, both small and great, lying before the cape of Florida, the bay of Mexico, and Tierra firma, to the coasts and inlands of Newe Spaine, Tierra firma and Guiana, up the mighty rivers of Orenoque, Dessekebe, and Marannon, to every part of the coast of Brasil, to the river of Plate, through the streights of Magellan forward and backward, and to the south of the said streights as far as 57 degrees: and from thence on the back side of America along the coastes, harbours and capes of Chili, Peru, Nicaragua, Nueva Espanna, Nueva Galicia, Culiacan, California, Nova Albion, and more northerly as farre as 43 degrees. Together with the two renowned and prosperous voyages of Sir Francis Drake and Mr. Thomas Candish round about the circumference of the whole earth, and divers other voyages intended and set forth for that course. Collected by Richard Hakluyt, preacher, etc. Imprinted at London by George Bishop, Ralfe Newberie and Robert Barker. Anno Dom. 1600."

This and the preceding volume, as we have already stated, are dedicated to "Sir Robert Cecil, principall secretarie to Her Majestie." In the dedication to the second volume, Hakluyt strongly urges on the minister the expediency of colonizing Virginia, and refers to the circumstance of Cecil having consulted him, in 1597, "touching the state of the country of Guiana, and whether it were fit to be planted by the English?" In the dedication to the third volume, Hakluyt takes an opportunity to refer to the subject of a lectureship on navigation for the benefit of English mariners, and to urge its establishment, referring to the good example of Spain in this respect.

But Hakluyt was not satisfied with labouring himself, and encouraging others to labour; he endeavoured to provide against the time when professional or other cares might interfere with his great pursuit. In the dedication of the third volume he says:

"As I long since foresaw that my profession of divinity, the care of my family, and other occasions, might call and divert me from these kind of endeavours, I therefore have for three years past encouraged and furthered in these studies of cosmography and foreign histories my honest, industrious, and learned friend, Mr. John Pory; one of special skill and extraordinary hope to perform great matters in the same and beneficial to the commonwealth."

The result of this encouragement was a translation

of the *History of Africa* by John Leo, commonly called Leo Africanus, which Mr. Pory published in the year 1600, with the title—

"A geographical historie of Africa, written in Arabicke and Italian, by John Leo, a More, borne in Granada and brought up in Barbarie, etc. Before which out of the best ancient and moderne writers is prefixed a generall description of Africa, and also a particular treatise of all the maine lands and isles undescribed by John Leo. And after the same is annexed a relation of the great princes and the manifold religions in that part of the world. Translated and collected by John Pory, lately of Gonevill and Caius College in Cambridge. Londini, Impensis Georg. Bishop, 1600." Fol.

In his dedication to Sir Robert Cecil, the translator refers to the interest Hakluyt took in the work, in the following terms: "M. Richard Hakluyt, who out of his mature judgement in these studies, knowing the excellencie of this storie above all others in the same kinde, was the only man that mooved me to translate it."

Pory was not the only person whom Hakluyt encouraged to make translations of works bearing upon his favorite pursuit. Parke, in the preface to his translation of the *History of China*, from the Spanish of Gonzalez de Mendoza, bears the following testimony to his active zeal:

"Which labours I have undertaken at the earnest request and encouragement of my worshipfull friend Master Richard Hakluyt, late of Oxforde, a gentleman, besides his other manifolde learning and languages, of singular and deepe insight in all histories of discoverie and partes of cosmographie. And also for the zeale he beareth to the honor of his countrie and countrimen brought the same [*i. e.* Gonzalez de Mendoza's work] first above two years since over into this court," etc.

Again, about the year 1612, P. Erondelle published a translation of part of Lescarbot's *Histoire de la Nouvelle France*, under the title of—

" Nova Francia, or the description of that part of New France which is one continent with Virginia. Described in the three late voyages and plantation made by Monsieur de Monts, Monsieur de Pont-Gravé, and Monsieur de Poutrincourt, into the countries called by the French men La Cadie, lying to the south west of Cape Breton. Together with an excellent treatise of all the commodities of the said countries, and maners of the naturall inhabitants of the same, etc. London, printed for Andrew Webb." 4to.

From the preface we learn that Hakluyt was also the instigator of this work.

" Gentle reader, the whole volume of the navigations of the French nation into the West Indies (comprised in three bookes) was brought to me to be translated by Mr. Richard Hackluyt, a man who for his worthy and profitable labours, is well known to most men of worth not only of this kingdome but also of forrain parts, and by him this part was selected and chosen from the whole worke, for the particular use of this nation, to the end that comparing the goodnesse of the lands of the northern parts heerein mentioned with that of Virginia, which (though in one and the selfe same continent, and both lands adjoining) must be far better by reason it stands more southerly neerer to the sunne, greater encouragement may be given to prosecute that generous and goodly action in planting and peopling that country to the better propagation of the Gospel of Christ, the salvation of innumerable souls, and general benefit of this land, too much pestred with over many people.... If a man that sheweth foorth effectually the zealous care he hath to the wellfare and common good of his country deserveth praises of the same, I refer to the judgement of them that abhor the vice of ingratitude (hatefull above all to God and good men) whether the said Mr. Hakluyt (as well for the first procuring of this translation, as for many workes of his set out by him for the good and everlasting fame of the English nation) deserveth not to reape thankes."

In the following year, 1601, Hakluyt gave to the world a translation, from the Portuguese, of a work by Antonio Galvam, entitled—

" Tratado dos varios e diversos caminhos por onde nos tempos passados a pimenta e especiaria veyo da India as nossas partes e assim de todos os descubrimentos antigos e modernos que saõ feitos atè a era de 1550. Com os nomes particulares das pessoas que os fizeraõ em que tempos e suas alturas. Lisboa por Joaõ Barreira, 1563." 8vo.

This work was edited and published, after the author's death, by Francesco de Sousa Tavares. To the English version Hakluyt gave the title—

" The discoveries of the world from their first originall unto the yeere of our Lord 1555. Briefly written in the Portugall tongue by Antonie Galvano, Governour of Ternate, the chiefe island of the Malucos : corrected, quoted, and now published in English by Richard Hakluyt, sometimes student of Christchurch in Oxford. Londini, Impensis G. Bishop. 1601." 4to.

This translation was not his own, as he himself states in the dedicatory epistle to Sir Robert Cecil. His words are—

" Now touching the translation, it may please you, sir, to

be advertised that it was first done into our language by some honest and well affected marchant of our nation, whose name by no means I could attain unto, and that, as it seemeth, many yeeres ago. For it hath lien by me above these twelve yeeres. In all which space, though I have made much inquirie and sent to Lisbon, where it seemeth it was printed, yet to this day I could never obtain the originall copie; whereby I might reforme the manifold errours of the translator."

He then proceeds to describe the trouble it cost him to verify the facts from the original histories, and to annex the marginal quotations to the work.

His last publication was a translation of Fernando de Souto's discoveries in Florida, which he printed under the following title:

"Virginia richly valued by the description of the maine land of Florida her next neighbour: out of the foure yeeres continuall travell and discoverie for above one thousand miles east and west of Don Ferdinando de Soto, and six hundred able men in his companie. Wherin are truly observed the riches and fertilitie of those parts abounding with things necessarie, pleasant and profitable for the life of man: with the natures and dispositions of the inhabitants. Written by a Portugall gentleman of Elvas emploied in all the action, and translated out of Portugese by Richard Hakluyt. At London, printed by Felix Kyngston for Matthew Lownes, 1609." 4to.

This work was evidently intended to encourage the young colony in Virginia, and procure support for the undertaking. The hardships, naturally attendant upon the first attempts at colonization in Virginia, had been greatly increased by mismanagement, and

INTRODUCTION. xxxiii

the losses and discouragement of the settlers had arrived at such a height that, but for the opportune arrival of Lord Delawarr in the month of June, 1610, the colony would have been abandoned; the settlers being actually on their way to the sea coast when they were met by their new governor, with supplies of stores and men. It was, probably, for the purpose of again stimulating the exertions of the colonists, depressed by much suffering, and of procuring the additional support, of which they stood so much in need, that in the year 1611 the title of the *Virginia richly valued*, was altered as follows:

" The worthye and famous historie of the travailes, discovery, and conquest of that great continent of Terra Florida, being lively paraleld with that of our now inhabited Virginia. As also the comodities of the said country, with divers excellent and rich mynes of golde, silver, and other metals, etc., which cannot but give us a great and exceeding hope of our Virginia, being so neere of one continent, etc. London, printed for Matthew Lownes, 1611." 4to.

The preface is addressed " To the right honorable the right worshipfull counsellors, and others, the cheerefull adventurers for the advancement of that Christian and noble plantation in Virginia", whom, perhaps, it was found necessary to excite by a direct reference to "riche mynes of golde, silver, and other metals." It will be evident from all that has been said, that Hakluyt took a deep interest in the success of the Virginian colony. Robertson, in his *History of America*, vol. iv, p. 171, 10th edit., bears honorable testimony to our author, in the following words : " The

f

most active and efficacious promoter of this (the colonization of Virginia) was Richard Hakluyt, prebendary of Westminster, to whom England is more indebted for its American possessions than to any man of that age."

The esteem in which he was held by mariners is evidenced by the fact, that in a voyage of discovery made by Hudson in the year 1608, at the charge of the Muscovy company, a promontory, on the continent of Greenland, was named Hakluyt's Headland;[1] and three years later, in a voyage of discovery to Pechora, in Russia, made at the expense of the same company, by William Gourdon, a river was named by the navigators Hakluyt's River.[2]

We have already mentioned that his estate descended to his son, who is reported to have squandered it. His unpublished manuscripts, sufficient to have formed a fourth volume to his Collection, had a better fate, by falling into the hands of Purchas, who inserted them, in an abridged form, in his *Pilgrimes*. It is to be regretted that this compiler should have adopted the plan of curtailing all his narratives; we get more facts, within a given compass, it is true, but this advantage is more than compensated by the loss of the interest, and indeed confidence, which a genuine unabridged narrative always inspires. Purchas, however, was fully able to appreciate the merit of such a

---

[1] *Purchas*, vol. iii, p. 464. The name of Hakluyt's Headland no longer exists, nor can the locality be identified.

[2] *Purchas*, vol. iii, p. 531. This river cannot be identified at the present day.

man as Hakluyt, and has not neglected to give him the praise he deserves; "thereby", says Oldys, "concurring with those writers of established judgment who have distinguished, according to his deserts, the surpassing knowledge and learning, diligence and fidelity, of this naval historian."

In Wood's *Athenæ Oxonienses*, edit. Bliss, a reference to three of Hakluyt's manuscripts, in the Selden Collection, is given as follows : viz.,—

1. "Notes of certain commodities in good request in the East Indies, the Moluccas, and China." 2. "The chiefe places where sondry sorte of spices do growe in the East Indies, gathered out of sondry the best and latest authors by R. Hackluyt." 3. "The remembrance of what is good to bring from the Indyes into Spayne, being good marchandize and bowght by him that is skillfull and trusty."

These manuscripts the Editor has printed in the Appendix to this work. There is every reason to conjecture that these notes were drawn up for the use of some body of merchants; the nature of the notes themselves, and the language used in several places, leave little room for doubt on this point. The question is, for whose use were they intended? It is not probable that they were framed for the Muscovy Company, which had been incorporated by Philip and Mary as far back as the year 1554, and, in all probability, stood in little need of such assistance. But in the year 1600, the date of the Notes, Queen Elizabeth granted a charter to an association of merchants, with whose gigantic growth there is no parallel in the history of commercial success. This association, "The United

Company of Merchants of England trading to the East Indies", commonly called "The East India Company",[1] sent out their first venture in the same year. Notes such as those drawn up by Hakluyt, contain precisely the information which would be required by men about to trade to the East; and when we look at the coincidence in the dates of the charter and the notes, we cannot but come to the conclusion that it was for the use of the East India Company that Hakluyt framed them.[2]

We now turn to the discussion of Hakluyt's first publication, the *Divers Voyages touching the Discoverie of America*. This work is of extreme rarity; when perfect it contains two maps, facsimiles of which are given with this edition. We are not aware of the existence of more than five copies of the book; and of these two only contain both the maps, and a third has one map. The two perfect copies are in the British Museum. One of these was acquired in the year 1841, at the sale of the library of the late Mr. George Chalmers, and is the most interesting of all, having the autograph signature of the author subscribed to the

[1] This is now their legal title by the 3rd and 4th Wm. IV, c. 85, s. 111.

[2] The Editor's acknowledgments are due to Thomas Rundall, Esq. of the East India House, for his kindness in searching in the archives of the Company for evidence of these notes having been communicated to it. Memoranda of "What the Indies do vent", etc. were found by that gentleman, but not in such a form as to identify them with the "Notes". This want of success, however, can hardly be considered to affect the question.

"Epistle Dedicatorie", and of which signature a fac-simile is here given.

The second is contained in the Grenville Collection. A third copy is in the Bodleian Library, at Oxford: this copy has only one map, that by Michael Lok. A fourth copy is in the possession of Mr. Edward A. Crowninshield, of Boston, with the maps supplied in fac-simile; and the fifth is in the library of Mr. James Lennox, of New York, the maps being also supplied in fac-simile.[1]

It may be said of this, as of every other work of

[1] At a meeting of the Society of Antiquaries, held in the month of March 1850, a copy of Michael Lok's map was exhibited by Mr. Payne Collier, and a letter read, addressed by that gentleman to the president, comprising "Some observations on Richard Hakluyt, and American discoveries." Speaking of the "Divers Voyages", Mr. Collier says: "Another copy has come to light, from which the map before the society has been extracted for exhibition this evening; and I apprehend that a third copy of the volume is preserved in the cabinet of a chary lover of old books, who was glad to obtain it at a high price, although it has not either of the maps that properly belong to it." Unfortunately, the names of the lucky possessors, or supposed possessors of these copies, are not given by Mr. Collier. The map, so exhibited, makes the *fourth* known, and not, as Mr. Collier supposes, only the *second*.

which Hakluyt was either the author or promoter, that it had a direct and practical object. At the period when he commenced his geographical studies there was but one English book in existence presenting even a limited view of maritime discovery; viz., Eden's *Historie of Travayle;* and this was confined to a translation of four decades of *Peter Martyr*, of Oviedo's *History of the West Indies*, and of extracts from various writers on geographical subjects, as Ziglerus, Paulus Jovius, Haiton, Herberstein, and others. The English, in general, knew little of what had been accomplished by their own countrymen, and still less of the labours of foreigners. Merchant adventurers collected information for the purposes of their traffic, but they had no interest in making it public, and a gold-mine, or a galleon, was in general the real object of expeditions professing to aim at higher purposes. With this spirit pervading all classes, it is not surprising that Hakluyt should express himself in the following language, in his epistle dedicatory to Sir Robert Cecil, prefixed to the English translation of Galvam's work:

"Now if any man shall marvel that, in these discoveries of the world for the space almost of fower thousand yeeres here set downe, our nation is scarce fower times mentioned, he is to understand that when this author ended his discourse (which was about the yeere of grace 1555) there was little extant of men's travailes. And for aught I can see there had no great matter yet come to light if my selfe had not undertaken that heavie burden, being never therein entertained to any purpose untill I had recourse unto yourselfe, by whose speciall favour and bountifull patronage I have been often much encouraged and as it were revived. Which travailes of our men, because as yet they be not come to ripenes, and have been made for the most part to places first discovered by others, when they shall come to more perfection and become more profitable to the adventurers, will then be more fit to be reduced into briefe epitomes by myselfe or some other endued with an honest zeale of the honor of our country."

And, again, in the preface to the first volume of the second edition of his General Collection, he says,—

" For the bringing of which into this homely and rough-hewn shape which here thou seest, what restlesse nights, what painefull dayes, what heat, what cold, I have endured; how many long and changeable journeys I have travailed; how many famous libraries I have searched into; what varietie of ancient and moderne writers I have perused; what a number of old records, patents, privileges, letters, etc., I have redeemed from obscuritie and perishing: into how manifold acquaintance I have entred; what expenses I have not spared; and yet what faire opportunities of private gaine, preferment and ease I have neglected, albeit thyselfe canst hardly imagine, yet I by daily experience do finde and feele, and some of my entier friends can sufficiently testifie," etc.

At the period when this was written the history of travel was in truth to the English reader all but a blank, and it is not too much to say, that when our author wished to enlist the sympathies of his countrymen in favour of his enlightened views for the moral and political improvement of the nation, he found few or no evidences to which he could point in support of his proposals.

Hakluyt was an ardent advocate for emigration. But

emigration to the states of a foreign power would give strength to such power at the expense of England. In order to be beneficial it must be connected with a sound system of colonization; and he naturally looked towards the vast continent of America as the only field upon which any such system could be carried out with effect. Here again he had to find information not only for the nation at large, but for those through whom the accomplishment of his designs was to be effected. For this purpose he brought together various accounts showing the discovery of the whole of the east coast of North America. The materials for this collection had to be gathered from various sources. One only was printed to his hand, viz. Ribault's discovery of Florida, and this, he informs us, was so rare, that had he not reprinted it, it would have utterly perished. The rest were either in manuscript or printed in a foreign language. A very slight examination of this little work will show that it is skilfully put together for the object in view. After a list of writers of geography and another of travellers, we have a short chapter showing the great probability of a passage to India by the north-west. This is followed by the epistle dedicatorie to "Master Phillip Sydney, Esquire," in which the author explains his views upon many subjects: The letters patent granted by King Henry VII to John Cabot and his three sons for exploring unknown regions: and, A note of Sebastian Cabot's voyage to the coast of North America. We then have a declaration of the Indies and lands discovered unto the emperor and the king of Portugal, written by Robert Thorne, and showing that the northern part of America remained for "King Henrie the Eight to take in hande"; and The booke made by Master Robert Thorne, being an information of the parts of the world discovered by him [the Emperor Charles V] and the king of Portingale; and also of the way to the Moluccaes by the north. This is followed by the relation of John Verazzani, in which he gives an account of his voyage of discovery along the eastern coast of America from about South Carolina to Newfoundland. Then come the Discoverie of the Isles of Frisland, etc., made by Nicolas Zeno and his brother Antonio; and The discovery of Florida by Captain John Ribault. Having thus given the reader the fullest particulars then known respecting the coast of America, he proceeds with notes given to Arthur Pett and Charles Jackman, sent by the merchants of the Muscovy Company for the discovery of the north-east streight, "not altogether unfit for some other enterprises of discoverie hereafter to be taken in hande." These notes are evidently framed with a view to commercial enterprise, but they are followed by "Notes to bee given to one that prepared for a discoverie", which are drawn up as instructions to colonists. The whole is wound up by the "Names of certain commodities growing in part of America not presently inhabited by any Christians from Florida northward", containing a goodly list of objects available both for the necessaries and the luxuries of life.

In a work so suggestive as this before us, it is difficult to avoid the innumerable temptations to discursiveness which beset almost every page. Minute annotation would, however, be out of place in the present instance. No more notes, therefore, have been given than appeared to be necessary for the proper elucidation of the text, reserving for this Introduction such further remarks as might be desirable for the purpose of illustration. These will now be made, in as concise a form as possible, upon the several pieces, in the order in which they occur in the Collection.

Our author commences with "The names of certaine late writers of Geographie, with the yeere wherein they wrote", and "The names of certaine late travaylers, both by sea and by lande, which also for the most part have written of their owne travayles and voyages."

In order to make these lists really useful, the works of the respective authors should be enumerated. This deficiency it is now proposed to supply, giving in every instance the title of the first edition, where it could be ascertained.

1. Ismail Ibn Ali Abulfeda. The work which entitles him to a place in this list is named "Takuwimu l-boldan" (*i. e.*, The description of the countries), and is the most complete and best geographical work in Arabic. Portions have been published from time to time by European scholars, as follows:

 i. Descriptio Chorasmiæ et Mawaralnahræ (*i.e.*, regionum extra Oxum). Arabice cum versione J. Gravii. Londini, 1650. 4to.

II. Descriptio Peninsulæ Arabiæ (printed with the Descriptio Chorasmiæ), Arab. Lat.; in vol. 3 of Geographiæ veteris Scriptores Græci minores. [Edited by J. Hudson.] Oxoniæ, 1698-1712. 8vo.
III. Tabula Syriæ, Arabice cum versione Latina et notis J. B. Koehler, et cum observationibus J. J. Reiskii. Lipsiæ, 1766. 4to.
IV. Descriptio Ægypti, Arab. Lat. et cum notis J. D. Michaelis. Gœttingæ, 1776. 8vo.
V. Tabulæ quædam geographicæ ... nunc primum Arabice ed. F. T. Rinck. Lipsiæ, 1791. 8vo.
VI. Descriptio regionum Nigritarum, Arabice. Printed at the end of Makrizi, Historia Regum Islamiticorum in Abissinia ... cum versione Latina F. T. Rinck. Lugduni Batavorum, 1790. 4to.

2. Sir John Mandeville. He wrote an account of his travels in the east. This work is said to have been composed originally in French in the year 1355, at Liege, to which place he had retired some years before his death. We give the titles of four editions (in as many languages), which were printed prior to the year 1500.

> Ce livre est eppelle mādeville et fut fait et compose par monsieur jehan de mandeville chevallier natif dāgleterre de la ville de saīct aleī. Et parle de la terre de promission cest assavoir de jerusalem et de pluseurs autres isles de mer et les diverses et estranges choses qui sont es dites isles. *End.* Cy finist ce ʻtresplaisant livre nome Mandeville....Et fut fait lā 1480 le un jour davril. Fol. This is supposed by Brunet to be the first edition in any language.

The first Italian edition is without title, but has the following colophon:

Explicit Johannes d' Mādevilla impressus Mediolani ductu et auspiciis magistri Petri de corneno pridie Callendas augusti 1480. Johane Galeazio Maria Sfortia Vicecomitte Duce nostro invictissimo ac principe Jucondissimo. 4to.

Itinerarius domini Johānis de mādeville militis. Printed about the year 1480. 4to.

It is not certain whether the first English edition was that printed by Wynkyn de Worde in 1499, or that by Pynson, without date. Pynson's, however, was probably earlier than 1499; it has no title, but the colophon is as follows:

Here endeth the boke of John Maimdvyle knyght of wayes to Jerusalem and of marveylys of ynde and of other countrees. Emprented by Rychard Pynson. 4to.

3. Albert Krantz. His historical and geographical works are—

I. Poloniæ et reipublicæ descriptio. Erfurti, 1575; fol.
II. Vandalia. Coloniæ, 1519; fol.
III. Regnorum aquilonarium Daniæ, Sueciæ, Norvagiæ, Chronica. Francofurti ad Moenum, 1575; fol.
IV. Saxonia. Francofurti ad Moenum, 1575; fol.

4. Pietro Martire Anghiera. His works are—

I. Opera. Legatio Babylonica; Oceani decas (one only); Poemata; Epigrammata. Hispali, per Jacobū Corumberger, 1511; fol.
II. De Orbe novo decades tres (with the Legatio Babylonica). Alcala, 1516; fol.
III. De Orbe novo decades (VIII). First complete edition. Compluti, 1530; fol.
IV. De nuper sub Carolo repertis insulis, simulq: incolarum moribus, R. Petri Martyris Enchiridion, Dominæ Margaritæ Diui Max. Cæs. filiæ dicatum. Basileæ, 1521; 4to.

v. Opus epistolarū Petri Martyris Anglerii Mediolanēsis Protonotarii aplíci atq : a cōsiliis rerū Indicarū nūc p̃mū et natū et mediocri cura excusum : quod q̃dē præter stili venustatē nostrorū qq; tēporum historie loco esse poterit. Cōpluti, 1530; fol.

5. Gonsalvo Hernandez de Oviedo y Valdez. He wrote—

 i. La historia general y natural de las Indias Occidentales. Toledo, 1526; fol.
 ii. La historia del estrecho de Magallanes ; which also forms book xx of the preceding work. Printed separately, 1552 ; fol.
 iii. Navegacion del rio Marañon. Printed in Ramusio; vol. 3, p. 415, edit. 1565.

6. Robert Thorne. What he wrote appeared for the first time in the " Divers voyages".

7. Girolamo Fracastoro. His geographical writings are comprised in his letters to Giambattista Ramusio, in which, amongst other subjects, he discusses at considerable length the periodical risings of the Nile.—Ramusio, vol. i, fol. 284 b. Edit. 1550.

8. Reinerus Gemma. He wrote a cosmography, also " Charta, qua continetur totius orbis descriptio", and " De principiis astronomiæ et cosmographiæ ac usu globi a se editi"; all which occur in the following work :

 i. Cosmographia Petri Apiani per Gemmam Frisium....jam demum ab omnibus vindicata mendis, ac nonnullis quoque locis aucta. Additis ejusdem argumenti libellis ipsius Gemmæ Frisii. Antverpiæ, Gregorio Bontio, 1550 ; 4to.

II. De Astrolabo Catholico Liber; which is inserted in Joannes Bellerus's edition of the Cosmographia of Appianus and Gemma, printed at Antwerp in 1584; 4to.

9. Antonio de Mendoza. His papers and despatches were used by Herrera in the composition of his "Historia general de los hechos de los Castellanos en las islas y tierra firme del mar Oceano"; and he also, while viceroy, caused a work to be written, entitled "De las cosas naturales y maravillosas de Nueva Hispaña", the authorship of which has been generally attributed to him.

10. Gerard Mercator. Besides the numerous maps and charts laid down by him, he published—

I. Tabulæ geographicæ ad mentem Ptolemæi restitutæ et emendatæ. Lovanii, 1589; fol.
II. Chronologia a mundi exordio ad annum 1568, ex eclypsibus & observationibus astronomicis ac Bibliis sacris; opus Onuphrio Panvinio probatum. Coloniæ, 1568; fol.
III. De usu annuli Astronomici. Lovanii, 1552.
IV. He edited also Globi terrestris Sculptura, 1541. And,
V. Globi cœlestis Sculptura. Lovanii, 1551.
VI. Galliæ tabulæ geographicæ. Germaniæ tabulæ geographicæ. Duysburgi Clivorum, 1585; fol.
VII. Italiæ, Sclavoniæ et Græciæ tabulæ geographicæ. Duisburgi, 1589; fol.
VIII. Atlas, sive cosmographicæ meditationes et fabrica mundi et fabricati figura. Duisburgi Clivorum, 1595; fol.

11. Giovanni Battista Guicciardini. He published a map, entitled—

Universi terrarum orbis imago, maxima forma; quam aquila biceps, alis expansis, comprehendit. Antverpiæ, 1549.

INTRODUCTION. xlvii

12. Giovanni Battista Ramusio.[1] He compiled three volumes of voyages and travels; the first was published anonymously, the second and third with his name. The first volume, which appeared in 1550, has the following title—

> Primo volume delle navigationi et viaggi nel qual si contiene la descrittione dell' Africa, et del paese del Prete Janni, con varii viaggi del mar Rosso a Calicut et insin all' Isole Molucche dove nascono le spetierie et la navigatione attorno il mondo. In Venetia, appresso gli heredi di Lucantonio Giunti, l'anno 1550.

The second volume appeared in 1559; and the third, three years earlier, viz., in 1556. That which is called the second volume was not published until two years after Ramusio's death. The titles of these volumes, as taken in an abridged form from the editions of 1574 and 1565, are as follows:

> Secondo volume delle navigationi, etc. Nel quale si contengono l'Historia delle cose de' Tartari e diversi fatti de' loro imperatori....varie descrittioni di diversi auttori dell' Indie Orientali, della Tartaria, della Persia, Armenia, Mengrelia, Zorzania, e altre provincie, &c. Et il viaggio della Tana. Con la descrittione de' nomi de' popoli, città, fiumi et porti d'intorno al mar Maggiore, &c. In Venetia nella stamperia de' Giunti, 1574; fol.
>
> Terzo volume delle navigationi, &c. Nel quale si contengono le navigationi al mondo nuovo, agli antichi incognito, fatte da Don Christoforo Colombo....con gl' acquisti fatti da lui e accresciuti poi da Fernando Cortese, da Francesco Pizarro et altri valorosi capitani, &c.

[1] Ramusio was born at Trevigi in 1485, and not at Venice in 1486, as erroneously stated in Note 11, at the foot of p. 3.

Le navigationi fatte dipoi alle dette Indie poste nella parte verso maestro Tramontana dette hora la Nuova Francia, &c. In Venetia nella stamperia de' Giunti, 1565; fol.

The materials for a fourth volume had been collected, but were destroyed by fire at the printer's.

13. Sebastian Münster. He was the author of—

I. Cosmographei oder Beschreibung aller Länder, Heerschaften, fürnemsten Stetten, Geschicten, Gebreuchen, Hantierungen, etc. Zum dritten mal trefflich sere gemeret und gebessert. Basil, H. Petri, 1550; fol.

The first edition was printed at the same place, and by the same printer, in 1541. From this work Richard Eden translated—

A treatise of the newe India with other new founde landes and ilandes, as well eastwarde as westwarde, as they are knowen and found in these oure dayes, after the descripcion of Sebastian Munster in his boke of universall cosmographie. London, by Edward Sutton, 1553; 8vo.

II. Tabulæ novæ ad geographiam Ptolemæi adjectæ.

III. Descriptio Germaniæ pro tabula Nic. Cusæ intelligenda, cum canone ejusdem tabulæ. Printed in Schardius, Historicum opus, commonly called Rerum Germanicarum Scriptores. Tom. i. Basileæ; fol.

14. Tommaso Giunti. The only connexion he appears to have had with the history of maritime discovery, was as one of the printers of Ramusio's Collection of Voyages and Travels. In 1559, after the death of Ramusio which occurred in 1557, Tommaso Giunti printed a second volume of the Collection, with a preface laudatory of Ramusio. At the end of the account of the Discovery of the Isles of Frisland,

etc., *post*, p. 90, this passage occurs: " This discourse was collected by Ramusio, secretarie to the state of Venice (*or by the printer, Thos. Giunti*). John Baptista Ramusio died in Padua in July 1557."

15. Clement Adams. See *post* under Richard Chancellor, No. 41.

16. Oronce Finé. His works are—

   i. De mundi sphæra sive cosmographiæ libri v. Parisiis, 1530; fol.

   ii. Nouvelle description de la France (a map). Paris, 1525.

   iii and iv. Two other maps, entitled, respectively; Nova descriptio terrarum ad intelligentiam utriusque testamenti maxime conducentium. Parisiis, 1536: And; Orbis totius recens et integra descriptio ad cordis humani effigiem. Parisiis, 1536.

17. Abraham Ortel. His geographical works are—

   i. Theatrum orbis terrarum. Antwerp, 1570; fol.

   ii. Synonymia geographica. Antwerp, 1578; 4to.

   iii. Thesaurus geographicus. Antwerp, 1596; fol.

   iv. Italiæ antiquæ specimen. Antwerp, 1584; fol.

   v. Gallia Cisalpina. Antwerp, 1590; fol.

   vi. Itinerarium per nonnullas Galliæ Belgicæ partes, ab Ortelio et Joanne Viviano descriptum. 1584; 12mo.

   vii. Parergon, sive veteris Geographiæ aliquot tabulæ; item nomenclator Ptolemaicus. Antwerp, 1595; fol.

   viii. Descriptio civitatum in agro Leodiensi. In number 2 of M. Z. Boxhornii autores præcipui de Leodiensi republica. Amsterdam, 1633; 16mo.

   ix. Tabula veteris et novæ Hispaniæ. In the Hispania illustrata. Tom. 1. Franckfort, 1603; fol.

18. Jeronimo Osorio. He wrote, inter alia—

De rebus Emmanuelis regis Lusitaniæ virtute et auspicio gestis libri duodecim. Ulyssiponæ, 1571; fol.

This work contains an account of the discoveries and conquests by the Portuguese in the East Indies.

19. André Thevet. He laid down several maps, and also wrote—

 I. Cosmographie du Levant. Lion, Jean de Tournes, 1556; 4to.
 II. Les singularités de la France Antarctique, autrement nommée Amerique, et de plusieurs terres et isles découvertes de nostre temps. Anvers, C. Plantin, 1558; 8vo.
 III. Cosmographie universelle. Paris, Lhuillier, 1575; fol.
 IV. Le grand insulaire et pilotage.
 V. Description de plusieurs isles.
 VI. Second voyage dans les terres australes et occidentales.

The last three works are in manuscript, in the Bibliothèque du Roi, at Paris.

20. François Belleforest. He edited, with great additions and numerous alterations, Münster's Cosmography, under the title—

La Cosmographie universelle de tout le monde....Auteur en partie Munster, mais beaucoup plus augmentée, ornée et enrichie par F. de Belleforest, tant de ses recherches, comme de l'aide de plusieurs memoires par hommes amateurs de l'histoire et de leur patrie. 2 vols. Paris, chez Michel Sonnius, 1575; fol.

21. Sir Humfrey Gilbert. He wrote—

A discourse of a discovery for a new passage to Cataia. Imprinted at London, by Henry Middleton, for Richard Ihones. 1576, Aprilis 12; 4to.

In this work there is a curious map, with the title

"A general map, made onelye for the particular declaration of this discovery"; in which all impediments in the way of the north-west passage are cleared away in a most summary manner.

22. Dionysius Settle. He wrote—

> A true reporte of the last [or rather the second] voyage into the west and northwest regions, &c., 1577, worthily atchieved by captaine Frobisher, of the sayde voyage the first finder and generall. With a description of the people there inhabiting, and other circumstances notable. London, by Henrie Middleton, 1577; 8vo.

Two editions of this work were printed in the year 1577.

23. George Best. He wrote an account of the three voyages of Sir Martin Frobisher for the discovery of the north-west passage, under the title of—

> A true discourse of the late voyages of discoverie, for the finding of a passage to Cathaya by the north-weast, under the conduct of Martin Frobisher, generall; devided into three bookes. In the first wherof is shewed his first voyage, wherein also, by the way, is sette out a geographical description of the worlde, and what partes thereof have bin discovered by the navigations of the Englishmen. Also, there are annexed certayne reasons to prove all partes of the worlde habitable, with a generall mappe adjoyned. In the second is set out his second voyage, with the adventures and accidents thereof. In the thirde is declared the strange fortunes which hapned in the third voyage, with a severall description of the countrey and the people there inhabiting. With a particular card thereunto adjoyned of meta incognita, so farre forth as the secretes of the voyage may permit. London, 1578; 4to.

24. Nicholas Chancellor. He drew up—

The second journal of Arthur Pet and Charles Jackman, in their discoverie northeastward, in the yeere 1580, with two barkes, the one called the William, the other the George.—Hakluyt, vol. i, p. 476.

25. The Rabbi Benjamin Ben Jonah. He wrote an account of his travels in Hebrew; the first edition of which in that language was published at Constantinople, at the Soncino press, in 1543, in 8vo. The earliest Latin edition has the following title:

Itinerarium Benjamini Tudelensis, in quo res memorabiles quas ante quadringentos annos totum fere terrarum orbem notatis itineribus dimensus vel ipse vidit vel a fide dignis suæ ætatis hominibus accepit, breviter atque dilucide describuntur; ex Hebraica Latinum factum, Bened. Aria Montano interprete. Antwerpiæ, 1575; 8vo.

26. Marco Polo. His work comprises an account of the travels of his father Nicolò, his uncle Maffeo, and himself, in the east. There has been much discussion, whether the account of these travels was written originally in Italian or in Latin; but it appears to be now generally admitted, that it was composed by Marco in the Venetian dialect, and not in the Latin language. Transcripts and translations were, however, speedily multiplied; and in the year 1477, the first printed copy issued from the press. This, however, was neither in Latin nor in Italian, but in German. The following is the title:

Hie hebt sich an das puch des edelñ Ritters vñ landtfarers Marcho polo. In dem er schreibt die grossen wunderlichen ding dieser welt. Sunderlichen von den grossen künigen vnd keysern die da herschen in den selbigen landen vnd von irem volck vnd seiner gewonheit da selbs. *End.* Diss hat gedruckt Friez Creüssner zu Nurm̄berg, 1477; fol.

The first edition in Italian was printed at Venice by "Zoanne Baptista da Sessa" in the year 1496, with the following title:

Marco Polo da Veniesia de le merauegliose cose del mondo; 8vo.

The Latin edition, like many books printed in the fifteenth century, has no title-page, but begins as follows:

In nomine dn̄i nri ihū xpi filii dei viui et veri amen. Incipit plogus ī libro dn̄i marci pauli de venecijs de cōsuetudinibus et cōdicionibus orientaliū regionū. It was printed about the year 1490; 4to.

27. Hatto. He drew up an account of various places in the east. His work is said to have been written in the French language, and it has been translated into many others. We give the titles of four editions (*i. e.*, two in French, one in Latin, and one in English), all of which were printed within a short time of each other, and between each of which there is more or less variation. That which immediately follows is supposed to be the earliest.

L'hystori merveilleuse, plaisante et recreative du grād empereur de Tartarie seigneur des Tartres nōme le grād Can. Cōtenāt six livres ou parties: Dont le premier traicte des singularitez et conditions des xiiii Royaulmes de Asye subjectz audict grand Chan. Le second parle des empereurs qui....ont regné et encore a present regnent en Asie....Le tiers descript q̄lle chose on doibt faire avāt que commencer la guerre. Le quart parle du voyage q̄ fist ung religieux des freres pscheurs allant....oultre mer prescher les mescreās....Le cinqesme cōtiēt commēt ung aultre religieux des freres mineurs alla oultre mer pour prescher les infidelles. Et fust jusques en la terre prebstre Jan....Le sixiesme p̱le du pays de surye et des villes sur mer degipte du desert du mōt de Synay darabe &c. Imprimée nouvellement a Paris en l'an 1529, pour Jehan sainct denys; fol.

In the commencement of this edition, it is stated that the author, after having for a long time followed the profession of arms under his uncle the king of Armenia, became a monk of the Premonstratensian Order in the kingdom of Cyprus in the abbey of the Epiphany, in which he wrote this book in the year 1310. And that this book was translated from Latin into French by Jean de Londit, a Benedictine monk of the abbey of St. Bertin, at St. Omer, in the year 1351.

Another French edition, printed without date, but certainly within a few years of the above, differs from it materially both in language and substance, and is entitled as follows:

Les fleurs des hystoyres de la terre Dorient. Cōpillees par frere Haycon seigneur du corc et cousin germain du roy Darmenie par le cōmandement du pape. Et sont divisees en cinq parties. La premiere partie contient la situation des royaulmes Dorient. La seconde parle des seigneurs q̇ en orient ont regne depuis lincarnation de nr̄e seigneur. La tierce partie parle des tartarins. La quarte p̱le des sarrazins et des turcz depuis le p̱mier jusq̇s aux presens q̇ ont conqueste rhodes, hongrie et dernieremēt assailly Austriche. La v. parle de Sophy roy de Perse et du prince Tamburlan. Nouvellement imprimee a Paris. 4to. With the device of Denis Janot on the verso of the last leaf.

The earliest Latin translation has the following title:

> Liber historiarum partium Orientis sive passagium terræ sanctæ, Haythono ordinis præmonstratensis authore: scriptus anno Redemptoris nostri 1300. Haganoæ, per Johan. Sec., anno 1529; 4to.

The preface to this edition, after stating that it was compiled by Haytho, adds :— "Which I, Nicholas Salconi, by command of Pope Clement V, first wrote in the French language in the city of Poitiers, as the said Friar Haytho verbally dictated it to me, without note or copy. And from the French I have translated it into Latin in the year 1307."

Not later than the same year (1529), Richard Pynson printed an English translation in folio, corresponding very closely with the Latin edition, but with the addition of matter not found in any of the three editions above mentioned. The title is—

> Here begynneth a lytell cronycle translated and imprinted at the cost and charge of Rycharde Pynson, by the cōmaundement of the ryght high and mighty prince Edwarde duke of Buckingham, yerle of Gloucestre Staffarde and of Northampton.

It is stated in the colophon, that this chronicle was translated out of French.

28. *Nicolò and Antonio Zeno.* The account of the travels of these brothers was published in the year 1558. The following is the title of the work in which it is found:

> Dei Commentarii del viaggio in Persia di M. Caterino Zeno il K. e delle guerre fatte nell' imperio Persiano dal tempo

di Ussuncassano in quà. Libri due. Et dello scoprimento dell' Isole Frieslanda, Eslanda, Engrovelanda, Estotilanda, et Icaria fatto sotto il Polo Artico da due fratelli Zeni, M. Nicolò il K. e M. Antonio. Libro uno. Con un disegno particolare di tutte le dette parti di Tramontana da lor scoperte. In Venetia, per Francesco Marcolini, 1558; 12mo.

29. Nicolò di Conti. He communicated his travels in the east to Poggio Bracciolini, by whom they were committed to writing in the Latin language, and form the fourth book of his *Historia de varietate fortunæ*, first published in 1723, by D. Georgi, from a manuscript in the Ottoboni Library. Georgi says in his preface, that this fourth book was published separately about 1492 : " Quartus vero continet elegantem ...Indiæ...descriptionem quam a Nicolao de Comitibus cive Veneto qui tum ex iis oris venerat Florentiæ hausit. Hic porro liber separatim prodiit circa annum 1492." No authority is given for this latter assertion; nor does an edition of 1492 appear to be known. Ramusio has inserted a translation into his Collection, vol. i, p. 365, edit. 1550; but his translation was made from a Portuguese version by Valentin Fernandez.

30. Cristoforo Colombo. The letters of Columbus comprise accounts of his first, third, and fourth voyages of discovery to the West Indies. The first letter, which was written in Spanish on the 14th of March 1493, was translated into Latin and published in the same year, with the title :

Epistola Christofori Colom: cui etas nostra multum debet; de insulis Indie supra Gangem nuper invētis. Ad quas perquirendas octavo antea mense auspiciis et ere invictissimorum Fernandi ac Helisabet Hispaniar̃ regū missus fuerat; ad magnificum dn̄m Gabrielem Sanches; eorundem Serenissimorum Regum Tesaurariū missa: Qua' generosus ac litteratus vir Leander de Cosco ab Hispana idiomate in Latinū cōvertit; tertio kaleñ Maii, 1493. Pontificatus Alexandri Sexti anno primo. Impressit Romæ Eucharius Argenteus anno dñi 1493; 4to.

The remaining letters, and also a memorial relating to the second voyage, and addressed to Ferdinand and Isabella, are printed in " Navarrete, Colleccion de los viages y descubrimientos que hicieron por mar los Españoles desde fines del siglo 15." Madrid, 1825; 8vo.

31. Sebastian Cabot. Hakluyt refers to " Mappes and Discourses drawne and written by himself (Cabot), which are in the custodie of the Worshipful Master William Worthington, etc." (*post* p. 26); but they are no longer to be found. The " Navigatione nelle parti settentrionali", generally attributed to him, and inserted in the second volume of Ramusio, edit. 1583, is nothing more than the Journal of Stephen Burrough's " Navigation and discoverie toward the river of Ob." This was first noticed by Mr. Biddle, in his Memoir of Cabot. We also find in Hakluyt, p. 259, edit. 1589: " Ordinances, instructions, and advertisements of and for the direction of the intended voyage for Cathaye, compiled .... the 9 day of May in the yere of our Lord God 1553."

32. Vasco da Gama. He wrote—

Relaçaō da viagem a India em a anno de 1597. MS.

33. Duarte Barbosa. He wrote an account of his

travels in the east, which has been translated into Italian, and inserted in the first volume of Ramusio's Collection, p. 288. Ramusio's translation was made from a copy of the Portuguese manuscript, original then at Lisbon.

34. Fernando de Magalhaens. He wrote—
 i. Roteiro da sua navegacaõ (MS.).
 ii. Mandado escrito em o canal de todos os Santos a 21 de Novembro de 1520 em o qual ordena a todos os capitaens a advirtaõ em tudo que for conveniente ao bom successo da Jornada que hia porseguiendo. Published in Barros, Decad. 3, da India, liv. 5, cap. 9.

35. Joaõ de Barros. He wrote—

Primeira decada da Asia, dos feitos que os Portuguezes fizeraõ no descubrimento e conquista dos mares e terras do Oriente. Lisboa, 1552; fol. Secunda decada da Asia, &c. Lisboa, 1553; fol. Terceira decada da India, &c. Lisboa, 1563; fol.

At his death he left a fourth Decade unfinished in manuscript, which was completed many years afterwards by Joaõ Baptista Lavanha, by order of Philip II of Portugal, and published at Madrid in 1613, in fol. Amongst his unpublished works are—

 i. Decada da Africa.
 ii. Geographia universalis.
 iii. Historia natural do Oriente.
 iv. Summario que trata das provincias do mundo em especial das Indias assi de Castella como das de Portugal, &c.

36. Jacques Cartier. We have accounts of three voyages made by J. Cartier. The first account which

was printed was of the second voyage, undertaken in the year 1535. The title is as follows:

Brief recit et succincte narration de la navigation faicte es ysles de Canada, Hochelage, et Saguenay et autres, avec particulieres meurs, langaige, et cerimonies des habitans d'icelles : fort delectable a veoir. Paris, par Ponce Roffet dict Faucheur et Anthoine le Clerc, freres, 1545 ; 8vo.

In 1598, the first voyage appeared under the title—

Discours du voyage de Jacques Cartier aux terres neufves de Canada, Norimbergue, Hochelage, Labrador, et pays adjacens dites Nouvelle France, en 1534. Rouen, Raph. du Petit, 1598 ; 8vo.

The Journal of the third voyage is printed in the third volume of Hakluyt's Collection. It does not appear that any of these journals were written by Cartier himself; indeed, the presumption is the other way.

37. Frances Vasques de Coronado. The third volume of Ramusio (p. 354, edit. 1565) contains—

Sommario di due sue lettere del viaggio fatto da Fra Marco da Nizza alle sette città di Cevola.

38. Juan Gaetano. He wrote—

Relatione del discoprimento dell' Isole Molucche per la via dell' Indie occidentali. In vol. i of Ramusio, fol. 403 ; edit. 1550.

39. François Xavier. Much geographical information is contained in his letters, written during his long residence in the east. The first publication was entitled—

Copie d'une lettre missive envoiée des Indes par monsieur maistre François Xavier a son prevost monsieur Egnace de Layola. Paris, Jehan Corbon, 1545; 8vo.

In 1600, Horatius Tursellinus printed at Mentz a collection of the letters of Xavier, under the title—

Francisci Xaverii epistolarum libri quatuor in Latinum conversi ex Hispano. 8vo.

And in 1661, Petrus Possinus printed at Paris the remainder, with the title—

S. Francisci Xaverii....Indiarum apostoli epistolæ novæ XVIII nunc primum ex autographis partim Hispanicis partim Lusitanicis Latinitate et luce donatæ. 12mo.

40. Sir Hugh Willoughby. In Hakluyt, vol. i, p. 265, edit. 1589, we find—

The true copie of a note found written in one of the two ships, to wit the Speranza, which wintered in Lappia, where sir Hugh Willoughby and all his companie died, being frozen to death. Anno 1553-4. O. S. This note is said to have been in the handwriting of sir Hugh Willoughby, and contains the names of the ships and their respective companies; the juramentum, or othe ministred to the captaine; the othe ministred to the maister of the ship, &c.; followed by a journal of the voyage from the 10th of May to the 18th of September.

41. Richard Chauncellor. He wrote—

The book of the great and mighty emperor of Russia and Duke of Moscovia, and of the dominions, orders and commodities thereunto belonging.—Hakluyt, vol. i, p. 237; edit. 1598.

" The newe navigation and discoverie of the kingdome of Moscovia by the north-east in the yeere 1553", is said to have been drawn up by Clement

Adams, from the dictation of Chancellor.—Hakluyt, vol. i, p. 270, edit. 1589; where the account is given in Latin and English.

42. Antonio Galvam. He was the author of a work entitled—

> Tratado dos varios e diversos caminhos por onde nos tempos passados a pimenta e especiaria veyo da India as nossas partes, e assim de todos os descubrimentos antigos e modernos que saõ feitos atè a era de 1550, &c. Lisboa, por Joao Barreira, 1563; 8vo.

He is also said to have written a work entitled—

> Historia dos Molucas, da natureza e descubrimento daquellas terras.

But it was never printed entire, and the original is not known to be now in existence; a great part, however, is said to have been inserted by Damiaõ de Goes, in his " Chronica del rey D. Manoel".

43. Stephen Burrough. He wrote—

> The navigation and discovery toward the river Ob (i. e. Obe), intending the discovery of the north-east passage: and, The voyage, an. 1557, from Colmogro to Wardhouse, which was sent to seeke the Bona Speranza, the Bona Confidentia, and the Philip and Mary, which were not heard of the yeere before. In Hakluyt, vol. i, p. 274-290.

44. William Burroughs. All that we appear to have of this navigator's writings, are the following short pieces:

> I. The copie of a letter sent to the emperour of Moscovie by Christopher Hodsdon and William Burrough, anno 1570, informing him that William Burroughs had taken five ships of the freebooters.—Hakluyt, vol. i, p. 425; edit. 1589.

II. The deposition of Mr. Wm. Burrough to certaine interrogatories ministred unto him concerning the Narve, Kegor, &c., to what king or prince they doe appertaine and are subject, made the 23 of June 1576.—Ibid. p. 438.

III. Certaine reasons to dissuade the use of a trade to the Narve aforesayd, by way through Sweden.—Ib. 439.

IV. The opinion of Master Wm. Burrough sent to a friend requiring his judgement for the fittest time of the departure of our ships towards S. Nicholas in Russia.—Ib. 487.

45. Anthony Jenkinson. He wrote the accounts of his several voyages, as follows:

I. The first voyage made by master Anthony Jenkinson from the citie of London toward the land of Russia, begonne the twelfth daye of Maye in the yeere 1557.

II. The voyage, wherein Osepp Napea, the Moscovite ambassadour to Queen Maria, returned home into his countrey. And a large description of the manners of the countrey, &c.

III. The voyage of mr. Anthony Jenkinson, made from the citie of Mosco in Russia, to the citie of Boghar in Bactria, in the yere 1558.

IV. A compendious declaration of the Journey of M. Anth. Jenkinson into the land of Persia, passing thorow Russia, Moscovia, and Mare Caspium. Anno 1561.

V. The voyage of Anthony Jenkinson into Russia the third time, an. 1566.

VI. The voyage of Anthony Jenkinson into Russia the fourth time, an. 1571.

These several accounts are printed in Hakluyt, vol. i, pp. 310, 314, etc.

46. Jean Ribault. He wrote, in French, an account of his voyage to Florida in the year 1562. This

appears to be no longer extant; but the title of the English translation, published in 1563, and which Hakluyt has reprinted in this collection, is given at p. 17 *post*.

47. Luke Ward. He wrote—

> The voyage intended towards China, wherein Mr. Edward Fenton was appointed generall. Written by Mr. Luke Ward, his vice-admiral and captaine of the Edward Bonaventure, begun anno Dom. 1582. In Hakluyt, vol. iii, p. 757; edit. 1600.

48. Edward Heyes. He wrote—

> A report of the voyage and successe thereof attempted in the yeere 1583, by Sir H. Gilbert, knight, with other gentlemen, intended to discover and to plant Christian inhabitants upon those large and ample countries extended northward from the Cape of Florida; written by Mr. Edward Haies, the principal actor in the same voyage. In Hakluyt, vol. iii, p. 143; edit. 1600.

" A very late and great probabilitie of a passage of the north-west part of America in fifty-eight degrees of northerly latitude", refers most probably to Hudson's Straits. It is well known that the Spaniards made some feeble attempts to discover the north-west passage, but whether the expedition here referred to as sent out by one Anus Cortereal be one of them, or whether such an expedition was ever sent out at all, it is impossible now to ascertain. Hakluyt was a man of easy faith, and too apt to repeat accounts as he received them, without stopping to verify or correct them. This " late probabilitie" would doubtless be an important addition to the eight reasons mentioned in his epistle to Sir Philip Sidney, and as such, not lightly to be rejected. It is much to be regretted, however, that he has not informed us who the "singularly grave and experienced man of Portingale", his informant, was. The eight reasons alluded to in proof of the probability of a north-west passage are: 1. The opinion of Cabot that all the north part of America is divided into islands. 2. That the passage is laid down in the map by Verazzani. 3. The story of Gil Gonsalva, recorded by Franciscus Lopes de Gomara, which, however, amounts to no more than a statement that Gil Gonçalez de Avila in 1522 explored the western coast of Mexico from Capo Blanco to Capo de Fonseca, for the purpose of finding a strait which it was said by the pilots existed thereabouts, and by which they could pass from the South Sea to the Atlantic Ocean.[1] 4. The report of the people of Saguinay to Jacques Cartier, that upon their coasts westward there was a sea the end whereof was unknown to them. 5. The assertion, by the inhabitants of Canada, that it is a month's space to sail to a land where cinnamon and cloves are growing. 6. That the people of Florida stated to Ribault that they might sail from the river of May unto Cevola and the South Sea through their country in twenty days. 7. The experience of Frobisher and Drake, one on the west coast of America, and the other on the east. 8. The opinion, or rather conjecture, of Mercator, that there must be a short way

[1] Lopez de Gomara. *La Historia general de las Indias*, fol. 258. Anvers, 1554. 12mo.

open into the west. It is not necessary at the present day to enter into any arguments to show the utter futility of these eight reasons. In the year 1582, however, the case was widely different : enough had been discovered to whet the appetite. To say nothing of the pretended voyages of the Zeni at the end of the fourteenth century, which were then universally received as genuine, Sebastian Cabot, there is great reason to believe, penetrated as high as 67 degrees of north latitude, discovering Hudson's Straits and Fox's Channel, in his search after the north-west passage to India. Gaspar Cortereal, in 1500, explored the eastern coast of America with the same object, and discovered the St. Lawrence, and also Hudson's Straits. Jacques Cartier in 1534 found the St. Lawrence, and explored it as high as Montreal, and from the statements of the natives, great expectations were entertained that the passage so ardently desired had been at length discovered. Frobisher, in his first voyage, in 1576, discovered in latitude 63 the strait which long bore his name, and has subsequently been called Lumley's Inlet; and in his second and third voyages, made in the two following years, he penetrated further into the strait, and also made his way into Hudson's Straits, although with no better success than on his former voyages. The time mentioned by Hakluyt, "not above eight yeres past", would be about 1574, and as the attention of navigators had since that time been always directed to Frobisher's Straits, this apparently new discovery might well be considered by him worthy of special mention.

The next piece in the collection is the epistle dedicatorie to "Master Philip Sydney, Esquire". It is well known that Sir Philip Sidney took a great interest in whatever tended to the honour and advantage of his native country, and it cannot be supposed that he looked with only ordinary interest upon the efforts made by such men as Frobisher and Drake for enlarging the limits of geographical knowledge. Although little is said by his biographers upon this point, it is more than probable that he occupied a prominent place among those who favoured the various adventurers in search of gold mines and new worlds. In October 1576, Frobisher returned from his first voyage in search of a north-west passage. His supposed success, both on this point and in the discovery of gold ore, caused great excitement in England, and Sidney wrote to his early friend and watchful adviser, Hubert Linguet, in such glowing terms of Frobisher and this expedition, as to draw from him (Linguet) a long and striking reply, in which he says : " Si vera sunt quæ de vestro Forbissero scribis, ille haud dubie obscurabit non solum Magellani sed etiam ipsius Christophori Columbi famam..... Ego vero ad te respicio qui hanc ob rem exaltas perinde ac si patria esset optime consultum, cum præsertim superiore vere in te animadverterim cupiditatem aliquam suscipiendæ ejusmodi navigationis." Linguet was right in his conjecture that Sidney contemplated undertaking one of these voyages of discovery. There can be little doubt that he entered into arrangements with Sir Humphrey Gilbert, taking from him an assignment of part of his interest under the letters patent granted to him by Queen Elizabeth in 1578.[1] He also, at a later period, made secret preparations for associating himself with Sir Francis Drake in his second expedition, of which he (Sidney) was to have had the principal direction, and had even engaged to equip a naval and land armament, and to make a vigorous attack upon the Spanish settlements in America. He was only prevented carrying this design into effect by the express command of the queen. It was not without reason, therefore, that Hakluyt addressed to Sir Philip Sidney a collection of documents, the object of which was to induce his countrymen to make permanent settlements in America: and we find that when in 1584 a bill was brought into parliament for confirming the letters patent granted by the queen to Sir Walter Raleigh for discovering remote heathen lands, it was committed, on the second reading, to the care of Sir Philip Sidney jointly with Hatton, then vice-chamberlain, Sir Francis Drake, and others.[2]

Full as this epistle is of various and most important topics, the author has laid out his views in so clear and concise a manner as to render any additional explanation here altogether superfluous. One of the points upon which he insists is "the title which we have to that part of America which is from Florida to 67 degrees northwarde, by the letters patentes graunted to John Gabote and his three sonnes, Lewis,

---

[1] See *Gentleman's Magazine*, Feb. 1850, p. 116, et seqq.
[2] Zouch's *Life of Sydney;* Linguet, *Epist. ad P. Sydneium,* p. 176-177.

Sebastian and Santius, with Sebastian's owne certificate to Baptista Ramusius of his discoverie of America, and the testimonie of Fabian our old chronicler." This forms the subject of the next division of the collection before us.

The honour of having discovered North America is claimed by most English writers for John Cabot, or Gabota, a Venetian, who was residing in Bristol as a merchant in the year 1594. In the preceding year all Europe had been astonished by the unlooked-for discoveries of Columbus, and Cabot, who appears to have possessed a bold and adventurous spirit, conceived the idea of following in the same track. With this object in view, he solicited the sanction of the king, Henry VII, to his undertaking, and on the 5th of March 1496,[1] the letters patent above referred to were granted to John Cabot and his three sons. The expedition did not sail until the following year, and no very intelligible details of the voyage are in existence. There are, however, several accounts more or less contradictory. Hakluyt has inserted no less than six in his general collection. Perhaps the most precise is that which was inscribed in Latin by Clement Adams upon a map drawn by Sebastian, and engraved by Adams, but which is no longer in existence. This notice runs as follows: " In the year of our Lord

[1] This patent is sometimes said to have been granted in 1495, which would be correct according to the computation of the civil year at that period, viz., from the 25th of March; but as Henry VII commenced his reign on the 22nd of August 1485, the 5th of March in the eleventh year of his reign would fall in the year 1496, according to the historical computation.

1497, John Cabot, a Venetian, and his son Sebastian, discovered that country, which no one before his time had ventured to approach, on the 24th of June, about five o'clock in the morning. He called the land Terra primum visa, because, as I conjecture, this was the place that first met his eyes in looking from the sea. On the contrary, the island which lies opposite the land, he called the island of St. John—as I suppose, because it was discovered on the festival of St. John the Baptist. The inhabitants wear beasts' skins and the intestines of animals for clothing, esteeming them as highly as we do our most precious garments. In war their weapons are the bow and arrow, spears, darts, slings, and wooden clubs. The country is steril and uncultivated, producing no fruit ; from which circumstance it happens that it is crowded with white bears and stags of an unusual height and size. It yields plenty of fish, and these very large, such as seals and salmon : there are soles also above an ell in length ; but especially great abundance of that kind of fish called in the vulgar tongue baccalaos. In the same island also breed hawks, so black in their colour that they wonderfully resemble ravens; besides which there are partridges and eagles of dark plumage." The map upon which this account was inscribed was engraved in the year 1549,[1] fifty-two years after the event recorded took place; but it has been suggested with much plausibility[2] that Adams may have been

---

[1] Purchas, vol. iii, p. 807.
[2] Tytler, *Historical View of the Progress of Discovery on the more Northern Coasts of America*, p. 23. Edinb. 1832, 12mo.

employed by Sebastian Cabot himself to engrave this map in order to gratify Edward VI, with whom he was in great favour, and that this account of the discovery of Newfoundland may have been supplied by Sebastian.

The author of the Memoirs of S. Cabot argues with great show of reason, that the land first visited by John Cabot was Labrador, and not the island of Newfoundland. The name of the vessel which first touched the shores of America was the Matthew, of Bristol. The fact of this discovery having been made by John Cabot and not Sebastian, is alluded to in a second patent granted to " John Kabotto, Venetian", giving him license to sail with six ships " to the land and isles of late found by the said John in our name and by our commandment." It is not our object to enter into any examination of the various accounts extant respecting the voyages of the Cabots, father and son; neither do we purpose attempting to settle the respective claims of these two great men to the discovery of the North American continent. To an impartial mind the quotations given above would, in all probability, prove sufficiently conclusive. The author of the Memoirs of S. Cabot however takes a far different view of the question, and we cannot therefore quit this part of our subject without noticing the pertinacity and ingenuity with which he endeavours to set aside John Cabot, and disputes all evidence calculated to disprove his theory in favour of Sebastian.[1] The

[1] See *Memoir of Sebastian Cabot,* cap. x, where the author treats this subject at some length, and brings forward many interesting particulars.

extract given by Hakluyt from Fabyan, must refer to the voyage made by Sebastian after the second patent had been granted to his father.

The next paragraph of Hakluyt's work refers to three savage men, said to have been brought home by Sebastian in 1498, and presented to the king. Here again Mr. Biddle steps in to defend his protégé,[1] and contends that these men were not brought home by Cabot, repelling with great energy the charge that he would be guilty of so cruel an act as carrying off the aborigines of the country. This cruel act, he contends, must have been perpetrated by "three Portuguese", who, jointly with Richard Warde, Thomas Ashehurst, and John Thomas, obtained letters patent from Henry VII in 1501, conferring upon them the same powers, and couched in the same terms as we find in the letters patent granted to John Cabot and his sons in 1496.

While upon this part of our subject, it may not be out of place to give a list of the several patents granted by the sovereigns of England for the discovery and planting of unknown lands.

The first is the patent granted by Henry VII in 1496 to John Cabot and his sons, as mentioned above, and which is printed in this collection, *post*, p. 19.

On the 3rd of February 1498, Henry VII granted a second patent to John Cabot alone. This patent has often been referred to, but was printed for the first time in the Memoir of Sebastian Cabot by Mr. Biddle, who discovered this interesting document in

[1] *Memoir of S. Cabot*, p. 229.

the Rolls' chapel. It is of much importance in examining the question of the first discovery of America, and we therefore give it at length.

Memorandum quod tertio die Februarii anno regni Regis Henrici Septimi xiii ista Billa delibata fuit Domino Cancellario Angliæ apud Westmonasterium exequenda.

TO THE KINGE.

Please it your highnesse of your most noble and habundaunt grace to graunte to John Kabotto, Venecian, your gracious Lettres Patents in due fourme, to be made accordyng to the tenor hereafter ensuyng, and he shall continually praye to God for the preservacion of your moste noble and roiall astate longe to endure.

H. R.

REX.

To all men to whom theis presenteis shall come send gretyng: knowe ye that we of our grace especiall and for dyvers causis us movying, we have geven and graunten, and by theis presentis geve and graunte to our welbeloved John Kabotto, Venecian, sufficiente auctorite and power, that he by him, his deputie or deputies sufficient, may take at his pleasure VI Englisshe shippes in any porte or portes or other place within this our realme of England, or obeisance, so that and if the said shippes be of the bourdeyn of cc tonnes, or under, with their apparail requisite and necessarie for the safe conduct of the said shippes, and them convey and lede to the londe and isles of late founde by the seid John in oure name and by our commaundemente, paying for theym and every of theym as and if we should in or for our owen cause paye and noon otherwise. And that the said John, by hym, his deputie or deputies sufficiente, maye take and receyve into the said shippes, and every of theym, all such maisters, maryners, pages, and other subjects, as of their owen free wille wole goo and passe with him in the same shippes to the seid londe or iles without anye impedymente, lett, or perturbance, of any of our officers or ministres or subjects, whatsoever they be, by theym to the seyd John, his deputie, or deputies, and all other our seid subjects, or any of theym passinge with the seid John in the seid shippes to the seid londe or iles, to be doon, or suffer to be doon or attempted. Geving in commaundement to all and every our officers, ministers, and subjects, seying or herying theis our Lettres Patents without any ferther commaundement by us to theym, or any of theym, to be geven to perfourme, and socour the said John, his deputie, and all our said subjects so passyng with hym, according to the tenor of theis our Letters Patentis. Any Statute, Acte, or Ordennance, to the contrarye made or to be made in any wise notwithstanding.

The next patent, in order of date, was granted by Henry VII on the 19th of March 1501, to Richard Warde, Thomas Ashehurst, and John Thomas, of Bristol, and John Fernandus, Francis Fernandus, and John Gunsolus, subjects of the King of Portugal. This document also was first brought to light by Mr. Biddle. It was discovered by him in the Rolls' chapel, and is printed in the Appendix to his Memoir of Cabot. As it is not likely to become very generally known through either of these channels we have thought it advisable to give it here at length. It is as follows:

Memorandum quod xix die Marcii, anno regni Regis Henrici Septimi xvi, ista Billa delibata fuit Domino Custodi Magni Sigilli Angliæ apud Westmonasterium exequenda.

TO THE KYNG OUR SOVEREYNE LORD.

Please it your Highness of your most noble and habundaunt

l

lxxiv INTRODUCTION.

Grace to graunt unto your welbeloved subjects Richard Warde, Thomas Asshehurst, and John Thomas, merchants of your Towne of Bristowe, and to John Fernandus, Francis Fernandus, and John Gunsolus, Squyers, borne in the Isle of Surrys under the obeisaunce of the Kynge of Portingale, your gracious Lettres Patentis, under your Greate Seale, in due forme to be made according to the tenour hereafter ensuying; and that this Byll, sygned with your gracious hand, may be to the Reverend Fader in God, Henry, Byshop of Salesbury, Keeper of your Greate Seale, sufficient and immediate warrant for the making, sealyng, accomplysshyng, of your said Lettres Patentes, and they shall duryng ther lyves pray to God for the prosperous contynuance of your most noble and ryall astate.

H. R.

Rex universis et singulis ad quos præsentes Literæ Nostræ pervenerint Salutem : Notum sit vobis et manifestum quod ex certis considerationibus nos moventibus de advisamento Consilii Nostri, concessimus et licentiam dedimus, prout per Præsentes concedimus et licentiam damus, pro Nobis et hæredibus nostris quantum in Nobis est, dilectis subditis nostris Ricardo Warde, Thomæ Asshurst, et Johanni Thomas, mercatoribus villæ nostræ Bristolliæ ac dilectis nobis Johanni Fernandus, Francisco Fernandus, et Johanni Gunsolus, armigeris in insulis de Surrys sub obediencia Regis Portugaliæ oriundis, et eorum cuilibet ac cujuslibet eorum hæredibus, attornatis, factoribus, seu deputatis ac eis et eorum cuilibet plenam ac liberam auctoritatem, facultatem et potestatem committimus navigandi et se transferendi ad omnes partes, regiones et fines Maris Orientalis, Occidentalis, Australis, Borealis et Septentrionalis, sub banneris, et insigniis nostris cum tot et tantis et talibus navibus sive batellis quot sibi placuerint et necessariæ fuerint, cujuscunque portagii quilibet navis sive batella extiterit, cum magistris, contromagistris, marinariis pagettis aliisque hominibus pro gubernatione, salva custodia et defensione navium et batellarum prædictarum competentibus requisitis et necessariis, ad custus et onera dicti Ricardi et aliorum prædictorum et pro hujusmodi salariis, vadiis et stipendiis prout inter eos poterunt concordare ad inveniendum, recuperandum, discoperiendum et investigandum insulas, patrias, regiones sive. provincias quascunque gentilium et infidelium in quacunque mundi parte positas quæ Christianis omnibus ante hæc tempora fuerunt et in præsenti sunt incognita.

Ac hujusmodi banneras et insignia nostra in quacunque villa, oppido, castro, insula seu terra-firma a se sic noviter inventis affigendi, ipsasque villas, oppida, castra, insulas et terras firmas pro nobis et nomine nostro intrandi et capiendi et ea tanquam vasalli nostri ac gubernatores, locatenentes et deputati nostri, eorumque dominio, titulo, dignitate et præeminencia eorundem nobis semper reservatis, occupandi, possidendi et subjugandi.

Et insuper quandocumque, imposterum, hujusmodi insulæ patriæ, terræ et provinciæ per præfatos Ricardum et alios prævocatos adeptæ, recuperatæ et inventæ fuerint, tunc volumus et per præsentes concedimus quod omnes et singuli tam viri quam fœminæ hujus regni nostri cæterique subditi nostri et insulas hujusmodi sic noviter inventas visitare et in eisdem inhabitare cupientes et desiderantes, possint et valiant licite et impune ad ipsas patrias, insulas et loca cum eorum navibus, hominibus et servientibus, rebus et bonis suis universis transire et in eisdem sub protectione et regimine dictorum Ricardi et aliorum prænominatorum morari et inhabitare, divitiasque, fructus et emolumenta patriarum, terrarum et locorum prædictorum adquirere et obtinere.

Dantes insuper et concedentes præfatis Ricardo, Thomæ et Johanni, Johanni, Francisco et Johanni et eorum cuilibet plenam tenore Præsentium potestatem et auctoritatem omnes et singulos homines, marinarios cæterasque personas ad insulas, patrias, provincias, terras firmas et loca prædicta ex causa prædicta, se divertentes et confluentes tam in comitiva dictorum Ricardi et aliorum prænominatorum quam in comitiva aliorum illuc imposterum recursum habere contingentium tam supra mare quam in insulis, patriis, terris-firmis et locis hujusmodi post quam inventa et recuperata fuerint regendi et gubernandi legesque ordinationes, statuta et proclamationes pro bono et quieto regimine et gubernatione dictorum hominum, magistrorum, marinariorum, et aliarum personarum prædictarum faciendi, stabiliendi, ordinandi et constituendi et superinde proclamationes faciendi ac omnes et singulos quos in hac parte contrarios et rebelles ac legibus, statutis et ordinacionibus prædictis inobedientes invenerint ac omnes illos qui furtum, homicidia, rapinas commiserint et perpetrarint aut aliquas mulieres insularum seu patriarum prædictarum, contra eorum voluntatem aut aliter, rapuerint et violaverint juxta leges et statuta per ipsos in hac parte ordinata castigandi et puniendi. Ac etiam concessimus præfatis Ricardo, Thomæ, Johanni, Johanni, Francisco et Johanni hæredibus et assignatis suis quod postquam aliquæ insulæ, provinciæ, terræfirmæ, regio seu provincia imposterum per ipsum Ricardum et alios prænominatos inventa fuerint tunc non licebit alicui seu aliquibus subdito seu subditis nostris durante termino decem annos proximo et immediate sequentes ad ipsas villas, provincias, insulas, terras-firmas et loca causa mercandisandi ac bona acquirendi *absque licentia nostra regia et* [the words in *italics* illegible, but supplied conjecturally from the corresponding paragraph in the subsequent patent of 9th December 1502] dictorum Ricardi et aliorum prænominatorum hæredum et assignatorum suorum cum suis navibus frequentare aut se divertere aut in eadem ingredi seu in eisdem pro aliquibus bonis acquirendi intromittere.

Et post terminum dictorum decem annorum quod nullus ex nostris subditis ad aliquam terram-firmam, insulam, patriam seu loca per ipsos Ricardum et Thomam et alios prædictos sic noviter inventa navigare et frequentare præsumat absque *licentia nostra prædicta et* [the words in *italics* supplied as before] prædictorum Ricardi et cæterorum sub pœna amissionis et forisfacturæ omnium bonorum, mercandisarum, rerum et navium quarumcunque ad ea loca sic noviter inventa navigare et in eadem ingredi præsumentium (videlicet) una medietas inde erit ad opus nostrum et alia medietas ad opus dictorum Ricardi et aliorum prænominatorum et hæredum suorum.

Et ultius ex abundanti gratia nostra concessimus et per Præsentes concedimus pro Nobis et hæredibus nostris, quantum in Nobis est, præfatis Ricardo, Thomæ, Johanni, Johanni, Francisco et Johanni et eorum quilibet mercandisas, mercimonia, aurum et argentum in massa, lapides preciosos et alia bona quæcumque de crescentia patriarum, insularumque et locorum prædictorum per ipsos sic recuperandorum et inveniendorum tam in dictis navibus et batellis quam aliis quibuscumque navibus exteris a dictis patriis, insulis, terrisfirmis et locis in hoc regnum nostrum Angliæ ad quemcunque portum seu alium locum ejusdem adducere et cariare et adduci seu cariari facere possit et valeat, eaque vendere et distribuere ad eorum proficium et advantagium, aliquo statuto, actu, ordinatione seu provisione inde in contrarium factis sive ordinatis nonobstantibus.

Ac Nos intime considerantes grandia custus et onera quæ circa præmissa facienda et perimplenda requiruntur, volentes igitur præfatis Ricardo, Thomæ et aliis memoratis personis gratiam provide facere specialem concessimus *(prout)* per Præsentes concedimus eisdem, hæredibus et assignatis suis quod ipsi et eorum quilibet hæredes et assignati sui prædicti de tempore in tempus durante termino quatuor annorum a tempore recuperationis et inventionis insularum, et provinciarum prædictarum proximo et immediate sequentes, mercandisas, mercimonia cæteraque bona in uno navi tantum cujuscunque portagii fuerit eskippata et onustata ac in hoc regnum nostrum Angliæ adducenda et transportanda in portu seu loco prædicto ad terram ponere, eaque vendere, exponere et pro libito suo distribuere possint de tempore in tempus, quolibet viagio, durante termino dictorum quatuor annorum, absque aliquibus custumis, subsidiis, seu aliis deveriis pro eisdem bonis mercimoniis et cæteris præmissis in dicta unica navi tantum contentis et eskippatis nobis aut hæredibus nostris infra dictum regnum nostrum Angliæ aliqualiter solvendis.

Proviso tamen quod Nobis de custumis, subsidiis, pondagiis et aliis deveriis Nobis pro cæteris mercandisis, mercimoniis et bonis in omnibus aliis navibus contentis debitis juxta consuetudinem in hoc regno nostro Angliæ hactenus usitatam fideliter respondeatur ut est justum. Et insuper volumus et concedimus per Præsentes quod quilibet capitalis magister, contra magister et marinarius cujuslibet navis ad aliquam terram-firmam, insulam, patriam, provinciam et locum prædictum frequentantis et navigantis habeant, gaudeant et percipiant de bonis et mercimoniis a dictis insulis, terris-firmis et provinciis in hoc regnum Angliæ adducendis custumas et subsidia sequentia, videlicet.

Quod quilibet magister habeat, gaudeat et percipiat subsidia et custumas, quolibet viagio, quatuor doliorum.

Et quilibet contramagister vel quarter-magister custumas et subsidia duorum doliorum.

Ac quilibet marinarius custumas et subsidia unius dolii.

Licet *sint caveata et eskippata* [the words in *italics* supplied as before] ut bona sua propria aut ut bona alicujus alterius personæ cujuscunque et hoc absque aliquibus custumis, subditis debitis seu deveriis infra hoc regnum nostrum Angliæ ad opus nostrum aut hæredum nostrorum pro eisdem doliis aliqualiter solvendis seu petendis.

Et si contingat aliquem vel aliquos mercatorem seu mercatores hujus regni nostri ad dictas insulas, patrias et loca sub licencia dictorum subdictorum nostrorum aut absque licencia causa habendi mercandisas et mercimonia adventare et laborare ad bona et mercimonia ab eisdem partibus in hoc regnum nostrum adducere, tunc volumus et concedimus, per præsentes, præfatis Ricardo, Thomæ, Johanni, Johanni, Francisco, Johanni hæredibus et assignatis suis quod ipsi durante termino decem annorum antedicto habeant de quolibet hujusmodi mercatore, solutis nobis custumis, subsidiis et aliis deveriis Nobis in hac parte debitis et consuetis, vicesimam partem omnium hujusmodi bonorum et mercimoniarum per ipsos a dictis insulis, patriis et locis quolibet viagio durante dicto termino decem annorum in hoc regnum nostrum Angliæ traducendorum et caricandorum habendam et capiendam hujusmodi vicesimam partem in portu ubi contigerit dicta bona discaricari et exonerari.

Proviso semper quod predicti Ricardus et alii prædicti, hæredes et assignati sui et non alii omnino imposterum durante dicto termino decem annorum sint Factores et Attornati in dictis insulis, terris-firmis et patriis pro quibuscunque hujusmodi mercatoribus aliisque personis illuc ex causa prædicta confluentibus in et pro eorum factis mercatoriis in eisdem.

Proviso etiam quod nulla navis cum bonis et mercandisis a dictis partibus sic noviter inventis carcati et onusta *postquam in aliquam portum hujus* [the words in *italics* supplied as before] Regni nostri adducta fuerint non exoneratur de eisdem bonis et mercandisis nisi in præsentia præfactorum Ricardi et aliorum prædictorum eorumve hæredum seu deputatorum ad hoc assignandum sub pœna forisfacturæ eorumdem bonarum et mercandisarum; unde una medietas ad opus nostrum et alia medietas præfatis Ricardo et aliis prænominatis et hæredibus suis applicentur.

Et si imposterum aliqui extran-*ei aut aliæ* [the part in *italics* supplied as before] personæ ad ipsas partes contra voluntatem ipsorum Ricardi et aliorum prænominatorum causa habendi divitias navigare et ea vi et armis ingredi ac dictos Ricardum et alios prædictos aut hæredes suos ibidem insultare ac eos expellere et debellare aut alias inquietare presumpserint quod tunc volumus ac eisdem subditis nostris tenore Præsentium damus et committimus ipsos extraneos licet sint subditi et vasalli alicujus principis Nobiscum in liga et amicitia existentis totis suis viribus tam per terram quam per mare et aquas dulces expugnandi, resistendi et gueriam contra eos levandi et faciendi eosque capiendi, subpeditandi et incarcerandi ibidem quousque fines et redemptiones eisdem subditis nostris facerint moratur aut alias secundum sanam discretionem ipsorum subditorum nostorum et hæredum suorum castigandi et puniendi.

At etiam præfatis subditis nostris cæterisque personis prædictis plenam tenore Præsentium potestatem damus et committimus sub se quoscumque capitaneos, locatenentes et deputatos in singulis civitatibus, villis, oppidis et locis dictarum insularum, provinciarum, patriarum et locorum prædictorum ad regendum et gubernandum omnes et singulas personas in eisdem partibus sub regimine et gubernatione dictorum subdictorum nostorum ibidem commorantium ac ad justitiam eisdem secundum tenorem et effectum ordinationum, statutorum et proclamationum prædictorum debite exequendum et administrandum per Literas suas Patentes sigillis eorum sigillandas, faciendi, constituendi, nominandi et substituendi. Et insuper concessimus et per Præsentes concedimus præfatis Ricardo, Thomæ, Johanni, Johanni, Francisco et Johanni ad terminum vitæ suæ et cujuslibet eorum diutius viventis officium Admiralli supra Mare in quibuscunque locis, patriis, et provinciis a se sic noviter inventis et imposterum inveniendis et recuperandis, ipsosque Ricardum, Thomam, Johannem, Johannem, Franciscum, Johannem et eorum quemlibet conjunctim et divisim Admirallos nostros in eisdem partibus facimus, constituimus, ordinamus et deputamus, per Præsentes dantes et concedentes eisdem et eorum cuilibet plenam tenore Præsentiarum potestatem et auctoritatem ea omnia et singula quæ ad officium

Admirallitatis pertinent faciendi, exercendi et exequendi secundum legem et consuetudinem maritimam in hoc regno nostro Angliæ usitatam.

Ac etiam postquam præfati Ricardus Warde, Thomas Ashhurst et Johannes Thomas, ac Johannes Fernandus, Franciscus Fernandus et Johannes Gunsolus aliquas terras-firmas, insulas, patrias et provincias, oppida, castra, civitates et villas per assistentiam nostram sic invenerint, obtinuerint, et subjugaverint tunc volumus et per Præsentes concedimus eisdem, hæredibus et assignatis suis, quod ipsi et hæredes sui habeant, teneant et possideant sibi, hæredibus et assignatis suis omnia et singula talia et tanta, terras-firmas, insulas, patrias, provincias, castra, oppida, fortallicia, civitates et villas qualia et quanta ipsi et homines tenentes et servientes sui possunt inhabitare, custodire, sustinere et manutenere: Habenda et Tenenda easdem terras, insulas et loca prædicta sibi, hæredibus et assignatis suis et cujuslibet eorum de nobis et hæredibus nostris imperpetuum per fidelitatem tantum absque aliquo compoto seu aliquo alio nobis aut hæredibus nostris proinde reddendo seu faciendo, Dignitate, Dominio, Regalitate, Jurisdictione, et Pre-eminentia in eisdem nobis semper salvis et omnino reservatis.

Et ultius concessimus præfatis Ricardo, Thomæ, Johanni, Johanni, Francisco, Johanni quod ipsi, hæredes et assignati sui prædicti dictas terras-firmas, insulas et provincias ipsis et hæredibus suis prædictis ut præmittitur sic concessas, postquam inventæ et recuperatæ sint, ac cum in plena possessione earundem fuerint teneant, possideant et gaudeant liberè, quiete, et pacifice absque impedimento aliquali nostri aut hæredum nostrorum quarumcunque. Et quod nullus ex subditis nostris eos eorum aliquem de et super possessione et titulo suis de et in dictis terris-firmis, insulis et provinciis se aliqualiter contra voluntatem suam expellat quovis modo *seu aliquis extraneus aut aliqui extranei virtute aut colore alicujus concessionis nostræ sibi Magno Sigillo Nostro per antea factæ aut imposterum faciendæ cum aliquibus aliis locis et insulis* ...... *et contiguis ac membris et parcellis præfatis insulis, terris-firmis provinciis et locis* .... *absque licentia* .... *subditorum nostrorum et aliorum prænominatorum aliquo modo intromittat nec intromittant.* [Through the words in *italics* the pen is drawn in the original, and a space then occurs, from which the writing has been carefully and completely erased.] Promittentes bona-fide et in verbo regio Nos ratum gratum et firmum habituros totum et quicquid præfati Ricardus, Thomas, Johannes, Johannes, Franciscus et Johannes et eorum quilibet pro præmissorum complemento fecerint fierique procuraverint in hac parte. Et quod Nos aut hæredes nostri nullo unquam tempore in futuro ipsos aut eorum aliquem hæredes et assignatos suos in jure, titulo et possessione suis inquietabimus, impediemus aut molestium eis faciemus nec per alios nostros subditos aut alios quoscunque quantum in nobis fuerit fieri seu procurari permittemus seu procurabimus, nec ipsos hæredes et assignatos suos pro aliqua causa imposterum emergente seu contingente ab eisdem terris-firmis, provinciis et locis nullo modo amovebimus aut amoveri seu expelli per subditos nostros procurabimus. Et ultius ex uberiori gratia nostra et mero motu nostro concessimus et per Præsentes concedimus pro nobis et hæredibus quantum in nobis est Johanni Fernandus, Francisco Fernandus et Johanni Gunsolus, Armigeris de Insulis de Surrys subditos Regis Portugaliæ oriundis et eorum cuilibet quod ipsi et eorum quilibet ac omnes liberi sui tam procreati quam procreandi in perpetuum sint indigeni et ligei nostri et hæredum nostrorum et in omnibus causis, querelis, rebus et materiis quibuscumque habeantur, pertractarentur, teneantur, reputentur et gubernentur tanquam veri et fideles ligei Nostri infra regnum nostrum Angliæ oriundi et non aliter nec alio modo. Et quod ipsi et omnes liberi sui prædicti omnimodo actiones reales, personales et mixtas in omnibus curiis, locis et jurisdictionibus nostris quibuscunque habere, exercere, eisque uti et gaudere ac eas in eisdem placitare et implacitari, respondere et responderi, defendere ac defendi possint et eorum quilibet possit in omnibus sicuti veri et fideles ligei nostri infra regnum nostrum prædictum oriundi. Et quod ipsi et eorum quilibet terras, tenementa, reditus, reversiones, servitia et alias possessiones quascunque tam in dominio quam in reversione infra dictum regnum nostrum Angliæ ac alia dominia et loca sub obedientia nostra perquirere, capere, recipere, habere, tenere, possidere et hæreditare sibi, hæredibus et assignatis suis imperpetuum vel alio modo quocunque, ac ea dare, vendere, alienare et legare cuicunque personæ sive quibuscunque personis sibi placuerit libere, quiete, licite et impune possint et quilibet eorum possit ad libitum suum adeo libere, integre et pacifice sicut possit et valeat aliquis ligeorum nostrorum infra regnum nostrum Angliæ oriundus. Ita tamen quod prædicti Johannes Fernandus, Franciscus et Johannes Gunsolus et omnes liberi sui prædicti solvant aut solvi faciant et eorum quilibet solvat seu solvi faciat talia custumas, subsidia et alia demandia pro bonis, mercibus, mercandisis et mercimoniis suis in Regnum nostrum Angliæ adducendis vel extra idem Regnum educendis qualia alienigeni nobis solvant aut solvere deberent vel consueverunt. Et quod idem Johannes Fernandus, Franciscus et Johannes Gunsolus et omnes liberi sui prædicti de cætero in futuro colore seu vigore alicujus statuti, ordinacionis sive concessionis in Parliamento nostro aut extra Parliamentum nostrum facti vel fiendi non arcteantur seu compellantur nec eorum aliquis arcteanetur, teneatur, seu compellatur ad solvendum, dandum vel supportandum nobis vel alicui hæredum nostrorum seu cuicunque alteri aliqua taxas, tallagia seu alia onera quæcunque pro terris, tenementis, bonis vel personis suis præterquam talia et tanta qualia et quanta alii fideles ligei nostri infra dictum regnum nostrum oriundi pro bonis, terris tenementis seu personis suis solvunt, dant, faciunt vel supportant aut solvere, dare, facere vel supportare consueverunt et teneantur, sed quod prædicti Johannes Fernandus, Franciscus et Johannes Gunsolus et omnes liberi sui prædicti habere et possidere valeant et possint et eorum quilibet valeat et possit omnia et omnimodo alia libertates, privilegia, franchesias et custumas ac eis uti et gaudere possint et eorum quilibet possit infra dictum regnum nostrum Angliæ, jurisdictiones et dominia nostra quæcunque adeo plene, libere, quiete, integre et pacifice sicut cæteri ligei nostri infra idem regnum nostrum oriundi habent, utunt et gaudent aut habere, possidere, uti et gaudere debeant et valeant aliquo statuto, acto, ordinacione vel aliqua alia causa, re, vel materia quacunque nonobstante.

Proviso semper quod præfati Johannes Fernandus, Franciscus et Johannes Gunsolus homagium ligeum Nobis faciant et eorum quilibet faciat ac lotto et scotto et aliis oneribus in regno nostro prædicto debitis et consuetis contribuant et eorum quilibet contribuat sicut alii ligei nostri infra dictum regnum nostrum oriundi faciunt.

Proviso etiam quod iidem Johannes Fernandus, Franciscus et Johannes Gunsolus solvant et eorum quilibet solvat nobis et hæredibus nostris tot et tanta custumas subsidia et alia deveria pro bonis et mercandisis suis prout alienigeni nobis solvere et reddere teneantur.

Et ulterius ex uberiori gratia nostra concessimus præfatis Ricardo, Thomæ, Johanni, Johanni, Francisco, et Johanni quod ipsi habeant Præsentes Literas Nostras in Cancellaria nostra absque aliquo fine seu feodo aut aliquibus finibus seu feodis pro eisdem Literis nostris aut aliqua parte eorundem aut pro Magno Sigillo nostro ad opus nostrum in Hannaperio dictæ Cancellariæ nostræ aliqualiter solvendis.

Et volumus et concedimus per Præsentes quod Reverendissimus in Christo Pater Henricus Episcopus Salisb. Custos Magni Sigilli nostri auctoritate præsentis Concessionis nostræ fieri faciat et sigillari tot et talia Brevia sub Magno Sigillo

nostro sigillando custodi sive clerico Hanaperii nostri dirigenda pro exoneratione dictorum finium et feodorum quot et qualia in hac parte necessaria fuerint et requisita, absque aliquo alio Warranto aut prosecutione penes Nos in hac parte faciendis.
In cujus, etc.

In the following year, viz., on the 9th of December 1502, Henry VII granted by his letters patent to Hugh Elyot, Thomas Ashehurst, John Gunsolus, and Francis Fernandus, and their heirs—" Auctoritatem, facultatem et potestatem navigandi et se transferendi ad omnes partes et fines maris orientalis, occidentalis, australis, borealis et septentrionalis sub banneris et insigniis nostris ... ad inveniendum, recuperandum, discooperiendum et investigandum insulas, patrias, regiones sive provincias quascunque gentilium et infidelium in quacunque mundi parte positas." It was enjoined that no one should be at liberty to visit the places discovered by the patentees for the purposes of trade for the period of forty years after such discovery, without the licence of the patentees.

Philip and Mary, by their charter dated the 6th of February, in the first and second years of their reign (1555),[1] incorporated William Marquis of Winchester, Henry Earl of Arundel, and others, by the name of Merchant adventurers of England for the discovery of lands, territories, isles, dominions and seignories unknown; and appointed Sebastian Cabot to be the first Governor of the Company. This Corporation was commonly called the Muscovy Company, and

[1] 1554 old style.

enjoyed under their charter most extensive privileges for exclusive traffic in northern parts. In the year 1566, Queen Elizabeth, in consequence of various traders having encroached upon the monopoly of the Muscovy Company, granted them a fresh charter of incorporation, by the name of the Fellowship of English Merchants for discovery of new trades.

Queen Elizabeth, by her letters patent, dated June 11th, in the twentieth year of her reign (1578), granted unto Sir Humphrey Gilbert, of Compton, in the county of Devon, and to his heirs and assigns for ever, free liberty and licence from time to time, and at all times for ever, to discover, find, search out, and view, such remote, heathen, and barbarous lands, countries, and territories, not actually possessed of any Christian prince or people, as to him, his heirs, and assigns, and to every or any of them, shall seem good, and the same to have, hold, occupy, and enjoy, to him, his heirs, and assigns, for ever.

By letters patent, dated the 6th of February, in the twenty-sixth year of her reign (1584), Elizabeth granted to Adrian Gilbert, of Sandridge, in the county of Devon, and to any other person, by him or his heirs to be assigned, and to those his associates and assistants whose names are written in a schedule thereunto annexed and to their heirs and to one assignee of each of them, and each of their heirs, free liberty, power, and full authority to depart out of the realm into all or any isles, countries, regions, provinces, and all manner of other places whatsoever, that by the northwestward, north-eastward, or northward, should be by him, his associates or assigns, discovered. The patent then grants the exclusive trade to all such places as aforesaid, and confers upon the said Adrian Gilbert and his associates the name of the " Colleagues of the fellowship for the discovery of the northwest passage".

By letters patent, dated 25th March, in the twenty-sixth year of her reign (1584), Elizabeth granted unto Sir Walter Raleigh, his heirs and assigns for ever, free liberty and licence from time to time, and at all times for ever, to discover, search, find out, and view, such remote, heathen, and barbarous lands, countries, and territories, not actually possessed of any Christian prince, nor inhabited by Christian people, as to him, his heirs, and assigns, should seem good, and to hold the same to him, his heirs, and assigns, for ever.

The two pieces next in order, are " The declaration of the Indies ... by Master Robert Thorne, merchant of London", the object of which is to induce Henry VIII to promote voyages of discovery for a passage to the East Indies, by the north, north-east, or north-west ; and " The Booke made by Master Robert Thorne ... being an information of the parts of the world discovered by [the emperor] and the king of Portingale: and also of the way to the Moluccaes by the north."

The subjects treated of in this latter piece are very various and of much interest, but they are not of a nature to call for remark here. The map which accompanies it is not mentioned by Hakluyt in his

Epistle Dedicatorie; it is, however, not only curious in itself, but derives an additional interest from the explanation of it given by Thorne.

The "Relation of John Verarzanus" comprises an account of his voyage along the coast of North America, from Florida as high as Cape Breton. The expedition consisted originally of four ships, fitted out by Francis I, and which sailed under the command of Verazzani in the year 1523. Their first operations were directed against the Spaniards, and for this purpose they cruised for some time off the coast of Spain. Three of the vessels were greatly damaged in a storm, and Verazzani, after refitting, proceeded alone on his voyage of discovery,—the details of which are comprised in this relation.

This is the earliest voyage embracing a description of the eastern coast of North America, of which any particulars are found recorded. Verazzani, however, was not the first by whom at least a great part of this coast had been visited. Peter Martyr (Dec. III, cap. VI) informs us that "These Northe seas have byn searched by one Sebastian Cabot. ... He furnished two shippes in England at his owne charges: and fyrst with three hundreth men directed his course so farre toward the Northe pole, that even in the mooneth of July he founde monstrous heapes of Ise swimming on the sea, and in maner continual day lyght. ... Thus seyng suche heapes of Ise before hym, he was enforced to tourne his sayles and folowe the Weste, so coastynge styll by the shore, that he was thereby broughte so farre into the southe by reason of the lande bendynge so muche southward, that it was there almoste equall in latitude with the Sea cauled Fretum Herculeum, havynge the north pole elevate in maner in the same degree. He sayled likewise in this tracte so farre towarde the weste, that he had the islande of Cuba [on] his lefte hande in maner in the same degree of longitude."[1] The statement by Gomara on the same subject is to the same purpose. He says:—" He armed two ships in England at the expense of King Henry VII, who was desirous of trading in the spicery as did the King of Portugal. Some say that he bore the cost himself, and that he promised King Henry to go by the north to Catayo, and to bring thence spices in less time than the Portuguese could accomplish it by the south. He also went for the purpose of ascertaining what kind of country the Indies would be to colonise. He took with him three hundred men, and directed his course for Cape Labrador, as high as fifty-eight degrees. ... Then Cabot yielding to the cold and the strangeness of the land, turned towards the west, and refitting at the Baccalaos, he ran along the coast as far as thirty-eight degrees, and thence returned into England."[2]

This was most probably the second voyage,—that made in 1498, after the granting of the second patent to John Cabot.

The map which accompanies this relation is twice referred to by Hakluyt in his Epistle Dedicatorie.

[1] Eden's Translation, 1555, 4to., fol. 118.
[2] Lopez de Gomara. *La Historia general de las Indias*, cap. 39, fol. 31. Anvers, 1554, 12mo.

Speaking of the practicability of the north-west passage (p. 11), he says : " Secondly, that Master John Verarzanus, which had been thrise on that coast, in an olde excellent mappe which he gave to King Henrie the Eight, and is yet in the custodie of Master Locke, doth so lay it out as it is to bee seene in the mappe annexed to the end of this boke, beeing made according to Verarzanus plat." And again (at p. 17): " The mappe is Master Michael Locke's, a man for his knowledge in divers languages, and especially in cosmographie, able to doe his countrey good, and worthie, in my judgment, for the manifolde good partes of him, of good reputation and better fortune."

The name of Michael Lock must always occupy a place in the history of maritime discovery. But little has appeared in print respecting him beyond the fact that he was consul at Aleppo for the Company of Merchants of Turkey. In the Cotton MSS. in the British Museum (Otho, E. VIII.) are various papers relating to his affairs with the Turkey Company, among which (fol. 41) is the following piece of autobiography. " My late father, Sr William Lok, knight, alderman of London, kept me at scholes of grammer in England till I was xiij yeres olde, which was A°. Dni. 1545, and he being sworn servant to King Henry the viiith his mercer and also his agent beyond the seas [in] dyvers affayres, he then sent me over seas to Flanders and France to learn those languages and to know the world. Synce which tyme I have contynued these xxxij yeres in travaile of body and study of mynde, following my vocation in the trade of merchandise, whereof I have spent the first xv yeres in contynuall travaile of body, passing through allmost all the cuntrees of Christianity. Namely out of England into Scotland, Ireland, Flanders, Germany, France, Spayne, Italy, and Greece, both by land and by sea, not without great labo^{rs}, cares, dangers and expenses of mony incident: having had the charge (as capitayn) of a great ship of burden 1000 tuns, by the space of more then iij yeres in dyvers voyages in the Levant seas, wherwithall I returned into England. In which travailes, besides the knowledge of all those famous common languages of those cuntries, I sought allso for the knowledge of the state of all their common wealths, chiefly in all matters apperteining to the traffique of merchants. And the rest of my tyme I have spent in England under the happy raigne of the Queenes Matie now being," etc. The remainder is injured by fire.

It appears from the same manuscript that he was a great promoter of the voyages of Martin Frobisher to discover a north-west passage to Cathay, acting as treasurer for the first three expeditions, and in two instances at least being left to make up a very considerable sum out of his own funds. This must have taken place some time before his engagement as consul or agent at Aleppo for the Turkey Company.[1]

Hakluyt speaks of three voyages made by Verazzani.[2] At present nothing is known of any other

[1] For further particulars respecting Lock, see Additional MSS. in the British Museum, Nos. 12497, 12503, 12504, and the *Life of Sir Julius Cæsar* (who was his stepson), 1810, 4to. pp. 8, 9.

[2] See *post* p. 11.

voyage than that the particulars of which are given in the following collection. Tiraboschi, vol. VII, p. 383, edit. 1827, mentions a manuscript account of a voyage by Verazzani in the following words : " Nella libreria Strozziana in Firenze oltre la relazion sopraccenata conservasi manoscritta una narrazione cosmografica assai bene distesa di tutti i paesi ch'egli avea in quel viaggio osservati, e da essa raccogliesi ch'egli ancora evea formato il disegno di tentar per que' mari il passaggio all' Indie orientali." A copy of this manuscript is now on its way to England, but we are informed that the particulars it contains are substantially the same as those of which we are already in possession. Annibale Caro, in one of his letters (*Lettere Familiari*, p. 7, edit. 1610) speaks of a brother of Verazzani as a discoverer of new lands. There may probably be a confusion between the two, but this point, as well as those of the connection, if any, of Giovanni with Henry VIII,[1] and the time and manner of his death, appear to be involved in the utmost obscurity.[2]

" The discoverie of the Isles of Frisland, Iseland, Engroveland, etc.," which follows next in the collection, has been passed over without any editorial annotation, a careful perusal of the account having led us to the perfect conviction that the story as a whole is a fabrication. Some of the materials of which it is composed may be true, but the true is so blended with the palpably false as to be no longer separable from it otherwise than by the application of a process of ana-

---

[1] See *post* p. 11.   [2] See *post* p. 93.

lyzation far too tedious for the present work. Palpably incredible, however, as this relation is, the genuineness of its details have been contended for by more than one modern writer of intelligence; and an amount of labour has been spent upon the investigation which could only be justified by the degree of credit the account enjoyed during a period of nearly two hundred years, and the influence this ill-placed faith exercised on the early progress of geographical knowledge. Although, as we have said above, the scope of the present work will not allow of a complete examination and exposure of all the points of this imposture, neither should we have thought it advisable to rest upon the bare denunciation of falsehood against it, had the subject not been treated so clearly and in so satisfactory a manner by Captain C. C. Zahrtmann, in the fifth volume of the Journal of the Royal Geographical Society of London, p. 102. In this most excellent paper the author contends:

First.—That there never existed an island of Frisland; but that what has been represented by that name in the chart of the Zeni is the Feröe Islands.

Second.—That the said chart has been compiled from hearsay information, and not by any seaman who had himself navigated in those seas for several years.

Third.—That the "History of the voyages of the Zeni"—more particularly that part of it which relates to Nicolò—is so replete with fiction, that it cannot be looked to for any information whatever as to the state of the North at that time.

Fourth.—That both the history and the chart were most probably compiled by Nicolò, a descendant of the Zeni, from accounts which came to Italy in the middle of the sixteenth century, being the epoch when information respecting Greenland first reached that country, and when interest was awakened for the colony which had disappeared.

It is not our purpose to follow Captain Zahrtmann through his chain of proofs in support of these several positions. His arguments appear to us most conclusive; and they are easily accessible to all who take sufficient interest in the subject to desire to follow out the investigation.

At the period when Ribault wrote his account of "the true and last discoverie of Florida," and for a very long time afterwards, the name of Florida was applied to that vast tract of country extending from Canada to the Rio del Norte. The present boundaries of the state were not definitively fixed until the year 1795, when they were settled by treaty with Spain.

Ribault, in the early part of his narrative, says that "many from time to time have gone about to finde out this great lande, and to inhabit there, who neverthelesse have alwaies failed, and beene put by from their intention and purpose; some by fear of shipwrackes, and some by great windes and tempestes, that drove them backe to their marveilous griefe." That this assertion was substantially true, not only of the district then known as Florida, but also of the entire country from Mexico northwards, will appear from the following facts. Of the voyage of Sebastian Cabot in 1498, but slight particulars have come down to us: supposing, however, that he left some of his three hundred men as colonists on any part of the American coast, it is certain that the settlement never took root. The voyage of Verazzani produced no result. Jacques Cartier in the years 1534 and 1535 visited the higher parts of North America. In the first voyage he discovered the gulph of St. Lawrence, and in the second the river of that name, up which he sailed three hundred leagues, and took possession of the country (which he called New France,) in the name of his sovereign Charles IX. In both voyages he wintered in the country, returning home in the spring, but made no settlement. In the year 1540 he was dispatched thither again by Francis I, with five ships, for the purpose of extending his discoveries in Canada and Hochelaga, to which latter district he gave the name of Montreal. It was now determined that the work of colonization should be vigorously prosecuted, and that Cartier should be followed as speedily as possible by François de la Roche, Sieur de Roberval, as governor of Canada, with emigrants, and all necessary stores. Cartier arrived in Canada in August 1540, and waited until 1542 for Roberval (who had been detained in France by various obstacles), when finding himself reduced to great extremities, he returned to France. Roberval arrived in Canada this same year and planted his colony, shortly after which he also returned to France, and the colony was totally neglected. In 1549 Roberval again embarked for the St. Lawrence, accompanied by his brother and many emigrants, but they were never heard of afterwards. Another attempt at colonization on the American coast was made in the year 1555, under the auspices of the Admiral Coligny, who was actuated by the double object of promoting the welfare of his native country, and of providing for the Protestants of France a refuge from religious persecution, of which he foresaw they would ere long stand in great need. The Chevalier de Villagagnon, who had embraced the tenets of the Reformed Church, was chosen to command the expedition, which consisted of two ships. In this instance Villagagnon selected South America, and landing at the river Janeiro, constructed a fort, to which he gave the name of his patron Coligny. This fort was soon washed away by the sea. Three ships arrived at the settlement in the year 1557, carrying colonists, and also fourteen missionaries sent out by the Church of Geneva; but Villagagnon had in the mean time abandoned the Protestant religion, and returned to his old faith. The settlers, treated by him with harshness, became discouraged, and the greater number returned home in the following year. Many of those who remained were murdered by the Portuguese, who compelled the few survivors to quit the colony in the year 1560. This attempt having proved abortive, Coligny, anxious to carry out his project of colonization, selected Jean Ribault as the captain of an expedition to the coast of North America.

INTRODUCTION. xcvii

A man more fit for his purpose could not have been chosen. The account of this voyage which Hakluyt has printed, is of the most interesting character; but it breaks off with the departure of Ribault from the shores of Florida on his return to France, leaving his readers in ignorance of the fate of the small band of brave men he left behind him. Fortunately we possess an account of this same voyage, and of two which succeeded it, edited and published by Basanier at the instigation and expense of Hakluyt in the year 1586, and translated and published by Hakluyt himself in the following year.[1] From this work we learn[2] that when Ribault had explored the coast and neighbouring country, as described in his own Account, and while at Port Royal, he called his men together, and addressed them in the following terms: " I thinke there is none of you that is ignoraunt of howe greate consequence this our enterprise is, and also howe acceptable it is to our young king; therefore, my friends, as one desiring your honour and benefite, I woulde not fayle to advertise you all of the exceeding greate good happe which shoulde fall to them, which as men of valure and worthy courage, would make triall in this our first discoverie of the benefites and commodities of this newe lande: which should be, as I assure myselfe, the greatest occasion that ever could happen unto them to arrise unto the title and degree of honour. And for this cause I was desirous to propose unto you, and set downe before yeour eies,

[1] See *ante* p. xix.
[2] We quote from Hakluyt's translation.

the eternall memorie which of right they deserve,
which forgetting both their parents and their countrey,
have had the courage to enterprise a thing of such
importance, which even kinges themselves understanding to be men aspiring to so high degree of magnani-
mitie, and increase of their majesties, doe not disdaine
so wel to regarde, that afterwardes, employing them
in matters of weight and of high enterprise, they make
their names immortal for ever. How beit I woulde
not have you persuade yourselves, as manie do, that
you shall never have such good fortune, as not being
knowen neither to the king nor the princes of the
realme, and besides descending of so poore a stock that
few or none of your parents having ever made profession of armes have beene knowen unto the great
estates. For albeit that from my tender yeeres I my
self have applied al my industry to follow them, and
have hazarded my life in so many dangers for the
service of my prince, yet could I never attaine ther-
unto (not that I did not deserve this title and degree
of government) as I have seen it happen to many others,
only bicause they descended of a noble race, since
more regard is had of their birth than of their vertue.
For well I knowe that if vertue were regarded, there
would more be found better to deserve the title, and
by good right to be named noble and valiant. I will
therfore make sufficient answeare to such proposi-
tions and suche thinges as you maye object against
mee, laying before you the infinite examples which
we have of the Romaines: which, concerning the
point of honour, were the first that triumphed over

the world. For how many find we among them which for their so valiant enterprises, not for the greatnesse of their parentage, have obtayned the honour to triumph. If we have recourse unto their ancestors, wee shall finde that their parentes were of so meane condition, that by labouring with their handes they lived verie basely. As the father of Ælius Pertinax, which was a poor artisant; his grandfather likewise was a bondman, as the historiographers do witnesse: and neverthelesse, being moved with a valiant courage he was nothing dismayed for al this, but rather desirous to aspire unto high things, he began with a brave stomache to learne feates of armes, and profited so well therein, that from steppe to step he became at length to be emperour of the Romaines. For all this dignitie he despised not his parentes; but contrariwise, and in remembrance of them hee caused his father's shoppe to be covered with a fine wrought marble, to serve for an example to men descended of base and poore linages, and give them occasion to aspire unto high things notwithstanding the meanness of their ancestors. I will not passe over in silence the excellencie of prowes of the valiant and renowned Agathocles, the sonne of a simple potter; and yet, forgeting the contemptible estate of his father, he so applied himself to vertue in his tender yeeres, that by the favour of armes he came to be king of Sicilia; and for all this title he refused not to be counted the sonne of a potter. But the more to eternise the memorie of his parents and to make his name renowned, he commanded that he should be served at the table with vessels of gold and silver and others of earth; declaring thereby that the dignitie where in he was placed came not unto him by his parents, but by his owne vertue onely. If I shall speak of our time, I will lay before you onely Rusten Bassha, which may be a sufficient example to all men; which, though he were the sonne of a poor heardman, did so apply his youth to all vertue, that being brought up in the service of the great Turke he seemed so to aspire to great and high matters in such sorte, that growing in yeeres he increased also in courage, so farre foorth that in fine for his excellent vertues he married the daughter of the great Turke his prince. How much then ought so many worthy examples to move you to plant here? Considering also that hereby you shalbe registered for ever as the first that inhabited this strange countrey. I pray you therefore all to advise your selves therof and to declare your minds freely unto me, protesting that I will so well imprint your names in the king's eares, and the other princes, that your renowme shall hereafter shyne unquenchable through our realme of Fraunce."

This speech excited the greatest enthusiasm among his men, and the volunteers to remain were so numerous that the only difficulty was whom to select. Twenty-eight men were ultimately chosen, at the head of whom he placed Albert de la Pierria, "a souldier of long experience, and the first that from the beginning did offer to tarry". His next care was to find a fit place for the settlement, and after some search he fixed upon a spot generally supposed to be the site of the present town of Beaufort. Here he erected a fort, to which he gave the name of Charlesfort, after the reigning sovereign of France; and having supplied it abundantly with stores of all kinds, resigned it to the settlers with the following observations: " Captayne Albert, I have to request you, in the presence of all men, that you would quite yourselfe so wisely in your charge, and governe so modestly your small company which I leave you, which with so good cheere remayneth under your obedience, that I never have occasion but to commend you, and to recount unto the king, as I am desirous, the faithful service which before us all you undertake to doe him in his New France: And you, companions, quoth he to the souldiers, I beseech you also to esteeme of Captayne Albert as if it were myselfe that stayed here with you; yeelding him that obedience which a souldier oweth unto his generall and captayne, living as brethren one with another without all dissension, and in so doing God will assist you and bless your enterprises." After this admirable exhortation Ribault and his company took leave of the settlers and returned into France.

Albert and his companions now set themselves diligently to work to fortify their position. This necessary work accomplished, they spent their time in exploring the country and forming friendships with the Indians. All this was wisely and prudently done: but unfortunately they neglected one most important duty; they made no provision for their future sustenance. As a natural consequence, when the stores

left them by Ribault were exhausted, they were forced to apply for assistance to the natives. This appeal was responded to readily and with great liberality, and they had just begun to feel themselves at ease as regarded the means of existence, when their fort accidentally caught fire and was burnt to the ground. Again the Indians came forward, and lent their aid with such hearty good will that in twelve hours their fort was rebuilt. Want of provisions was for some time their principal ground of complaint, but at length dissensions arose among them, the administration of the affairs of the colony by Albert became unpopular, and the hostile feeling arose at last to so great a height that he was put to death, and a man named Barré chosen as captain in his place. The account of this tragedy, as given by Laudonnière, is as follows:—
" But misfortune, or rather the just judgment of God, would have it that those which coulde not be overcome by fire nor water, shoulde be undone by their owne selves. This is the common fashion of men, which cannot continue in one estate, and had rather to overthrowe themselves than not to attempt some new thing daily. We have infinite examples in the auncient histories, especially of the Romanes, unto which number this little handful of men, being far from their countrey and absent from their countriemen, have also added this present example. They entred therfore into partialities and dissentions which began about a souldier named Guernache, which was a drummer of the French bands ; which, as it was told me, was very cruelly hanged by his owne captaine

and for a small fault; which captaine also using to threaten the rest of his souldiers which staied behind under his obedience, and peradventure, as it is to be presumed, were not so obedient unto him as they should have bin, was the cause that they fell into a mutiny, because that many times hee put his threatnings in execution; whereupon they so chased him that at the last they put him to death. . . . . . . They assembled themselves together to choose one to be governour over them, whose name was Nicholas Barré, a man worthy of commendation, and one which knew so well to quite himself of his charge, that all rancour and dissention ceased among them and they lived peaceably one with another."

This account was derived by Laudonnière from the mutineers themselves, whose interest it was to throw all the blame upon the murdered man. But Williams, in his *Territory of Florida* (New York, 1837, 8vo.) presents us with a somewhat different version of the story. He says (p. 170) : " Albert visited the Indian princes in his neighbourhood, cultivating their friendship and paying every attention to their wants, and such was his success that they readily supplied his people with provisions, and made them many presents of pearls, crystals, silver, etc. The colonists, however, were licentious, lazy and quarrelsome, and to preserve peace between them and the natives, he was obliged to exercise a very strict discipline; this they would not endure. Among the colonists was one Lachan [query, La Chère], who was a popular demagogue : he endeavoured to reduce some of the Indians to slavery, which Albert would not permit, and compelled him to do justice to the natives. A mutiny was the consequence, in which Albert lost his life. The Indians then refused to supply them with provisions, and none being likely to arrive from France, the colonists resolved to leave the fort and return to their country, etc."

Whatever may have been the circumstances by which Albert was led to adopt those measures of severity which cost him his life, his murder doubtless increased the difficulties of the settlers, and rendered it necessary that they should devise means for quitting Florida. With great labour, none of them being acquainted with the art of ship building, they constructed a small pinnace; the natives supplied them with cordage, and the sails they made out of their shirts and the sheets of their beds. In this ill-constructed vessel they put to sea, scantily supplied with provisions even for an uninterrupted voyage. Again the consequences of their want of foresight fell heavily upon them. When they had made about one-third of their voyage, the wind, which had hitherto been favourable, fell, and they lay becalmed for three weeks, making in all this time only about twenty-five leagues. Their provisions were soon exhausted, and after experiencing all the ordinary sufferings of famine, they were forced to the crowning horror, that of sacrificing one for the safety of the rest. A man named La Chere voluntarily offered himself. Before it became necessary to sacrifice a second victim, they were picked up by an English vessel, who, after putting the most feeble on shore (we are not told on what land) carried the rest to England, where they were presented to Queen Elizabeth.

The civil war which raged in France at the time of Ribault's return prevented the government from giving any attention to the settlement in Florida; but on the restoration of peace, Laudonnière was appointed to command three ships fitted out for the purpose of carrying succours to Albert and his companions. They set sail on the 22nd of April 1564, and arrived on the coast of Florida on the 22nd of June following. On this occasion, finding the settlement at Charlesfort abandoned, they selected a spot for their plantation near the mouth of the river May (now called the St. John), where they erected a fort, to which they gave the name of Fort Caroline in honour of Charles IX of France. They do not appear to have taken any wiser measures for a permanent settlement than those adopted by Albert, spending their time like him in exploring the country, and also suffering like their predecessors from want of provisions. After the lapse of more than a year, during which time they were often reduced to the brink of starvation, the men became clamorous to return to France, but two of their vessels having been carried away several months previously by some of their mutinous companions, they no longer possessed the means of transport.

On the 3rd of August, 1565, however, Sir John Hawkins came upon the coast, and through his humanity and kindness the suffering Frenchmen were put in a condition to escape from this wretched condition. The following is the account given by Laudonnière of the generous conduct of the British commander, who voluntarily offered them a free passage to France, and ultimately, at the desire of Laudonnière, sold them one of his ships. " We therefore tooke a viewe of the shippe which the generall would sell, whom we drewe to such reason that he was content to stand unto mine owne men's judgment, who esteemed it to be worth seven hundred crowns, wherof we agreed very friendly. Wherfore I delivered him in earnest of the summe two bastards, two mynions, one thousand of iron and one thousand of powder. This bargaine thus made he considered the necessity wherein we were, having for all our sustenance but myl and water: whereupon being moved with pitie, he offred to relieve me with twenty barrels of meale, six pipes of beanes, one hogshead of salt, and a hundred of waxe to make candels. Moreover, forasmuch as he sawe my souldyers goe barefoote, he offred me besides fifty payres of shoes, which I accepted, and agreed of a price with hym, and gave hym a byll of mine hand for the same, for which untill this present I am indebted to hym. He did more than this: for particularly he bestowed uppon myselfe a great jare of oyle, a jare of vynagre, a barill of olyves, and a great quantitye of ryce, and a barill of white biscuit. Besides he gave diverse presents to the principall officers of my companye according to their qualities; so that I may saye that wee receaved as manye courtesies of the generall as it was possible to receive of any man living."

Having made all necessary preparations, they were

about to depart on the 28th of August, when several vessels were discovered making for the shore. This proved to be Ribault, who had returned to Florida with seven ships, carrying emigrants and stores, and with authority to supersede Laudonnière in the government of the colony. About a week after his arrival, six large Spanish ships appeared on the coast, and anchored in the road, where four of the French ships lay which were too large to enter the river. The Frenchmen, distrusting the intentions of the Spaniards, slipped their cables, and stood out to sea. The Spaniards immediately gave chase, and fired upon them, but finding the French too fast for them, they returned to the coast, and entered a river about eight leagues from the River May, named by Ribault, in his first voyage, the Dolphins. The French vessels soon afterwards returned to their former position off the mouth of the River May. Ribault was at this time on shore with Laudonnière, who was confined by fever. When the arrival of the Spaniards was reported to Ribault, he determined to attack them with the three ships that were in the river, notwithstanding the remonstrances of Laudonnière, whose objections he silenced by producing a letter from the Admiral Coligny, containing these words:—" While I was sealing this letter, I received certain advice, that Don Pedro Melendes is departing from Spain to go to the coast of New France. See that you suffer him not to encroach upon you, and that you do not encroach upon him." On the 10th of September Ribault departed on this expedition, taking with him almost every man accustomed to bear arms, and thus depriving Laudonnière of all means of offering effective resistance to the Spaniards should they attack him, as he fully anticipated they would do. He endeavoured as far as he was able to repair and strengthen the fort, but a violent storm commenced immediately after Ribault's departure, and continued with such severity, that the works were greatly impeded. The same cause, however, which checked their defensive operations, gave them a delusive sense of security, as they imagined the Spaniards would never attempt an attack during such tempestuous weather. In this, however, they were fatally mistaken. On the 20th of September, the Spaniards suddenly appeared, having been guided overland by a deserter named François Jean, and captured the fort after a very slight resistance—the greater part of those who attempted to defend it were slain, and Laudonnière himself escaped with difficulty to the woods. The only chance of safety consisted in reaching the French ships, which lay at the mouth of the river. To accomplish this he had to wade through the marshes, and passed the night standing up to his neck in water, supported in the arms of one of his soldiers: in the morning he got safely on board, and succeeded in picking up about eighteen or twenty others, the rest being all butchered by the Spaniards. Dismal as was the fate of Laudonnière and his company, that of Ribault was yet more disastrous. The storm which we have already mentioned as having arisen immediately after his departure from the River May, wrecked all his ships, and he and his men, to the number of about six hundred, escaped with difficulty to shore in the neighbourhood of the spot where the Spaniards had encamped. It is said, that even under these unfavourable circumstances, Ribault might have attacked the enemy with a prospect of success, but his men were discouraged. One party of two hundred gave themselves up, and were forthwith led by tens behind a sand-hill and butchered in cold blood. Three days afterwards, Ribault and one hundred and fifty more surrendered, and were in like manner murdered. Lescarbot, in his *Histoire de la Nouvelle France*, says, that Ribault was flayed alive, and his skin sent into Spain. Of the remainder, twenty escaped to the woods, and were never heard of afterwards; and the rest, being too insignificant to cause any fear to the Spaniards, were spared. The French settlement was thus utterly destroyed by the Spaniards, who, it must be borne in mind, were at this time at peace with France. They attached labels to their murdered victims, on which were inscribed the words, " Not as Frenchman, but as heretics"— the poor Frenchmen being Huguenots. These atrocious deeds were bitterly revenged by Dominique de Gourgues, who in the year 1567, fitted out a private expedition, and in his turn utterly annihilated the settlement raised by the Spaniards on the ruins of Fort Caroline—hanging those who were not destroyed by the sword, to whom he attached labels, with the words, " Not as Spaniards, but as murderers". The particulars of this expedition are of high interest, but the scope of the present work does not permit us to carry any further the history of the colonization of America.

On the 14th day of September 1585, Sir Francis Drake sailed from England on his voyage to the West Indies, in command of twenty-five ships. He first directed his course to the coast of Spain, and anchored within the isles of Bayona, now called the islands of Cies, at the mouth of the Bay of Vigo. His appearance caused the greatest consternation among the Spaniards; and the Marquis of Santa Cruz, High-Admiral of Spain, drew up suggestions for the necessary defences, both on the coast of Spain, and for the Spanish possessions in the East and West Indies. A translation of a small part of this plan, in the handwriting of Hakluyt, is now in the possession of Mr. Henry Stevens. By the kind permission of this gentleman, we are enabled to present the members of the society with a fac-simile of this highly interesting fragment, of which we also append a transcript for the benefit of those of our readers to whom the handwriting of the sixteenth century may not be familiar.

"That the castles of this citie, river, and teritorie, bee victuayled: and that they bee provided of powder, mach, and leade, and al things els touchinge artillerie: as I have craved the same in my supplications, wch I sent unto his ma^{tie} the seventh of March this present yere 1585.

<small>Eight galies belonge to the river of Lisbon & six to ye river of Sivil.</small> "That the galies bee provided for fower monethes, and that sixe more bee brought from Spayne unto this river wth 120 soldiers in every galie, that they may bee devided

That the castles of this citie, river, and territorie bee strength=
ned: and that they bee provided of powder, march and leade,
and of enough tonnage artillerie: as I haue evabed for
same in my supplicationt wch I sent vnto his ma^{tie} the first
of march this present yere 1588.

That the galies bee provided for some monthes, and that
there more bee brought from Spayne vnto this river w^{th}
120 pieces in every galie, that they may bee devided among
those that were aforce in the river of Lisbon. And in case
that it fall out that the English army goe not to the In=
dies, and overrun it selfe in this kingdome, it may bee
English shipps, wch well doe the one and the other, wee shal bee
enforced to make knotes army for the safe conduct of the
Indian fleete of twelve shipps, fower patashes and fifteene
hundred soldiers to the marines.

All that thinge seem^{e} vnto mee to bee most fitt for his ma^{tie}
service to bee prepared wth greate diligence and care, and he
provide money needfull for the same, w^{thout} proferringe the
one before the other, but that al may bee don w^{thout} omitting
of any parte. Yet I refeure my selfe w^{holy} to better ad=
vise and vpor iudgment. Written in Lisbon the 26 of
october after the Spanish arromphe, 1588.

the Ende — Translated out of Spanish by
Richard Hakluyt younger

left margin: That galies bee=
tonge to the river
of Lisbon, and 6.
to the river of Sivil.

(Endorsed.)

The opinion of Don Alnaro
Baçan, marshes of Santa Cruz
and late Admiral of Spayne
tong^{my} the Army of Fra^{aurel}
Drake lying at the y^{sles} of
Bayona on the cost of Galizia
declaring w^{hat} harme hee might
doo in the west Indies.

J. W. Randall.

amonge those eight wch are here in this river of Lisbon. And in case that it fall out that the English army goe not for the Indies, and occupie it selfe in this kingdome, because there bee English ships wch will doe the one and the other, wee shall bee enforced to make another army for the safe conduct of the Indian fleete of twelve ships, fower pataches, and fifteene hundred soldiers, beside mariners.

" Al these things seeme unto me to bee necessarie for his ma^ties service to bee prepared wth greate diligence and care, and to provide money needful for the same without preferringe the one before the other, but that al may bee don without omittinge of any parte. Yet I referre myselfe wholely to better advice and riper judgment. Written in Lisbon the 26 of October, after the Spanish accompte, 1585.

THE ENDE.

Translated out of Spanish by Richard Hakluyt, preacher.

(*Endorsed.*)

" The opinion of Don Alvaro Baçan, Marches of Santa Cruz, and late Admiral of Spayne, touching the army of Francis Drake, lying at the yles of Bayona, on the cost of Galizia, declaring what harme hee might doe in al the West Indies."

The document of which the above is a portion is printed entire in Hakluyt's *General Collection*, vol. iii, p. 532. Edit. 1600.

DIVERS

voyages touching the discouerie of America *and the Ilands adiacent* vnto the same, made first of all by our *Englishmen and afterwards by the Frenchmen and Britons.*

And certaine notes of aduertisements and obseruations, necessarie for such as shall heereafter make the like attempt.

With two Mappes annexed heereunto for the plainer understanding of the whole matter.

Imprinted at London

for Thomas Woodcocke, *dwelling in paules Church-Yard,* at the signe of the blacke beare.

1582.

THE NAMES OF CERTAINE LATE WRITERS OF GEOGRAPHIE, WITH THE YEERE WHEREIN THEY WROTE.

The yeere of
our Lorde.
1300. Abelfada Ismael, Prince of Syria, Persia, and Assyria.[1]
1320. John Mandeuill, Englishman.[2]
1500. Albertus Crantzius of Hamburge.[3]
1520. Peter Martyr, Millanoyse.[4]
1525. Gonsaluo Ouiedo, Spaniarde.[5]
1527. Robert Thorne, Englishman.
1530. Hieronymus Fracastor, Italian.[6]
1539. Gemma Frisius.[7]
1540. Antonie di Mendoza, Spaniard.[8]
1541. Gerardus Mercator, Fleming.[9]
1549. John Baptista Guicchardine, Florentine.[10]
1553. John Baptista Ramusius, hee gathered many notable things.[11]
1554. Sebastian Munster, Germane.[12]
1554. Thomas Giunti, Venetian.[13]
1555. Clement Adams, Englishman.
1555. Orontius Finæus, Frenchman.[14]

([1]) Ismail Ibn Ali Abulfeda, King of Hammah, in Syria, born in the year 1273. ([2]) Sir John Mandeville, born at St. Albans. ([3]) Albert Krantz, a native of Hamburg. ([4]) Pietro Martire Anghiera, born at Arona in 1455. ([5]) Gonsalvo Hernandez de Oviedo y Valdez, born at Madrid about 1478. ([6]) Girolamo Fracastoro, a native of Verona, born in the year 1483. ([7]) Reinerus Gemma, born at Dockum, in Friesland, in 1508. ([8]) Antonio de Mendoza, Viceroy of Mexico. ([9]) Gerard Mercator, born at Rupelmond, in 1512. ([10]) Giovanni Batista Guicciardini. ([11]) Giovanni Batista Ramusio, born at Venice in 1486. ([12]) Sebastian Münster, born at Ingelheim in 1489. ([13]) Tommaso Giunti, a celebrated printer at Venice. ([14]) Oronce Finé, born at Bri-

1564. Abraham Ortelius, Fleming.[15]
1574. Hierome Osorius, Portingall.[16]
1575. Andreas Theuet, Frenchman.[17]
1575. Francis Belforest, Frenchman.[18]
1576. Humfrey Gilbert Knight, Englishman.[19]
1577. Dionyse Settle, Englishman.
1578. George Beste, Englishman.
1580. Nicolas Chauncellor, Englishman.

ançon in the year 1494. ([15]) Abram Ortel, a native of Antwerp, was born in the year 1527. ([16]) Jeronimo Osorio, born at Lisbon in 1506. ([17]) André Thevet, a native of Angoulême. ([18]) François Belleforest, born at Sarzan, near Samatan, in 1530. ([19]) Sir Humphrey Gilbert, born in Devonshire in 1539.

THE NAMES OF CERTAINE LATE TRAUAYLERS, BOTH BY SEA AND BY LANDE, WHICH ALSO FOR THE MOST PART HAUE WRITTEN OF THEIR OWNE TRAUAYLES AND VOYAGES.

The yere of our Lorde.

1178. Beniamin Tudelensis, a Iewe.[1]
1270. Marcus Paulus, a Venetian.[2]
1300. Harton, an Armenian.[3]
1320. John Mandeuile Knight, Englishman.
1380. Nicolaus and Antonius Zeni, Venetians.
1444. Nicolaus Conti, Venetian.
1492. Christopher Columbus, a Genoway.[4]
1497. Sebastian Gabot, an Englishman, the sonne of a Venetiā.[5]
1497. M. Thorne and Hugh Eleot of Bristowe, Englishmen.
1497. Vasques de Gama, a Portingale.[6]
1500. Gasper Corterealis, a Portingale.[7]
1516. Edoardus Barbosa, a Portingale.[8]
1519. Fernandus Magalianes, a Portingale.[9]
1530. John Barros, a Portingale.[10]
1534. Jaques Cartier, a Briton.[11]
1540. Francis Vasques de Coronado, Spaniarde.
1542. John Gaeton, Spaniarde.[12]

([1]) Benjamin Ben Jona, born at Tudela in the first half of the twelfth century. ([2]) Marco Polo, a native of Venice. ([3]) Hatto, Hayto, Aithonus, Aythonus, Haithonus, or Aytonus, Prince of Gorigos, in Cilicia. ([4]) Cristoforo Colombo, a native of Genoa, born about the year 1447. ([5]) Sebastian Cabot, born at Bristol about the year 1467. ([6]) Vasco da Gama, born at Sines, in Portugal. ([7]) Gaspar Cortereal, born at Lisbon. ([8]) Duarte Barbosa, a native of Lisbon. ([9]) Fernando de Magalhaens. ([10]) Ioaō de Barros, was born at Viseu, in Portugal, in the year 1496. ([11]) Jacques Cartier, born at St. Malo. ([12]) Juan Gaetano.

1549. Francis Xauier, a Portingale.[13]
1553. Hugh Willowbie knight and Richard Chauncellor, Eng.
1554. Francis Galuano, a Portingale.[14]
1556. Steuen and William Burros, Englishmen.[15]
1562. Antonie Jenkinson, Englishman.
1562. John Ribault, a Frenchman.
1565. Andrewe Theuet, a Frenchman.
1576. Martin Frobisher, Englishman.[16]
1578. Francis Drake, Englishman.[17]
1580. Arthur Pet and Charles Jackmā, Englishmen.
1582. Edwarde Fenton and Luke Warde, Englishmen.
1582. Humfrey Gilbert knight, Edward Heyes, and Antonie Brigham, Englishmen.

([13]) François Xavier, Saint, born at the Castle of Xavier, at the foot of the Pyrenees, in 1506. ([14]) The person here meant appears to be Antonio Galvam, Governor of the Moluccas, born in 1503 at Lisbon; or, according to Barbosa Machado, in the East Indies. ([15]) Stephen Burrough, born at Northam, in Devonshire, in 1525. ([16]) Sir Martin Frobisher, born at Doncaster. ([17]) Sir Francis Drake, born near Tavistock, in Devonshire, in 1545.

A VERIE LATE AND GREAT PROBABILITIE *OF A PASSAGE BY THE NORTH-WEST* PART OF AMERICA IN FIFTY-EIGHT DEGREES OF NORTHERLY LATITUDE.

AN excellent learned man of Portingale, of singuler grauety, authoritie, and experience, tolde mee very lately, that one *Anus Cortereal*,[1] Captayne of the yle of Tercera, about the yeere 1574, which is not aboue eight yeres past, sent a Shippe to discouer the North-west passage of America, and that the same shippe arriuing on the coast of the saide America, in fiftie eyghte degrees of latitude, founde a great entrance exceeding deepe and broade without all impediment of ice, into whiche they passed aboue twentie leagues, and found it alwaies to trende towarde the South, the lande lying lowe and plaine on eyther side: And that they perswaded them selues verely that there was a way open into the south sea. But their victailes fayling them, and being but one shippe, they returned backe agayne with ioy. This place seemeth to lie in equal degrees of latitude with the first entrance of the sounde of Denmark, betweene Norway and the head land, called in Latin *Cimbrorum promontorium*,[2] and therefore like to bee open and nauigable a great part of the yeere. And this report may be well annexed unto the other eight reasons mentioned in my epistle dedicatorie, for proofe of the likelihood of this passage by the north-west.[3]

[1] *i.e.*, Ioaõ, or Ioannes.   [2] *Anglicê*, the Skaw.

[3] This statement is extremely vague. There can be no doubt but that the "great entrance" mentioned in the text was Hudson's Straits; but, unfortunately, we have no further account of this expedition. It is, to say the least, singular, that the names of Gaspar Cortereal and his descendant or relative Anus (or Joannes), should be connected with two independent discoveries of this great inland sea, at the distance of nearly eighty years from each other.

TO THE RIGHT WORSHIPFULL AND *MOST VERTUOUS GENTLEMAN MASTER* PHILLIP SYDNEY, ESQUIRE.

I MARUAILE not a little (right worshipfull) that since the first discouerie of America (which is nowe full fourescore and tenne yeeres), after so great conquests and plantings of the Spaniardes and Portingales there, that wee of Englande could neuer haue the grace to set fast footing in such fertill and temperate places as are left as yet vnpossessed of them. But againe, when I consider that there is a time for all men, and see the Portingales time to be out of date, and that the nakednesse of the Spaniards and their long hidden secretes[1] are nowe at length espied, whereby they went about to delude the worlde, I conceiue great hope that the time approcheth and nowe is, that we of England may share and part stakes (if wee will our selues), both with the spaniarde and the Portingale, in part of America and other regions, as yet vndiscouered. And surely if there were in vs that desire to aduaunce the honour of our countrie which ought to bee in euery good man, wee woulde not all this while haue foreslowne[2] the possessing of those landes, whiche of equitie and right appertaine vnto vs, as by the discourses that followe shall appeare most plainely. Yea, if wee woulde beholde with the eye of pitie how al our Prisons are pestered and filled with able men to serue their Countrie, which for small roberies are dayly hanged vp in great numbers, euen twentie at a clappe, out of one iayle (as was seene at the last assizes at Rochester), wee

---

[1] By "hidden secretes", it is presumed that the author alludes to the false pretence of religion used by the Spaniards as a cloak for their cruel oppression of the Indians; or, as he expresses it in a subsequent passage, "pretending to convert infidels, but seeking their goods."

[2] Foreslowne—Forborne, in the sense of *neglected*.

woulde hasten and further euery man to his power the deducting[1] of some Colonies of our superfluous people into those temperate and fertile partes of America, which, being within sixe weekes sayling of England, are yet vnpossessed by any Christians: and seeme to offer themselues vnto vs, stretching neerer vnto her Maiesties Dominions then to any other part of Europe. Wee reade that the Bees whe' they grow to be too many in their own hiues at home, are wont to bee led out by their Captaines to swarme abroad and seeke themselues a new dwelling place. If the examples of the Grecians and Carthaginians of olde time and the practise of our age may not mooue vs, yet let vs learne wisdome of these smal weake and vnreasonable creatures. It chaunced very lately that vpon occasion I had great conference in matters of Cosmographie with an excellent learned man of Portingale, most priuie to all the discoueries of his nation, who wondered that those blessed countries from the point of Florida Northward were all this while vnplanted by Christians, protesting with great affection and zeale, that if hee were nowe as young as I (for at this present hee is threescore yeeres of age) hee woulde sel all hee had, being a man of no small wealth and honour, to furnish a conuenient number of ships to sea for the inhabiting of those countries, and reducing those gentile people to christianitie. Moreouer, hee added, that John Barros, their chiefe Cosmographer, being moued with the like desire, was the cause that Bresilia was first inhabited by the Portingales:[2] where they haue nine baronies or lord-

^{The speech of a learned Portingale.}

^{Master John Barros, the causer of the inhabiting of Bresilia.}

---

[1] Deducting, *i. e.*, conveying.

[2] This statement must be received with caution. The coast of Brazil was discovered by Vicente Yañez Pinzon, in the year 1499, and possession taken for the crown of Portugal by Pedro Alvarez Cabral in 1500. The first settlement was made as early as the year 1503, by Amerigo Vespucci. Joaō de Barros, who was not born until the year 1496, held successively the offices of Captain or Governor of Fort St. George da Mina, Treasurer of the Colonial Department, and Factor or Agent-General for the Colonial Possessions of Portugal in India and Africa.

ships, and thirtie engennies or suger milles, two or three hundred slaues belonging to eche myll, with a Iudge and other officers and a Church: so that euery mill is as it were a little common wealth: and that the countrie was first planted by such men as for small offences were saued from the rope.[1] This hee spake not onely vnto mee and in my hearing, but also in the presence of a friend of mine, a man of great skill in the Mathematikes. If this mans desire might bee executed, wee might not only for the present time take possession of that good land, but also, in short space, by God's grace, finde out that shorte and easie passage by the North-

About 1539 he obtained the Captaincy (or in other words a grant) of a district in the Brazils called Maranham, but that was ten years after the attention of the Portuguese government had been steadily directed towards the colonization of the Brazils, and the system of dividing the country into captaincies had been adopted. His great work, the Decades, was not published until the year 1553, and these contained the history of the East and not of the West Indies. It appears, therefore, that neither his official nor his historical labours pointed towards the American continent; and although he *may* have influenced the movements of his government in this respect, there is no evidence on record to support the broad assertion contained in the text.—See Barbosa Machado, *Bibliotheca Lusitana*.—Southey's *History of the Brazils*, part I, page 32-48.

[1] The Portuguese and Spaniards, but particularly the former, set the example to modern Europe of transporting criminals to their colonies. The first legislative enactment in England, upon the subject of transportation, was the statute 39 Eliz. c. 4, by the fourth section of which it was enacted—that "if any rogues shall appear to be dangerous to the inferior sort of people, &c. they may lawfully bee banished out of this realme...... unto such parts beyond ye seas, as shall be at any time hereafter for that purpose assigned by the Privy Councell......or by any sixe or more of them." The practical interpretation of this act was given by James I, who, by a letter addressed to the Treasurer and Council of the Colony of Virginia in the year 1619, commanded them " to send a hundred dissolute persons to Virginia, which the Knight Marshal would deliver to them." Virginia appears thus to have been the first British settlement in America to which English criminals were transported; and the system was afterwards extended, particularly from the reign of Charles II, to Maryland, Delaware, North Carolina, South Carolina, Georgia, New Jersey, New York, and Pennsylvania.—See also Lang, *Transportation and Colonization*, p. 8, et seqq.

DEDICATORIE. 11

west, which we haue hetherto so long desired, and whereof
wee haue many good and more then probable coniectures : a
fewe whereof I thinke it not amisse heere to set downe,
although your worship knowe them as well as my selfe.
First, therefore, it is not to be forgotten that Sebastian
Gabot wrote to Master Baptista Ramusius, that he veryly
beleeued that all the north part of America is diuided into
Ilandes.[1]   Secondly, that master John Verazanus, which
had been thrise on that coast, in an olde excellent mappe
which he gaue to King Henrie the eight, and is yet in the
custodie of master Locke, doth so lay it out as it is to bee
seene in the mappe annexed to the end of this boke, beeing
made according to Verazanus plat.   Thirdly, the story of
Gil Gonsalua, recorded by Franciscus Lopes de Gomara,
which is saide to haue sought a passage by the Northwest,
seemeth to argue and proue the same.[2]   Fourthly, in the
second relation of Iaques Cartier, the 12 chapter, the people
of Saguinay doe testifie that vpon their coastes Westwarde
there is a sea, the ende whereof is vnknowne vnto them.[3]
Fiftly, in the end of that discourse is added this, as a special
remembrance, to wit, that they of Canada say that it is a
monethes space to saile to a lande where cinamon and cloues
are growing.[4]   Sixtly, the people of Florida signified vnto

[1] Ramusio, *Navigationi*, vol. iii, Preface, p. 6.

[2] For the passage referred to in the text, see Lopez de Gomara, *Historia general de las Indias*, fol. 258. Anvers, 1554, 12º.

[3] The following is the passage referred to in the text : "We understood of Donnacona and of others, that the said river is called the River of Saguenay ... and that beyond Saguenay the said river entereth into two or three great lakes, and that there is a sea of fresh water found ; and as they have heard say of those of Saguenay, there was never man heard of that found out the end thereof : for as they told us, they themselves were never there."—*Hakluyt*, vol. iii, p. 225. The river here meant is the St. Lawrence ; and the lakes and sea, Lakes Ontario, Erie, Huron, Michigan, and Lake Superior.

[4] *Hakluyt*, vol. iii, p. 232. This statement is far too vague to admit of any conjecture as to the land meant.

John Ribault (as it is expressed in his discourse heerewithall imprinted), that they might saile from the Riuer of May vnto Ceuola and the south sea through their countrie within twentie dayes. Seuenthly, the experience of captain Frobisher[1] on the hyther side, and Sir Fraunces Drake on the back side of America,[2] with the testimonie of Nicolaus and Anthonius Zeni, that Estotilanda is an Ilande,[3] doth yeelde no small hope thereof. Lastly, the judgement of the excellent Geographer Gerardus Mercator, which his sonne,

[1] Frobisher made three voyages in search of a north-west passage: the first in the year 1576, and the second and third in the two following years. On each occasion he penetrated far enough to excite hopes of ultimate success; but not so far as to meet with any of those discouraging circumstances which at a later period checked the spirit of adventure in this quarter, and it is to be hoped will at length be allowed their due weight in determining how far it is expedient to risk the lives of brave men in solving a geographical problem,—the explanation of which, however complete, can lead to no practical result. In the first voyage those straits were discovered which have since borne Frobisher's name: "He entered", the account says, "the same the one and twentieth of July, and passed above fifty leagues therein .. having upon either hand a great maine or continent."—*Hakluyt*, vol. iii, p. 58. In the third voyage, the ships missed Frobisher's Straits, and bearing to the south of Queen Elizabeth's Foreland, entered Hudson's Straits by mistake,—"of which mistaken straights, considering the circumstance, we have great cause to confirm our opinion, to like and hope well of the passage in this place. For the foresaid bay or sea, the further we sailed therein, the wider we found it, with great likelihood of endless continuance."—*Ib.* vol. iii, p. 80.

[2] The voyage of Drake, in which he discovered and took possession of California, under the name of New Albion, was performed in the years 1577-80. There is no circumstance connected with this voyage calculated to raise hopes of the practicability of the north-west passage, beyond the fact, that Drake sailed as high as the forty-eighth degree of north latitude, with the bold design of returning home by a north-east passage, and still found an open sea before him: at this point, however, the sufferings of his men from cold obliged him to turn southwards again. It is worthy of notice, that in the description of New Albion, contained in the account of this voyage, the following passage occurs: "There is no part of earth here to be taken up wherein there is not some probable show of gold or silver."—*Hakluyt*, vol. iii, p. 730.

[3] See *post*, under "The Discoverie of the Isles of Frisland, Iseland," etc.

Rumold Mercator, my friende, shewed mee in his letters, and drewe out for mee in writing, is not of wise men lightly to be regarded. His words are these—*Magna tametsi pauca de noua Frobisheri nauigatione scribis, quam miror ante multos annos nō fuisse attentatam. Non enim dubium est, quin recta et breuis via pateat in occidentem Cathaium vsq;. In quod regnū, si recte nauigationem instituant, nobilissimas totius mundi merces colligent et multis Gentibus adhuc idololatris Christi nomen communicabunt.* You write (saith hee to his sonne) great matters, though very briefly, of the new discouerie of Frobisher, which I wonder was neuer these many yeeres heretofore attempted. For there is no doubt but that there is a straight and short way open into the West, euen vnto Cathay. Into which kingdome, if they take their course aright, they shall gather the most noble merchandise of all the worlde, and shall make the name of Christ to bee knowne vnto many idolatrous and Heathen people. And heere, to conclude and shut vp this matter, I haue hearde my selfe of Merchants of credite, that have liued long in Spaine, that King Phillip hath made a lawe of late that none of his subiectes shall discouer to the Northwardes of fiue and fortie degrees of America: whiche may bee thought to proceede chiefly of two causes, the one, least passing farther to the North they should discover the open passage from the south sea to our north sea: the other, because they haue not people enough to possesse and keepe that passage, but rather thereby shoulde open a gappe for other nations to passe that way. Certes, if hetherto in our owne discoueries we had not beene led with a preposterous desire of seeking rather gaine then Gods glorie, I assure my self that our labours had taken farre better effecte. But wee forgotte that Godlinesse is great riches, and that if we first seeke the kingdome of God all other thinges will be giuen vnto vs, and that as the light accompanieth the Sunne, and the heate the fire, so lasting riches do waite vpon them that are zealous for the aduauncement

The iudgement of Gerardus Mercator, of a passage by the Northwest.

A lawe made of late by King Phillip.

of the kingdome of Christ and the enlargement of his glorious Gospell: as it is sayde, I will honour them that honour mee. I truste that nowe, being taught by their manifolde losses, our men will take a more godly course, and vse some part of their goods to his glorie: if not, he will turne euen their couetousnes to serue him, as he hath done the pride and auarice of the Spaniards and Portingales, who, pretending in glorious words that they made their discoueries chiefly to conuert Infidelles to our most holy faith (as they say) in deed and truth, sought not them but their goods and riches. Whiche thing, that our nation may more speedily and happily performe, there is no better meane, in my simple iudgemēt, then the increase of knowledge in the arte of nauigation and breading of skilfulnesse in the sea men: whiche Charles the Emperour, and the king of Spaine that nowe is, wisely considering, haue in their Contractation house[1] in Siuill, appointed a learned reader of the sayde art of Nauigation, and ioyned with him certayne examiners, and haue distinguished the orders among the sea men, as the groomet, whiche is the basest degree, the marriner, which is the seconde, the master the thirde, and the pilot the fourth, vnto the which two last degrees none is admitted without hee haue heard the reader for a certaine space (which is commonly an excellent Mathematician, of which number were Pedro di Medina,[2] which writte learnedly of the art of nauigation, and Alonso di Chauez[3] and Hieronimus di Chauez, whose works likewise

The co'tractatio' house at Siuill.

[1] Contractation-house, *i.e.*, the house in which agreements are made for the promotion of trade—the Exchange.

[2] Pedro de Medina, born at Seville. He wrote—1, *Arte de Navegar*, Seville, 1545, fol. 2, *Regimiento de Navegacion*, Seville, 1563, 4to. 3, *Libro de las Grandezas y Cosas memorables de Espana*, Seville, 1543, fol. 4, *Chronica breve de Espana*, Seville, 1548. 5, *Chronica de los Duques de Medina Sidonia*, MS. 6, *Dialogos de la Verdad sobre la Conversion del Pecador*, Valladolid, 1545, fol. 7, *Tabula Hispaniæ Geographica;* used by Ortelius, in his *Theatrum Orbis Terrarum*.

[3] Alonso de Chaves was a Spanish cosmographer, and one of the examiners of pilots (Herrera, *Historia general de los Hechos de los Castellanos*

I haue seene),[1] and being founde fitte by him and his assistantes, which are to examine matters touching experience, they are admitted with as great solemnitie and giuing of presents to the ancient masters and Pilots, and the reader and examiners, as the great doctors in the Vniuersities, or our great Sergeantes at the law when they proceed, and so are admitted to take charge for the Indies. And that your worshippe may knowe that this is true, Master Steven Borrows,[2] M. S^teuen Borrowes. nowe one of the foure masters of the Queene's nauie, tolde me that, newely after his returne from the discouery of Moscouie by the North in Queene Maries daies, the Spaniards hauing intelligence that he was master in that discouerie, tooke him into their cōtractation house at their making and

en las Isles y Tierra Firme del Mar Oceano, Dec. III, p. 219; IV, p. 30), but we cannot find any account of his works.

[1] Geromino de Chaves, a native of Seville. His works are— 1, *Tratado de la Esfera, que compuso el doctor Juan de Sacrobusto, con muchas adiciones, traducido con escolios y figuras*, Seville, 1545, 4to. 2, *Chronographia o Repertorio de los Tiempos*, Seville, 1554, 4to. 3, He was also the author of two maps : one of America, which was never published ; and the other of Seville and its territory, which was used by Ortelius, in his *Theatrum Orbis Terrarum.*

[2] The following inscription occurs on a monumental brass, in the middle aisle of Chatham Church, and is here given from a rubbing, with which we have been favoured by William Thomas Wright, Esq., of Gravesend : — " Here lieth buried the bodie of Steuen Borough, who departed this life ye xijth of July, in ye yere of our Lord 1584, and was borne at Northam, in Deuonshire, ye xxvth of Septemb', 1525. He in his life-time discouered Muscouia, by the Northerne sea passage to St. Nicholas, in the yere 1553. At his settyng foorth of England, he was accompanied with two other shippes, Sir Hugh Willobie beinge Admirall of the fleete, who, with all the Company of ye said two shippes, were frosen to death in Lappia ye same winter. After his discouerie of Roosia, and ye Coastes there to adioyninge — to wit, Lappia, Nova Zemla, and the Cuntrie of Samoyeda, etc. : hee frequented ye trade to St. Nicholas yearlie, as chiefe pilot for ye voyage, untill he was chosen for one of ye fowre principall Masters in ordinarie of ye Queen's Maties royall Navy, where in he continued beinge imployed as occasion required, in charge of sundrie sea seruises, till time of his death." This inscription is printed in the *Registrum Roffense*, p. 731.

admitting of masters and pilots, giuing him great honour, and presented him with a payre of perfumed gloues, woorth fiue or six Ducates. I speake all this to this ende, that the like order of erecting such a Lecture here in London, or about Ratcliffe, in some conuenient place, were a matter of great consequence and importance for the sauing of many mens liues and goods, which nowe, through grosse ignorance, are dayly in great hazerd, to the no small detriment of the whole realme.[1] For whiche cause I haue dealt with the right worshipfull sir Frances Drake, that seeing God hath blessed him so wonderfully, he woulde do this honour to him selfe and benefite to his countrey, to bee at the cost to erect such a lecture: Whereunto, in most bountifull maner, at the verie first, he answered, that he liked so well of the motion, that he would giue twentie poundes by the yeere standing, and twentie poundes more before hand to a learned man, to furnish him with instruments and maps, that woulde take this thing vpon him: yea, so readie he was, that he earnestly requested mee to helpe him to the notice of a fitte man for that purpose, which I, for the zeale I bare to this good actio', did presently, and brought him one, who came vnto him and conferred with him thereupon: but in fine he would not vndertake the lecture vnless he might haue fourtie pounde a yeere

Margin notes: A lecture of the art of nauigatio' necessarie for to be erected in London. The bountifull offer of Sir Fra'cis Drake toward furthering the art of Nauigation.

---

[1] In the course of nearly three hundred years, but little improvement, if any, appears to have been effected in this respect. In the year 1848, certain papers relating to the commercial marine of Great Britain were presented to both Houses of Parliament: they consist of answers addressed to Mr. Murray, of the Foreign Office, in reply to queries submitted to several of the British Consuls abroad—having a particular reference to the character and conduct of British shipmasters and seamen. Two sentences from these documents will suffice to show how closely the present state of things resembles that against which Hakluyt so strongly protests:—"There is no system of regular education for the merchant service of Great Britain; but in foreign countries this is much attended to" (page 1). Again:—"Is it justifiable, that the lives of thousands of persons should be jeoparded, because shipowners have a right to place incompetent persons in charge of vessels?" (page 142).

DEDICATORIE. 17

standing, and so the matter ceased for that time: howebeit, the worthie and good Knight remaineth still constant, and will be, as he told me very lately, as good as his worde. Nowe, if God shoulde put into the head of any noble man to contribute other twentie pounde to make this lecture a competent liuing for a learned man, the whole realme no doubt might reape no small benefite thereby. To leave this matter and to drawe to an ende I haue heare, right worshipfull, in this hastie worke first put downe the title which we haue to that part of America which is from Florida to 67 degrees northwarde by the letters patentes graunted to Iohn Gabote and his three sonnes, Lewes, Sebastian, and Santius, with Sebastians owne Certificate to Baptista Ramusius of his discouerie of America, and the testimonie of Fabian, our own Chronicler. Next, I have caused to bee added the letters of Mr. Robert Thorne to King Henrie the eight, and his discourse to his Ambassadour, doctor Ley, in Spaine, of the like argument, with the Kings setting out of two ships for discouerie in the 19 yere of his raigne. The' I have translated the voyage of Iohn Verarzanus from thirtie degrees to Cape Briton (and the last yeere, at my charges and other of my friendes, by my exhortation, I caused Iaques Cartiers two voyages of discouering the grand Bay, and Canada, Saguinay, and Hochelaga, to bee translated out of my Volumes, which are to be annexed to this present translation). Moreouer, following the order of the map, and not the course of time, I have put downe the discourse of Nicholaus and Antonius Zenie. The last treatise of Iohn Ribault is a thing that hath been alreadie printed, but not nowe to be had, vnlesse I had caused it to be printed againe.[1] The mappe is

[1] The title of the first edition of this treatise is " The whole and true discouerye of Terra Florida, (englished the Florishing lande) Conteyning aswell the wonderfull straunge natures and maners of the people, with the merueylous commodities and treasures of the country: As also the plesaunt Portes, Hauens and wayes therevnto. Neuer founde out before the last yere 1562. Written in Frenche by Captaine Ribauld, the fyrst

D

master Michael Lockes, a man, for his knowledge in diuers languages, and especially in Cosmographie, able to doe his countrey good, and worthie, in my iudgment, for the manifolde good partes in him, of good reputation and better fortune. This cursorie pamphlet I am ouer bold to present vnto your worshippe: but I had rather want a litle discretion then to bee founde vnthankful to him which hath been alwaies so readie to pleasure me and all my name.

Heere I cease, crauing pardon for my ouer boldnesse, trusting also that your worshippe will continue and increase your accustomed fauour towarde these godly and honourable discoueries.

Your worshippe's humble alwayes

to commaunde. R. H.

that whollye discouered the same. And nowe newly set forthe in Englishe the xxx of May. 1563. Prynted at London by Rouland Hall for Thomas Hacket." A copy is in the general library of the British Museum, but the work is of great rarity.

A LATINE COPIE OF THE LETTERS PATENTES
OF KING HENRIE THE SEUENTH, GRAUNTED
vnto Iohn Gabote and his three Sonnes, Lewes,
Sebastian, and Santius, for the discouering of
newe and vnknowen Landes.

HENRICUS *dei gratia rex Angliæ et Franciæ et dominus hiberniæ, omnibus ad quos præsentes literæ nostræ peruenerint, salutem. Notum sit et manifestum: quod dedimus et concessimus, ac per præsentes damus et concedimus pro nobis et hæredibus nostris dilectis nobis Ioanni Gaboto ciui Veneciarum, Lodouico, Sebastiano et Santio, filiis dicti Ioannis, et eorum et cuiuslibet eorum hæredibus et deputatis, plenam ac liberam authoritatē facultatem et potestatem nauigandi ad omnes partes, regiones et sinus maris orientalis, occidentalis, et septentrionalis, sub banneris, vexillis et insigniis nostris, cum quinque nauibus siue nauigijs cuiuscunque portituræ et qualitatis existant et cum tot et tantis nautis et hominibus quot et quantos in dictis nauibus secum ducere voluerint, suis et eorum proprijs sumptibus et expensis ad inueniendum, discoperiendum et inuestigandum quascunque insulas, patrias, regiones siue prouincias gentilium et infidelium quorumcunque in quacunque parte mundi positas, quæ Christianis omnibus ante hæc tempora fuerint incognitæ. Concessimus etiam eisdem et eorum cuilibet eorumque et cuiuslibet eorum hæredibus et deputatis ac licentiam dedimus ad affigendum prædictas banneras nostras et insignia in quacunque villa, oppido, castro, insula seu terra firma a se nouiter inuentis. Et quod prænominatus Ioannes et filii eiusdem seu hæredes et eorundem deputati quascunq; huiusmodi villas, castra, oppida et insulas a se inuentas quæ subiugari, occupari, possideri possint, subiugare, occupare, possidere valeāt tanquā vasalli nostri et gubernatores, locatenentes et deputati, eorundem dominium,* titulum et iurisdictionem earundem villarum, castrorum, oppidorum, insularum, ac terræ firmæ sic inuentorum nobis acquirendo. Ita tamen vt ex omnibus fructibus, proficuis, emolumentis, commodis, lucris, et obuentionibus ex huiusmodi nauigatione prouenientibus, præfatus Ioannes et filii ac hæredes, et eorum deputati teneātur et sint obligati nobis pro omni viagio suo, toties quoties ad portū nostrū Bristolliæ applicuerint (ad quem omnino applicare teneātur et sint astricti) deductis omnibus sūptibus et impensis necessariis per eosdem factis, quintam partem capitalis lucri facti, siue in mercibus siue in pecuniis persoluere. Dantes nos et concedētes eisdē suisq: hæredibus et deputatis, vt ab omni solutione custumarum omniū et singulorum bonorum ac mercium, quas secum reportarint ab illis locis sic nouiter inuentis, liberi sint et immunes. Et insuper dedimus et concessimus eisdem ac suis hæredibus et deputatis, quod terræ omnes firmæ, insulæ, villæ, oppida, castra et loca quacunq; a se inuenta, quot-quot ab eis inueniri contigerit, non possint ab aliis quibusuis nostris subditis frequentari seu visitari, absq: licentia prædictorum Ioannis et eius filiorum suorumq; deputatorum, sub pœna amissionis tā nauium, quam bonorum omniū quorumcunq; ad ea loca sic inuenta nauigare præsuentiū. Volentes et strictissime mandantes omnibus et singulis nostris subditis tam in terra quam in mari constitutis, vt præfato Ioanni et eius filiis, ac deputatis, bonā assistentiam faciant et tam in armandis nauibus seu nauigiis, quam in prouisione quietatus et victualium pro sua pecunia emendorum, atq: aliarum omnium rerum sibi prouidendarum pro dicta nauigatione sumenda, suos omnes fauores et auxilia impertiant. In

Martii 1495. cuius rei testimonium has literas nostras fieri fecimus patentes: teste me ipso apud Westmonasteriū quinto die Martii, anno regni nostri vndecimo.

THE SAME LETTERS PATENTS IN ENGLISH.

HENRIE, by the grace of God, king of England and France, and Lorde of Irelande, to all, to whom these presentes shall come, greeting. Be it knowen, that we haue giuen and granted, and by these presentes doe giue and grant for us and our heyres, to our well beloued John Gabote, citizen of Venice, to Lewes, Sebastian, and Santius, sonnes of the saide John, and to the heires of them and euery of them, and their deputies, full and free authoritie, leaue, and power, to sayle to all partes, countreys, and seas, of the East, of the West, and of the North, under our banners and ensignes, with fiue ships of what burden or quantitie soeuer they be: and as many mariners or men as they will haue with them in the saide ships, upon their owne proper costes and charges, to seeke out, discouer, and finde, whatsoeuer iles, countreyes, regions or prouinces, of the heathen and infidelles, whatsoeuer they bee, and in what part of the worlde soeuer they be, whiche before this time haue been vnknowen to all Christians. We haue granted to them also, and to euery of them, the heires of them, and euery of them, and their deputies, and haue giuen them licence to set up our banners and ensignes in euery village, towne, castel, yle, or maine lande, of them newely founde. And that the foresaid John and his sonnes, or their heires and assignes, may subdue, occupie, and possesse, all such townes, cities, castles, and yles, of them founde, which they can subdue, occupie, and possesse, as our vassailes and lieutenantes, getting vnto vs the rule, title, and iurisdiction of the same villages, townes, castles, and firme lande so founde. Yet, so that the foresaide John and his sonnes and heires, and their Deputies, bee holden and bounden of all the fruites, profites, gaines, and commodities, growing of such nauigation, for euery their voyage, as often as they shall arriue at our port of Bristoll (at the which port they shall be bounde and holden only to arriue), all manner of

Licence gra'ted to Iohn Gabot his sonnes and heires, to discouer lands vnder the king's banner.

To subdue and possesse those Landes as the kings vassalles.

The fift of all goods to be paid to the king.

necessarie costes and charges by them made being deducted, to pay vnto us in wares or money the fifth part of the Capitall gaine so gotten. Wee giuing and graunting vnto them and to their heires and Deputies, that they shall bee free from all paying of customes of all and singuler such merchandize as they shall bring with them from those places so newely founde.

Freedome from all customes.

None but they and their assignes may trauaile thither.

And, moreouer, wee haue giuen and graunted to them, their heires and Deputies, that all the firme landes, Iles, Villages, Townes, Castles, and places, whatsoeuer they be, that they shall chaunce to finde, may not of any other of our subiectes bee frequented or visited without the licence of the foresayd John, his sonnes, and their deputies, under paine of forfayture as well of their shippes as of all and singuler goods of all them that shall presume to sayle to those places so founde. Willing and most straightly commaunding all and singuler our subiectes, as well on lande as on sea, appointed officers, to giue good assistāce to the aforesaid John and his sonnes and deputies, and that as well in arming and furnishing their ships or vessels, as in prouision of quietnesse, and in buying of victualles for their money, and all other thinges by them to be prouided, necessarie for the saide nauigation, they doe giue them all their helpe and fauour. In witnesse whereof, wee have caused to bee made these our letters patentes. Witnesse our selfe at Westminster, the fifte day of March, in the xi yeere of our reigne.

The 5 of March 1594.

A NOTE OF SEBASTIAN GABOTES VOYAGE OF
Discouerie, taken out of an old Chronicle, written by
Robert Fabian, sometime Alderman of London,
which is in the custodie of John Stowe, Citizen,
a diligent searcher and preseruer of Antiquities.

THIS yeere the King (by meanes of a Venetian, whiche made himselfe very expert and cunning in knoweledge of the circuite of the worlde and Ilandes of the same as by a Carde and other demonstrations reasonable hee shewed), caused to man and victuall a shippe at Bristowe, to search for an Ilande, whiche hee saide hee knewe well was riche and replenished with riche commodities. Which Ship, thus manned and victualed at the kinges cost, diuers merchants of London ventured in her small stockes, being in her as chiefe Patrone the saide Venetian. And in the companie of the saide shippe sayled also out of Bristowe three or foure small ships fraught with sleight and grosse merchandizes, as course cloth, Caps, Laces, points, and other trifles, and so departed from Bristowe in the beginning of May: of whom in this Maiors time returned no tidings. *In the 13 yere of king Henrie the VII. 1498.* *Note.* *Bristow.* *William Purchas, Maior of London.*

Of three sauage men which. hee brought home and presented vnto the king in the XVII yeere of his raigne.

This yeere also were brought vnto the king three men, taken in the new founde Iland,[1] that before I spake of in William Purchas time, being Maior. These were clothed in beastes skinnes, and ate rawe fleshe, and spake such speech that no man coulde understand them, and in their demeanour like to bruite beastes, whom the king kept a time after. *Three sauage men brought into England.* *Rawe flesh. Beastes skins.*

[1] Ilands.—Stowe, *Annals*, p. 485. Edit. 1615.

Of the which vpon two yeeres past after I saw two apparelled after the maner of Englishmen, in Westminster pallace, which at that time I coulde not discerne from Englishemen, till I was learned what they were. But as for speech, I heard none of them vtter one worde.

John Baptista Ramusius, in his preface to the thirde volume of the nauigations,[1] writeth thus of Sebastian Gabot :—

In the latter part of this volume are put certaine relations of John de Verarzana, a Florentine, and of a great Captaine[2] a Frenchman, and the two voyages of Jaques Cartier, a Briton,[3] who sailed vnto the lande set in fiftie degrees of latitude to the north, which is called New France : and the which landes hitherto it is not throughly knowne whether they doe ioyne with the firme lande of Florida and *Noua Hispania*, or whether they be separated and diuided all by the Sea as Ilands : and whether that by that way one may goe by Sea vnto the countrie of Cathaio :[4] as many yeeres past it was written vnto me by Sebastian Gaboto, our countrie man Venetian, a man of great experience, and very rare in the art of

Sebastian Gabots letters to Ramusius.

[1] Page 6. Edit. 1565.

[2] The title of this piece is as follows :—" Discorso d'un gran capitano di mare Francese del luoco di Dieppa sopra le navigationi fatte alla terra nuova dell' Indie occidentali, chiamata la nuova Francia, da gradi 40 fino a gradi 47 sotto il polo artico, e sopra la terra del Brasil, Guinea, Isola di San Lorenzo e quella di Summatra, fino alle quali hanno navigato le caravelle e navi Francesi." Who the great captain may have been does not appear.

[3] *i. e.*, from Brittany.

[4] CATHAIA, or CATHAY, has been mentioned by writers as a great kingdom, as early as the thirteenth century : it is not easy, however, to ascertain what district was comprised under this appellation. The locality was the north of China ; but the notions of the early cosmographers appear to have been far from definite upon the subject.—See a learned dissertation, by Andreas Müller, entitled *Disquisitio Geographica et Historica de Chataja*, in which he discusses " Quænam Chataja sit, et an sit idem ille terrarum tractus quem Sinas et vulgo Chinam vocant, aut pars ejus aliqua?" Berolini, 1671, 4to.

SEBASTIAN GABOTES VOYAGE. 25

Nauigation and the knowledge of Cosmographie: who sayled along and beyonde this lande of Newe Fraunce, at the charges of King Henrie the seuenth, king of Englande. And hee tolde mee, that hauing sayled a long time West and by North beyonde these Ilandes vnto the latitude of 67 degrees and an halfe under the North Pole, and at the 11 day of June, finding still the open Sea without any manner of impediment, hee thought verily by that way to haue passed on still the way to Cathaio, which is in the East, and woulde haue done it, if the mutinie of the shipmaster and marriners had not rebelled, and made him to returne homewardes from that place.[1] But it seemeth that God doth yet still reserue this great enterprise for some great Prince to discouer this voyage of Cathaio by this way; which for the bringing of the spiceries from India into Europe were the most easie and shortest of all other wayes hetherto founde out. And, surely, this enterprise woulde bee the most glorious, and of most importance of all other, that can be imagined, to make his name great, and fame immortall, to all ages to come, farre more then can be done by any of all these great troubles and prise.

He calleth them Ilands.

Sebastion Gabot might haue sailed to Cathaio.

This voyage to Cathay reserued by God for some great Prince.

This way the shortest of all others.

This discouery were a most glorious enteprise.

[1] There is much contradictory evidence, and of an early date, as to the degree of north latitude actually reached by S. Cabot; and the natural consequence has been great discrepancy in the statements of later writers, according as they have followed one or other of the earlier authorities. The doubt is, whether he stopped short at 56 degrees, or had penetrated as high as 67, when compelled to turn back by the mutinous fears of his crew. There is a strong presumption in favour of his having actually discovered Hudson's Straits, and gained the 67th degree through Fox's Channel.—See Ramusio, *Navigationi*, vol. i, fol. 402. Edit. 1550. *Id.* vol. iii, fol. 417. Edit. 1565; the various statements in Hakluyt's *Principall Navigations*, vol. iii, p. 6-9, 25, 26. Edit. 1600; vol. iv, p. 417. Edit. 1811; Gomara, *Historia general de las Indias*, fol. 31. Edit. 1554; and also the *Memoir of S. Cabot*, by Biddle, where the subject will be found discussed at considerable length. It is to be regretted that this gentleman has not been as careful in the arrangement of the very valuable materials he has brought together, as he has been diligent in the collection of them: we can rarely be certain that we have got all the information contained in his book upon any given subject.

E

warres, which dayly are vsed in Europe among the miserable Christian people.

This much concerning Sebastion Gabotes discouerie may suffice for a present cast: but shortly, God willing, shall come out in print, all his owne mappes and discourses, drawne and written by himselfe,[1] which are in the custodie of the worshipfull master Williā Worthington,[2] one of her Maiesties Pensioners, who (because so worthie monumentes shoulde not be buried in perpetuall obliuion) is very willing to suffer them to be ouerseene and published in as good order as may bee, to the encouragement and benefite of our Countriemen.

William Worthington, Pensioner.

[1] Cabot's Maps and Discourses were never printed. See also *Memoir of S. Cabot*, page 221, where Mr. Biddle suggests that Worthington may have been a creature of Philip II of Spain, and have been employed by him for the purpose of gaining possession of all Cabot's charts and papers.

[2] William Worthington. One of the "ordinary gentlemen and pensioners" of King Edward VI, and "bailiff and collector of the rents and revenues of all the manors, messuages, and hereditaments, within the city of London and county of Middlesex, which did belong to colleges, guilds, fraternities, or free chapels."—Strype, *Ecclesiastical Memorials*, vol. ii, part II, page 234. Oxford, 1822.

A DECLARATION OF THE INDIES AND LANDES
discouered and subdued vnto the Emperour and the king
of Portugale; and also of other partes of the Indies *and
rich countries to be discouered, which the worshipfull
Master Robert Thorne, merchant of London* (who
dwelt long in the city of Siuil, in Spaine), exhorted
King Henrie the eight to take in hande.

MOST EXCELLENT PRINCE,

EXPERIENCE proueth that naturally all Princes bee desirous to extend and enlarge their dominions and kingdomes. Wherfore it is not to bee maruelled to see them euery day procure ye same, not regarding any cost, perill, and labour, that may thereby chaunce; but rather it is to bee marueiled if there be any prince content to liue quiet with his owne dominions. For surely the people would thinke he lacketh the noble courage and spirit of all other. The worlde knoweth that the desires of Princes haue beene so feruent to obtaine their purpose, that they haue aduentured and proued things to mans coniecture impossible, the which they haue made possible, and also things difficult haue made facil; and thus to obtaine their purpose, haue in maner turned vp and downe the whole worlde so many times, that the people inhabiting in the farthest regiō of the occident, haue pursued with great desires, labours, and perils, to penetrate and enter into the farthest regions of the Orient: And in likewise those people of the said partes of the Orient haue had no lesse labour and desire to enter and penetrate into the farthest land of the Occident, and so following their purchase [purpose?] haue not seased vntill they could passe no farther by reason of the great Seas. This naturall inclination is cause that scarsely it may bee saide there is any kingdome stable, nor king quiet, but that his owne imagination, or other Princes his neighbours, doe trouble him. God and nature hath prouided to your Grace, and to your Gracious progenitors, this Realme of Englande, and set it in so fruitefull a place, and within suche limites, that it shoulde seeme to bee a place quiet and aparted from all the foresaide desires. One speciall cause is, for that it is compassed with the Sea: by reason thereof it seemes, this notwithstanding, their desires and noble courages haue been most commonly like vnto others: and with marueilous great labours, costes, and perilles, they haue trauelled and passed the Seas, making warre not onely with kings and dominions nigh neighbours, but also with them of farre countries, and so hath wonne and conquered many riche and faire Dominions, and amplified this your Graces Realme with great victorie and glory. And also nowe of late, your Grace hauing like courage and desire, and not without iust cause to enlarge this your kingdome, and demaund your limites and tribute of the French king, which at that present hee restrained, your Grace in person passed with a great power into France,[1] putting your Grace's person to great paine and labour, and without doubt victoriously you had conquered the saide Realme of Fraunce as yee began, if your aduersarie had not reconciled him, and knowledged your Graces right and title: and so promised truely to pay the tribute then due, and fulfill your request in all thinges, and also desired your Grace for peace, the which of your clemencie you could not refuse.

Nowe I, considering this your noble courage and desire, and also perceiuing that your Grace may at your pleasure, to your greater glory, by a godly meane, with litle cost, perill, or labour to your Grace or any of your Subiectes, amplifie and inriche this your saide Realme, I knowe it is my bounde dutie to manifest this secrete vnto your Grace, which hitherto, as I

---

[1] Henry VIII passed over into France in the month of June, 1513.

suppose, hath beene hid: which is, that with a small number Note. of shippes there may bee discouered diuers newe landes and kingdomes, in the whiche, without doubt, your Grace shall winne perpetuall glory and your Subiects infinite profite. To which places there is left one way to discouer, which is into the North: For that of the foure partes of the worlde it seemeth three partes are discouered by other Princes. For out of Spaine they haue discouered all the Indies and Seas Occidentall, and out of Portugale all the Indies and Seas Oriental: So that by this part of the Orient and Occident they haue compassed the worlde. For the one of them departing towarde the Orient, and the other towarde the Occident, met againe in the course or way of the middest of the day, and so then was discouered a great part of the same Seas and coastes by the Spaniardes. So that nowe rest to bee discouered the said North partes, the which it seemeth to mee is onely your charge and dutie. Because the situation of this your Realme is thereunto neerest and aptest of all other: and also for that you haue alreadie taken it in hande: And, in Note. mine opinion, it will not seeme well to leaue so great and profitable an enterprise, seeing it may so easily, and with so little coste, labour, and daunger, bee followed and obteined: Though, heretofore, your Grace hath made theereof a proofe, and founde not the commoditie thereby as you trusted, at this time it shall bee no impediment. For there may bee nowe prouided remedies for thinges then lacked, and the inconueniences and lettes remooued that then were cause your Grace's desire tooke no full effect, which is, the courses to be chaunged, and followe the aforesaid new courses.[1] And con-

---

[1] In Hakluyt's *Collections*, vol. i, page 515, we find an account of "The voyage of Sir Thomas Pert and S. Cabota to Brasil, St. Domingo, and St. John de Porto Ricco, an. 1516." This is the only voyage of the kind in Henry VIII's reign, prior to the time when Thorne wrote this Declaration; and is, no doubt, the "proofe" referred to in the text. Hakluyt declares that the expedition failed through the cowardice of Sir Thomas Pert; but we are not informed whether the object were the discovery of new

cerning the marriners, shippes, and prouision, an order may be deuised and taken, meete and conuenient, much better then hetherto. By reason whereof, and by God's grace, no doubt your purpose shall take effect. Surely the coste heerein will bee nothing in comparison to the great profite. The labour is much lesse, yea nothing at all, where so great honour and glory is hoped for: and, considering well the courses, truly the dāger and way is shorter to vs thē to spaine or Portugall, as by euident reasons appeareth. And nowe to declare some thing of the commoditie and vtilitie of this Nauigation and discouering: it is very cleere and certaine that the Seas that commonly men say that without great danger, difficultie, and perill, yea, rather, it is impossible to passe, those same Seas bee nauigable, and without any such daunger but that shippes may passe, and have in them perpetuall cleerenesse of the day without any darknesse of the night: which thing is a great commoditie for the nauigants to see at all times rounde about them, as well the safegardes as daungers; and howe great difference it is betweene the commoditie and perilles of other, which lease the most parte of euery foure and twentie houres the saide light and goe in darknesse, groping their way, I thincke there is none so ignorant but perceiueth this more plainely then it can bee expressed: yea, what a vantage shall your Graces Subiects haue also by this light to discouer the strange landes, countries, and coastes, for if they that bee discouered to sayle by them in darkenesse is with great danger, muche more then the coastes not discouered be dangerous to trauell by night or in darknesse. Yet these dangers or darkenesse hath not letted the Spaniardes and Portingals and other to discouer many unknowen realmes to their great perill, which con-

Note.

regions, or a predatory excursion against the Spanish possessions. The "new courses" recommended by Thorne, evidently refer to the expediency of attempting a northern passage in preference to the more beaten track towards New Spain.

sidered (and that your Grace's Subiectes may haue the said lighte) it will seeme your Grace's subiects to bee without actiuitie or courage in leauing to do this glorious and noble enterprise. For they, being past this little way which they named so dangerous, which may bee ii or iii leagues before they come to ye Pole, and as much more after they passe the Pole, it is cleere that from thence foorth the Seas and landes are as temperat as in these partes, and that then it may be at the will and pleasure of the marriners to choose whether they will saile by ye coastes that bee colde, temperate, or hot. For they being past the Pole, it is plaine they maye decline to what parte they list. If they will goe towarde the Orient, they shall inioy the regions of all the Tartarians that extende towarde the midday, and from thence they may goe and proceede to the lande of ye Chinas, and from thence to the land of Cathaio oriental, which is of all the mayne lande most orientall that can bee reckoned from our habitation. And if from thence they doe continue their nauigation, following the coaste that returns towarde the occident, they shall fall in Melassa,[1] and so in all the Indees which we call oriental; and, following that way, may return hither by the Cape of Bona Speransa:[2] and thus they shall compasse the whole worlde. And if they will take their course after they be past the pole towarde the occident, they shall goe in the backe side of the new found lande, which of late was discouered by your Grace's subiectes, vntill they come to the backside and South seas of the Indees occidentalls. And so continuing their viage, they may returne thorowe the Straite of Magallanas to this countrey, and so they compasse also the worlde by that way, and if they goe this thirde way, and after they bee past the pole, goe right towarde the pole Antartike, and then decline toward the lands and Ilands situated betweene the Tropikes and vnder the Equinoctial, without

[1] Melassa—most probably the Malay peninsula.
[2] Cape of Good Hope.

doubt they shal find there ye richest lāds and Ilands of the worlde of Golde, precious stones, balmes, spices, and other thinges that wee here esteeme most: which come out of strang countreys, and may returne the same way.

By this, it appeareth your Grace have not onely a greate aduantage of the riches, but also your subiectes shal not trauell halfe of the way that other doe, which goe rounde about as aforesaide.

GRadus180. demercationis Portugalensiũ a terris isto ⊗ oppositis incipiunt, ac terminatur in gradus 160 huius cartæ versus orientem, secundum computationem Hispanorum. Et sic insulæ Tharsis & Ophir ditissimæ videntur extra illorum demercationem cadere. Portugalenses verò suam eleuationem a terris isto signo ⊗ oppositis incipere aiunt, & terminare in gradus 180. huius cartæ, ut videantur prædictas insulas utcũq; attingere, & gradus 180. demercationis Hispanorum a priore signo ⊗ secundum Hispanorum cõputationem. Vel incipiunt a posteriore secundum Portugalenses versus occidentem, & terminantur in gradus 160. secundum Hispanos, vel 180. secundum Portugalenses. Et sic, licet insulæ Tharsis & Ophir videntur attingere Portugalenses, tamen insulæ Capo verde dictæ, quæ intra supradicta signa ⊗ ✝ cadunt, videtur omittere. Et sic dum insulas Capoverde retinere volunt Portugalenses, illas Tharsis & ✝ Ophir non possunt attingere.

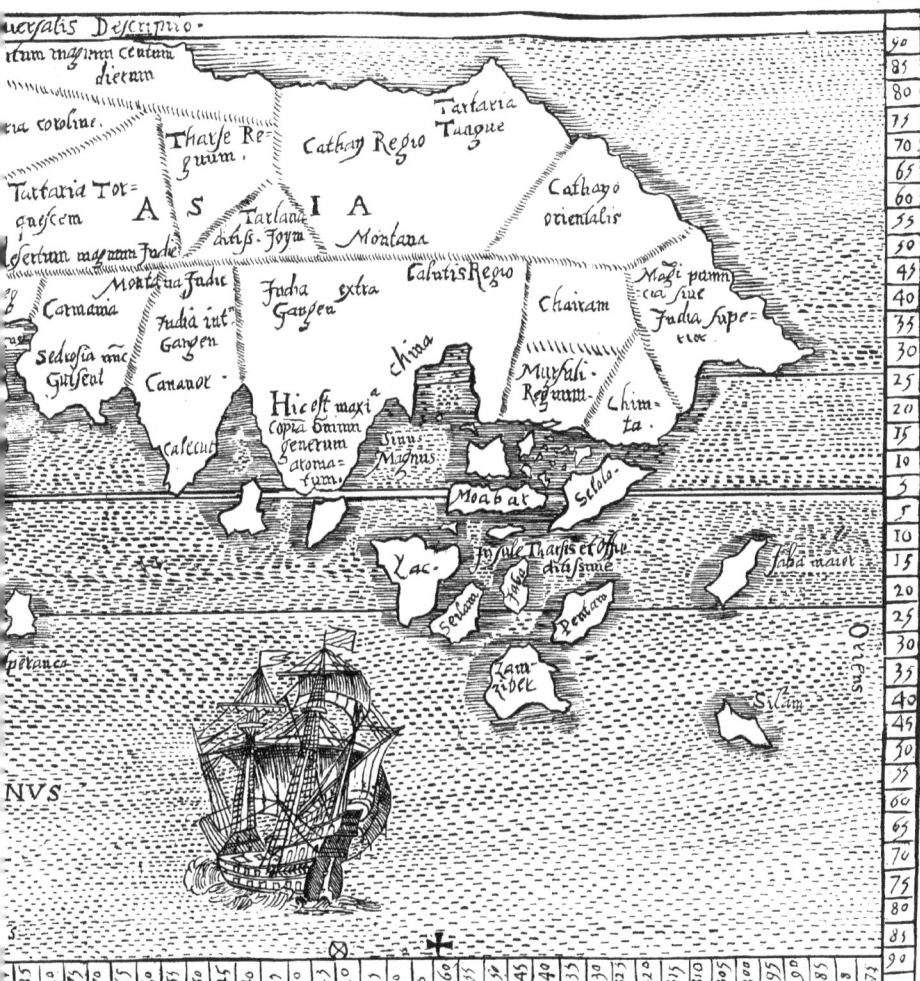

This is the forme of a Mappe sent 1527. from Siuill in Spayne by maister Robert Thorne marchaunt, to Doctor Ley Embassadour for king Henry the 8. to Charles the Emperour. And although the same in this present time may seeme rude, yet I haue let it out, because his booke coulde not well be vnderstood without the same. The imperfection of which Mappe may be excused by that tyme: the knowledge of Cosmographie not then beyng entred among our Marchauntes, as nowe it is.

THE BOOKE MADE BY THE RIGHT WORSHIPFUL

Master Robert Thorne, in the yeere 1527, in Siuill, to Doctour Ley,[1] Lorde Ambassadour for King Henrie the eight, to Charles the Emperour, being an information of the parts of the world discouered by him and the King of Portingale : And also of the way to the Moluccaes by the north.

RIGHT NOBLE AND REUERENDE IN, ETC. — I receiued your letters, and haue procured and sent to knowe of your seruant who your Lordeship wrote shoulde bee sicke in Merchena.[2] I can not there or els where heare of him, w'out he be returned to you or gone to S. Lucar and shipt. I can not iudge but that of some contagious sicknes he died, so that the owner of the house for defaming his house woulde bury him secretly and not be known of it. For such things haue oftē times happened in this countrey.

Also, to write to your Lordshippe of the newe trade of spicerie of the Emperour, there is no doubt but that the Ilandes[3] are fertile of cloues, nutmegs, mace, and cinnamon: And that the saide Ilandes, with other there about, abounde in gold, Rubies, Diamonds, Balasses,[4] Granates,[5] iacincts, and other stones and pearles, as al other lāds that are vnder and nere ye equinoctial. For we see where nature giueth any thing she is no nigarde. For as with vs and other, that are

---

[1] Dr. Edward Lee, chaplain and almoner to King Henry VIII, and afterwards archbishop of York.—Wood, *Athenæ Oxon.* vol. i, page 138. Edit. 1813.

[2] Marchena, near Seville.

[3] The Philippine Islands, discovered by Magellan for the crown of Spain, in the year 1521.

[4] The Balass ruby, of a faint red colour.

[5] Granate, or grenatite; prismatic garnet, of a shining, transparent, yellowish red.

aparted from the sayde equinoctiall, our mettalles be lead, tynne, and yron, so theirs be golde, siluer, and copper. And as our fruites and graines be aples, nuttes, and corne, so theirs bee dates, nutmegges, pepper, cloues, and other spices. And as wee haue iette, amber, cristall, iasper, and other like stones, so haue they rubies, diamonds, balasses, saphires, Iacincts, and other like. And though some say that of such precious mettals, graines, or kind of spices, and precious stones, the aboundance and quantitie is nothing so great as our mettals, fruites, or stones, aboue rehearsed: yet, if it be well considered how the quantitie of the earth vnder the equinoctiall to both the tropicall lines (in which space is founde the said golde, spices, and precious stones), to be as much in quantitie as almost all the earth from the tropickes to both the poles: it can not be denied but there is more quantitie of the said mettels, fruites, spices, and precious stones, then there is of the other mettels and other thinges before rehearsed. And I see that the preciousnesse of these thinges is measured after the distance that is betweene vs, and the things that we haue appetite vnto. For in this nauigation of the spicerie was discouered, that these Ilands nothing set by golde, but set more by a knife and a nayle of yron, then by his quantitie of Golde: and with reason, as the thing more necessarie for mans seruice. And I doubt not but to them shoulde bee as precious our corne and seedes, if they might haue them, as to vs their spices: and likewise the peeces of glasse that heare wee haue counterfayted, are as precious to them as to vs their stones: which by experience is seene daylie by them that haue trade thither. This of the riches of those countries is sufficient.

Touching that your Lordship wrote, whether it may be profitable to the Emperour or no, it may be without doubte of great profit: if, as the King of Portingall doth, he woulde become a marchant and prouide shippes, and their lading, and trade thither alone, and defende the trade of these

Ilands for himselfe. But other greater busines withholdeth him from this. But still, as nowe it is begunne to bee occupied, it would come to much. For the ships comming in safetie, there would thither many euery yeere, of whiche to the Emperour is due of all the wares and Juelles that come from thence the fift part for his custome cleare without any cost. And besides this, he putteth in euery flote a certayn quantitie of money, of whiche hee enioyeth of the gaines pounde and poundes, like as other aduenturers doe. In a flote of three shippes and a carauell, that went from this citie, armed by the marchauntes of it, which departed in Aprill last past, I and my partener haue 1400 Ducates, that Note. we employed in the sayde fleete, principally for that two Englishmen, friends of mine, whiche are somewhat learned in Cosmographie, shoulde goe in the same shippes, to bring mee certaine relation of the situation of the countrey, and to bee experte in the Nauigation of those seas, and there to haue informations of many other things and aduise that I desire to know especially. Seeing in these quarters are shippes and marriners of that countrey, and cardes by which they sayle, though much vnlike ours: that they should procure to haue the said Cards, and learne howe they vnderstande them, and especially to know what Nauigation they haue for those Ilandes Northwardes and Northeastwarde.

For if from the sayde Ilandes the Sea do extende without Note. interposition of lande, to sayle from the North poynt to the Northeast poynt, 1700 or 1800 leagues, they should come to the Newe founde Ilandes that wee discouered, and so wee shoulde bee neerer to the sayde spicerie by almost 2000 leagues then the Emperour or the king of Portingal are. And to aduise your Lordshippe whether of these spiceries of the King of Portingal or the Emperours is neerer, and also of the titles that eyther of them hath, and howe our Newe founde landes are parted from it (for that by writyng without some demonstration it were harde to giue any declaration of it),

I haue caused that your Lordeshippe shall receyue herewith a little Mappe or Carde of the worlde: the whiche I feare mee shall put your Lordshippe to more labour to understande then mee to make it, only for that it is made in so little roome that it cannot be but obscurely set out, y^t is desired to be seene in it, and also for y^t I am in this science little expert: Yet to remedy in part this difficultie, it is necessary to declare to your Lordshippe my intent, with which I trust you shal perceiue in this card part of your desire, if, for that I cannot expresse mine intent with my declaratiō, I doe not make it more obscure.

First, your Lordship knoweth that the Cosmographers haue deuided the earth by 360 degrees in latitude, and as many in longitude, vnder the which is comprehended al the roundnesse of the earth: the latitude beeing deuided into 4 quarters, ninetie degrees amount to euerie quarter, which they measure by the altitude of the poles, that is, the North and South starres, beeing from the line equinoctiall, till they come right vnder the North starre, the saide ninetie degrees: and as muche from the sayde line equinoctiall to the South starre bee other ninetie degrees. And asmuche more is also from eyther of the saide starres agayne to the equinoctiall. Which, imagined to be rounde, is soone perceiued thus 360 degrees of latitude to be consumed in the said foure quarters, of ninetie degrees a quarter, so that this latitude is the measure of the worlde from North to South, and from South to North. And the longitude, in which are also counted other 360, is counted frō West to East or from East to West, as in the card is set. The said latitude your Lordship may see marked and deuided in the end of this carde on the left hande. So that if you woulde know in what degrees of latitude any region or coast standeth, take a compasse and set the one foote of the same in the equinoctiall line right against the said region, and apply the other foote or compasse to the saide region or coast, and then set the sayd compasse at the ende of the

<small>To know the latitudes.</small>

carde, where the degrees are deuided. And the one foote of
the cōpasse standing in the line equinoctiall, the other will
shewe in the scale the degrees of altitude or latitude that the
sayd region is in. Also, the longitude of the worlde I have
set out in the nether part of the carde, contayning also 360
degrees: which begin to be coūted, after Ptolome and other
Cosmographers, from an head land, called *Capo verde*,[1] which
is ouer against a little crosse, made in the part occidentall,
where the diuision of the degrees beginneth and endeth in
ye same *Capo verde*. Nowe, to knowe in what longitude
any lande is, your Lordshippe must take a ruler, or a compasse, and set the one foote of the compasse upon the lande,
or coast, whose longitude you woulde knowe, and extende
the other foote of the compasse to the nexte parte of one of
the transuersall lines in the Orientall or Occidentall part:
which done, set the one foote of the compasse in the saide
transuersall lyne at the ende of the nether scale, the scale of
longitude and the other foote sheweth the degree of longitude that the region is in. And your Lordshippe must vnderstande, that this carde, though little, conteyneth the vniuersall
whole worlde betwixte the twoo collaterall lines, the one in
the Occidentall parte descendeth perpendicular vppon the 175
degree, and the other in the Orientall on the 170 degree, whose
distaunce measureth the scale of longitude. And that whiche
is without the two sayde transuersall lynes is onely to shew
howe the Oriental part is ioyned with the Occident, and Occident with the Orient. For that that is set without the line in

(marginal note: To know the Longitudes.)

---

[1] The meridian adopted by Ptolemy is not Cape Verde, but Ferro, the
most westerly of the Canary Islands, which were well known to the
ancients as the Insulæ Fortunatæ, although gradually forgotten after the
destruction of Carthage, the great maritime power of antiquity. Some
have fixed the first meridian at the island of St. Nicholas, near Cape
Verde; some at the island of Corvo, one of the Azores. The Dutch have
chosen the Peak of Teneriffe; others, the Isle of Palma, one of the Canaries; and the French have reckoned, within the last hundred years, both
from the Island of Ferro, and from Paris.

the Orient parte is the same that is set within the other line in
the Occidentall parte : and againe, that that is sette without
the line in the Occidentall part is the same that is set within
the line on the Orientall parte: To shewe that though this
figure of the worlde, in playne or flat, seemeth to haue an
ende, yet one imagining that this sayde carde were set vpon
a round thing, where the endes shoulde touche by the lines,
it would plainely appeare howe the Orient part ioyneth with
the Occident, as there without the lines it is described and
figured. And for more declaration of the said card, your
Lordship shall vnderstand, that beginning on the parte Occidentall within the lyne, the first land that is set out is ye
mayne land, and Iland of the Indies[1] of ye Emperour. Which
mayne lande or coast goeth Northwarde, and finisheth in the
lande that wee founde, which is called heere *Terra de Labrador*. So that it appeareth the sayde lande that wee founde,
and the Indies, to bee all one mayne lande. The sayd coast
from the saide Indies Southwarde, as by the carde your
Lordshippe may see, cōmeth to a certaine straite sea, called
Estrecho de todos Sanctos: by which straite Sea the Spaniardes Now called the streit of Magelane.
go to the spiceries, as I shall declare more at large : the
which straite sea is right against the three hundred fifteene
degrees of Longitude, and is of Latitude or altitude from the
Equinoctiall fiftie-three degrees. The first lande from the
sayd beginning of the carde towarde the Orient, is certaine
Ilandes of the Canaries, and Ilandes of *Capo verde*. But
the first mayne lande next to the line Equinoctiall, is the
sayde *Capo verde*, and from thence northwarde by the streite
of this sea of Italie.[2] And so followeth Spayne, Fraunce,
Flaunders, Almaine, Denmarke, and Norway, which is the
highest parte toward the North. And ouer against Flaunders are our Ilandes of England and Irelande. Of the landes
and coastes within the straites, I haue set out onelye the

---

[1] Mexico and the West Indies.   [2] The Straits of Gibraltar.

Regions, deuiding them by lynes of their lymittes, by whiche playnelie I thinke your Lordship may see, in what situatiō euery region is, and of what highnesse, and with what regions it is ioyned. I doe thinke few are lefte out of all Europe. In the partes of Asia and Affrica, I could not so well make the said diuisions: for that they be not so well knowen, nor neede not so muche. This I write, because in the sayde carde bee made the sayde lynes, and strikes that your Lordshippe should vnderstande wherefore they doe serue. Also, returning to foresayde *Capo verde*, the coast goeth Southwarde to a cape, called *Capo de bona speransa:*[1] which is right ouer agaynst the sixtye and sixtie-fifte degree of Longitude. And by this cape goe the Portingales to their spicerie. For from this cape towarde the Orient, is the Lande of Calicut, as your Lordshippe may see in the head lande ouer against the 130 degree. From the said Cape of *Bona Speransa* the coast returneth toward the line Equinoctiall, and passing foorth, entreth the read sea, and returning out, entreth againe into the gulfe of Persia, and returneth towarde the Equinoctiall line, till that it commeth to the headland called Callicut[2] aforesaide, and from thence the coast, making a Gulfe,[3] where is the riuer of Ganges, returneth towarde the line to a head lande called Malacha, where is the principall spicerie: And from this cape, returneth and maketh a great Gulfe,[4] and after, the coast goeth right toward the Orient, and ouer against this last gulfe and coast be manie Ilandes,[5] which be Ilandes of the spiceries of the Emperour. Upon which the Portingales and he be at variaunce. The said coast goeth towarde the Note. Orient and endeth right against the 155 degrees, and after returneth toward the occident Northwarde: which coast not yet plainely knowne, I may ioyne to the new found land found by vs, that I spake of before. So that I finishe with

[1] Cape of Good Hope. [2] Now called Cape Comorin.
[3] The Bay of Bengal. [4] The Gulf of Siam.
[5] The Philippine Islands.

this, a briefe declaration of the carde aforesayde. Well I knowe I shoulde also haue declared how the coastes within the streites of the Sea of Italie runne. It is plaine, that passing the streites on the Northside of that Sea after the Coast of Granado, and with that which pertaynes to Spayne, is the coast of that which Fraunce hath in Italie. And then followeth in one peece all Italie, which lande hath an arme of a sea, with a gulf, which is called *Mare Adriaticum*. And in the bottome of this gulfe is the citie of Venice. And on the other part of the said gulfe is Sclauonia,[1] and nexte Grecia, then the streites of Constantinople,[2] and then the Sea called *Euxinus*, which is within the saide streites: and comming out of the said straits, floweth toward Turcia maior. (Though now on both sides it is called Turcia.) And so the coast runneth Southward to Syria, and ouer against the said Turcia are the Ilādes of Rhodes, Candie, and Cyprus. And ouer against Italie are the Ilandes of Sicilia and Sardinia. And ouer against Spaine is Maiorca and minorca. In the ende of the gulfe of Syria is Iudea. And from thence returneth the coast toward the Occident, till it commeth to the streites where wee beganne, whiche all is the coast of Affricke or Barbarie. Also, your Lordshippe shall vnderstande, that the coastes of the Sea throughout all the world I haue coloured with yellow, for that it may appeare that all that is within the line coloured yellow, is to be imagined to be mayne land, or Iland: and all without the sayde line so coloured to bee Sea; whereby it is easie and light to know it. Albeit, in this little roome, any other description would rather haue made it obscure then cleere. Also, the sayd coasts of the Sea are all set iustly after the manner and forme

---

[1] Istria, Croatia, and Dalmatia, to which the term Sclavonia was formerly applied, as well as to that part of Europe which is known at the present day as Sclavonia Proper, situate between the Save, the Danube, and the Illova.

[2] The Dardanelles and Sea of Marmora.

as they lye, as the nauigation approoueth thē throughout all the carde, saue onely the coastes and Iles of the spicerie of ye Emperour, which is from ouer against the 160 to the 215 degrees of Longitude. For these coastes and situations of the Ilands, euery of the Cosmographers and pilots of Portingall and Spayne doe set after their purpose. The Spaniards, more towards the Orient, because they should appear to appertaiñe to the Emperour: and the Portingalles more toward the Occident, for that they should fall within their iurisdiction. So that the Pilots and nauigants thither, which in such cases should declare ye truth, by their industrie doe set thē falsely euery one to fauour his prince. And for this cause can be no certaine situatiō of y^t coast and Ilands til this difference betwixte them be verified. Nowe, to come to the purpose of your Lordshippes demaunde, touching the difference betweene the Emperour and the king of Portingall, to vnderstād it better, I must declare ye beginning of this discouering. Though, peraduēture, your Lordship may say, y^t in that I haue writtē ought of purpose, I fall in the Prouerbe, *A gemino ouo bellum :* But your Lordship commaunded me to be large, and I take licence to be prolixouse, and shal be, peraduenture, tedious, but your Lordship knoweth that *nihil ignorantia verbosius.* In the yeere 1484,[1] the king of Portingal minded to arme certaine caruelles to discouer this spicery. Then forasmuch as he feared that being discouered, euerie other prince would send and trade thither, so y^t the cost and peril of discouering should be his, and the profite common : wherefore, first, he gaue knowledge of this his mynd to all princes christened, saying, y^t he would seeke amōgst ye infidels newe possessiōs of regions, and therefore

[1] In this year Congo was discovered by Diego Cam, a Portuguese.— Barros, *Asia*, Dec. I, fol. 39. This was the first voyage in which stone pillars were used by the Portuguese to mark their discoveries ; they had previously used wooden crosses. We do not find in the different histories of Portuguese discovery, any account of the application to the various sovereigns of Europe, mentioned in the text.

would make a certain army : and y^t if any of thē would help in ye cost of ye said army, he should enioy his parte of the profite, or honour, that shoulde come of it. And as then this discouering was holden for a straunge thing and vncertaine. Nowe they say, that all the Princes of Christendome aunsweared, that they woulde bee no parte of such an army, nor yet of the profite y^t might come of it. After the which, he gaue knowledge to the Pope of his purpose, and of the answere of all the Princes, desiring him, y^t seeing that none would helpe in the costes, that hee woulde iudge all that shoulde be founde and discouered to be of his iurisdiction, and commaund that none other Princes should intermeddle therewith. The pope saide not, as Christ saith, *Quis me constituit iudicem inter vos?* He did not refuse, but making himselfe as Lorde and Iudge of all, not only graūted that all that should be discouered from Oriēt to Occidēt should be the kings of Portingall, but also, that vpon great censures no other Prince should discouer but he : And if they did, all to be the kinges of Portingall.[1] So he armed a fleete, and in the yeere 1487 was discouered ye Ilands of Calicut,[2] from

[1] See Barros, *Asia* (Dec. 1, fol. 14-39. Edit. 1628), as to the grants to this effect by various popes (beginning with Martin V, down to Sextus IV), of all that might be discovered by the Portuguese from Cape Bojador to the East Indies inclusive. Also, Dec. 1, lib. ii, cap. 4 ; and Navarrete, *Colleccion de Viages*, tom. ii, p. 23 *et seqq.*; as to the bulls of Pope Alexander VI, dated 2nd and 3rd May 1493, granting to Spain the whole of the western hemisphere, to commence at a line drawn from the north to the south pole, one hundred leagues westward from the Azores and Cape Verde Islands.

[2] What is here termed the discovery of the islands of Calicut, or in other words, the passage to the East Indies by the Cape of Good Hope, was not accomplished until the year 1498. But in 1487, the practicability of the passage was proved by Bartholomeu Diaz, who actually doubled the cape in that year.—Barros, *Asia*, Dec. 1, fol. 43. Edit. 1628. On the 8th of July 1497, Vasco da Gama set sail from Lisbon for the purpose of accomplishing the passage to the east by this route; and after exploring the eastern coast of Africa as far as Melinda, he steered across the Indian Ocean, and made land in India for the first time at the city of Calicut, on the 18th of May 1498.—*Id.* Dec. 1, fol. 63-73.

whence is brought all the spice he hath. After this, in the yeere 1492, the king of Spaine, willing to discouer landes towarde the Occident, without making any such diligence, or taking licence of the king of Portingale, armed certayne caruelles, and then discouered this India Occidentall, especially two Ilandes of the saide India, that in this carde I set foorth, named, the one *Ladominica*, and the other Cuba,[1] and brought certaine gold from thence. Of the which, when the king of Portingall had knowledge, he sent to the king of Spayne, requiring him to give him ye said Ilands. For that by the sentence of the Pope, all that should be discouered was his, and that he should not proceede further in the discouerie without his licence. And at the same time it seemeth, that out of Castill into Portingale had gone, for feare of burning, infinite number of Iewes that were expelled out of Spayne, for that they would not turne to be Christians, and carried with thē infinite number of gold and silver. So that it seemeth that the King of Spayne answered that it was reasō that the king of Portingall asked, and that to bee obedient to that which the pope had decreed, he would giue him the said Ilands of the Indies. Now, for as much as it was decreed betwixt ye said kings, y^t none should receiue ye others subiects, fugitiues, nor their goodes, therefore the king of Portingale should pay and returne to the king of Spaine a million of Golde or more, that the Iewes had carried out of Spaine to Portingale; and that so doing, he would giue these Ilandes, and desist from any more discouering. And not fulfilling this, he would not onely not giue these Ilands, but procure to discouer more where him thought best. It seemeth that the king of Portingale would not, or could not, with his ease pay this mony. And so not paying that, he coulde not let the King of Spaine to discouer : so that hee

---

[1] The island of Dominica was discovered by Columbus, on the 3rd of November 1493 ; and Cuba in the month of October 1492.—*Select Letters of Columbus*, edited by Major for the Hakluyt Society, pp. 2, 21.

enterprised not toward the Orient where he had begun and found the spicery. And consented to the king of Spaine, that touching this discouering, they should deuide the worlde betweene them two. And that all that should be discouered frō *Capo verde*, where this carde beginneth to be counted in the degrees of longitude, to 180 of the sayde scale of longitude, which is halfe the worlde toward the Orient, and finisheth in this carde right ouer against a little crosse made at the sayde 180 degrees, to be the king of Portingalles. And all the lande from the sayde Crosse towarde the Occident vntill it ioyneth with the other Crosse in the Orient, which conteineth the other hundreth and eightie degrees, that is the other halfe of the worlde, to bee the king of Spaynes. So that from the lande ouer agaynst the sayde hundreth and eightie degrees vntill it finish in the three hundred and sixtie on both the endes of the carde, is the iurisdiction of the king of Spayne. So after this manner they deuided the worlde betweene them.[1] Nowe, for that these Ilands of spicerie fall neere the terme and lymites betweene these Princes (for as by the sayde carde you maye see they beginne from one hundred and sixtie degrees of Longitude, and ende in 215), it seemeth all that falleth from 160 to 180 degrees shoulde bee of Portingall: and all the rest of Spayne. And for that their Cosmographers and Pilots could not agree in the situation of the said Ilands (for the Portingals set them al within their 180 degrees, and the Spaniards set them all without: and for that in measuring, all the Cosmographers of both partes, or what other that euer haue beene, cānot giue certaine order to measure yᵉ lōgitude of the world as

[1] See *ante*, p. 42, note 1. An agreement between Spain and Portugal was concluded on the 7th of June 1494, and is known as the Capitulation of Tordesillas. Its object was to secure to Portugal all that might be discovered within a line, to be drawn from the north to the south pole, at the distance of three hundred and seventy leagues from the Cape Verde Islands.—Navarrete, *Colleccion de Viages y Descubrimientos*, tom. ii, p. 130 *et seqq*.

théy do of ye latitude: for y^t there is no starre fixed frō East to West, as are ye starrs of the poles from North to South, but all mooueth with the mouing diuine) : no mañer can be found how certainely it may be measured, but by con- iectures, as the Nauigantes haue esteemed the way they haue gone. But it is manifest, that Spayne had the situation of all the landes from *Capo verde* towarde the Orient of the Portingales to their 180 degrees. And in all their cardes they neuer hitherto set the sayd Ilands within their limita- tiō of the sayd 180 degrees (Though they knew very well of the Ilandes) til nowe that the Spaniards discouered them. And it is knowne that the king of Portingale had trade to these Ilands afore, but would neuer suffer Portingale to goe thither from Calicut: for so much as hee knewe that it fell out of his dominion : least by going thither there might come some knowledge of those other Ilandes of the King of Spayne, but bought the cloues of Merchauntes of that countrie, that brought them to Calicut, much deerer then they would haue cost if he had sēt for thē, thinking after this maner it would abide alwaies secrete. And now that it is discouered he sendes and keepes the Spanierds from the trade all that he can. Also, it should seeme, that when this foresaide consent of the diuision of the worlde was agreed of betweene them, the king of Portingale had alreadye dis- couered certayne Ilandes that lye ouer against *Capo verde*,[1] and also certayne parte of the mayne lande of India towarde the South, from whence he fet Brasill, and called it the lande of Brasill.[2] So for that all shoulde come in his terme and

The longi- tudes harde to be founde out.

[1] The Cape Verde Islands were discovered by Antonio Nolle, a Geno- vese, in the service of the Infante Don Henry of Portugal. Geographers are not agreed as to the year in which this discovery was made : accord- ing to Chelmicki (*Corografia Cabo-Verdiana*, p. 2), it was in the month of May 1446 ; but we find it also assigned to the years 1440, 1445, 1449, 1450, and 1460.

[2] The natural conclusion to be drawn from this and the following pas- sage is, that the Portuguese had discovered Brazil before the agreement as to the three hundred and seventy leagues had been entered into. But

limites, hee tooke three hundred and seuentie leagues beyonde Capo verde: and after this, his 180 degrees, being his part of the worlde, shoulde beginne in the Carde right ouer against the 340 degrees, where I haue made a little compasse with a crosse, and shoulde finishe at the 160 degree, where also I haue made an other little marke. And after this computation without any controuersie, the Ilandes of the spicerie fall out of the Portingales domination. So that nowe the Spaniardes say to the Portingales, that if they woulde beginne their 180 degrees from the saide Capo Verde, to the intent they shoulde extende more towarde the oriente, and so to touche those Ilandes of the spicerie of the Emperour, which is all that is betweene the two crosses made in this carde, that then the Ilandes of Capo verde, and the lande of Brasill that the Portingales nowe obtaine, is out of the sayde limitation, and that they are of the Emperours. Or if their 180 degrees they count from the 370 leagues beyonde the sayde Capo verde, to include in it the sayde Ilandes and landes of Brasill, then plainely appeareth the saide 180 degrees shoulde finishe longe before they come to these Ilandes of the spicerie of the Emperour: As by this Carde your Lordeshippe may see. For their limittes shoulde beginne at the 340 degrees of this Carde, and ende at 160 degrees, where I haue made two little marks of the compasse with crosses in them.

this is not correct, the Capitulation of Tordesillas bearing date five years before the coast of Brazil was known. The name given to the country by the discoverers was Santa Cruz, which was afterwards changed to Brazil, from the immense quantity of the wood so called found there. There is early evidence to prove that the wood gave the name to the country, and not the country to the wood. The following passage occurs in the *Liber Radicum* of the Rabbi Kimchi, a Spaniard, who lived in the thirteenth century. "Algummim (2 Chron. ix, 10), alias Almugim (1 Kings, x, 12): both stand for the same, and in common language it is called Corallo; but some persons declare it to be a sort of wood used for dying, called in Arabic *Albakam*, and in common language *Brazil*."—Kimchi, *Lib. Rad. sub voce,* לצם.

So that plainely it shoulde appeare by reason, that the Portingales shoulde leaue these Ilandes of Capo verde, and land of Brasill, if they would haue part of the spicerie of the Emperours: or else holding these, they haue no parte there. To this the Portingales say, that they will beginne their 180 degrees from the selfe same Capo verde: for that it maye extende so muche more towarde the oriente, and touche these Ilandes of the Emperours: and woulde winne these Ilandes of Capo verde and lande of Brasill neuer the lesse, as a thinge that they possessed before the consent of this limitation was made.[1]

So none can verylye tell whiche hath the best reason.

They bee not yet agreed, *Quare sub Iudice lis est.* But without doubte, by all coniectures of reason, the sayde Ilandes fall all without the limitation of Portingale, and pertayne to Spaine, as it appeareth by the most parte of all the Cardes made by the Portingales, saue those they haue falsified of late purposely.[2] But nowe touching that your Lordeshippe

[1] See *ante*, page 9, note, as to the discovery of Brazil.

[2] In the year 1524, a serious effort was made to settle these differences, and commissioners from both crowns met at the boundary between Badajoz and Yelves. It had been previously agreed, that the Portuguese should be allowed the three hundred and seventy leagues mentioned in the text, and the points to be discussed were—1, Upon what medium the line of demarcation should be made, whether upon the marine chart, or upon the spherical map; 2, How they should fix the proper situation of the Cape Verde Islands; and 3, From which of the Cape Verde Islands they should commence the measurement of the three hundred and seventy leagues, for the line of demarcation. Difficulties immediately arose. There was found to be a difference of seventy leagues between the situation of places, as laid down in the maps produced by the Spaniards and the Portuguese. Again, the Portuguese wished to measure the three hundred and seventy leagues from La Sal, the most eastern of the Cape Verde Islands; the Spaniards, from San Antonio, the most western: the distance between the two being not less than seventy leagues. The Portuguese rejected both the marine charts and maps of the Spaniards, and endeavoured to confine the inquiry to the question of actual possession of the Spice Islands. The Spanish commissioners, on the other hand, insisted upon fixing the line of demarcation, affirming,

wrote, whether that which wee discouered toucheth any thing the foresayde coastes: once it appeareth plainely, that the Newe founde lande that wee discouered is all a mayne lande, with the Indies occidentall, from whence the Emperour hath all the golde and pearles: and so continueth of coaste more then 5000 leagues of length, as by this Carde appeareth. For from the saide newe landes it proceedeth toward the occidēt to the Indies, and from the Indies returneth toward the orient, and after turneth southwarde vp till it come to the straytes of Todos Sanctos, whiche I reckon to bee more then 5000 leagues.

<small>New found la'd discouered by the englishmen.</small>

<small>Note.</small>
So that to the Indians it shoulde seeme that wee haue some title, at least, that for our discouering wee might trade thither as other doe. But all this is nothing neere the spicerie.

<small>To sayle by the pole.</small>
Nowe then (if from the sayde newe founde landes the Sea bee Nauigable), there is no doubt, but sayling Northwarde and passing the pole, descending to the equinoctiall lyne, wee shall hitte these Ilandes, and it shoulde bee much more shorter way then eyther the Spaniardes or the Portingales haue. For wee bee distaunt from the pole but 39 degrees, and from the pole to the Equinoctiall bee 90, the which added together be 129 degrees, leagues 2480, and myles 7440. Where wee shoulde finde these Ilandes. And the Nauigation of the Spaniardes to the spicerie is, as by this Carde you may see, from Spayne to the Ilandes of Canarie, and from these Ilandes they runne ouer the lyne Equinoc-

<small>that the line of partition for the three hundred and seventy leagues must commence at the Island of San Antonio, and that the Moluccas, Sumatra, Malacca, the Philippine Islands, and also China, fell within the line of demarcation for Castille, by many degrees; and that their situation was not in the longitude affirmed by the Portuguese. In the midst of these discussions, the term for which the commission was appointed expired, and the commissioners ultimately came to the decision that they could decide nothing; and not knowing what better to do, left the matter to be settled by their respective sovereigns.—Herrera, *Historia de la Espana*, tom. i, Descripcion, p. 2, Dec. III, lib. vi, cap. 3-8; Navarrete, *Colleccion*, tom. iv, p. 310 *et seqq.*</small>

tiall Southwarde to the cape of the mayne lande of Indians, called the Cape of Sainte Augustine, and from this cape Southwardes to the straytes of Todos Sanctos, in the whiche Nauigation to the sayde straites is 1700 or 1800 leagues: and from these straytes, being past them, they returne toward the line Equinoctiall to the Ilandes of spicerie, whiche are distant from the sayde straites 4200 or 4300 leagues. ^{Or the straites of Magelen.}

The Nauigation of the Portingalles to the sayd Ilands is, departing from Portingale Southwarde towarde the Capo verde, and from thence to another Cape, passing the lyne equinoctiall, called Capo de bona speransa, and from Portingale to the cape is 1800 leagues, and from this cape to the Ilandes of spicerie of the Emperour is 2500 leagues.

So that by this nauigation amounteth all to 4300 leagues. So that as afore is sayde, if betweene our Newe founde landes, or Norway, or Islande, the Seas towarde the north be Nauigable, wee shoulde goe to these Ilandes a shorter way by more then 2000 leagues. And though wee went not to the saide Ilandes, for that they are the Emperours or Kinges of Portingale, wee shoulde by the way, and comming once to the line Equinoctiall, finde landes no lesse riche of Golde and spicerie as all other landes are vnder the saide line Equinoctiall: and also shoulde, if wee may passe vnder the North, enioye the Nauigation of all Tartarie. ^{Note.}

Which should bee no lesse profitable to our commodities of clothe, then these spiceries to the Emperour and king of Portingale. ^{Benefite to Englande.}

But it is a generall opinion of all Cosmographers, that passing the seuenth clyme,[1] the sea is all ice, the colde so ^{Obiection.}

---

[1] A climate is a space of the surface of the globe comprised between two circles parallel to the equator. The general rule for determining the region embraced by each climate has been a certain variance in the length of the longest day, so that the longest day at the parallel nearest to the equator shall exceed the longest day at the parallel nearest to the pole by the period of time fixed upon. Ptolemy made a quarter of an hour his rule; but most geographers, up to a period long subsequent to the time

much that none can suffer it. And hitherto they had all the like opinion, that vnder the lyne Equinoctiall for muche heate the lande was inhabitable.[1]

Answere. Yet since by experience is prooued no lande so much habitable nor more temperate. And to conclude, I thinke the same shoulde bee founde vnder the North if it were experimented. For as all iudge, *Nihil fit vacuum in rerum natura:* So I iudge there is no lande inhabitable nor Sea innauigable.

A true opinion. If I should write the reason that presenteth this vnto mee, I shoulde bee too prolixe, and it seemeth not requisite for this present matter. God knoweth that though by it I shoulde haue no great interest, yet I haue had and still haue no little

A voyage of discouerie by the pole. minde of this businesse: So that if I had facultie to my will, it should bee ye first thing that I woulde vnderstande,

M. Thorne and M. Eliot, discouerers of New found land euen to attempt, if our Seas Northwarde bee nauigable to the Pole, or no. I reason, that as some sicknesses are hereditarious and come from the father to the sonne, so this inclin-

when Thorne wrote, made half an hour the boundary of each climate, which would bring the "seventh clyme" mentioned in the text to about 50½ degrees north. This, however, would not at all bear out the assertion, that "it is a general opinion of all cosmographers, that passing the seventh clyme, the sea is all ice, the cold so much that none can suffer it." Geographers have been far from unanimous on the subject. Ricciolius, in his *Geographia et Hydrographia reformata*, page 268, Edit. Venetiis, 1672, fol. commences a very learned disquisition, "De climatum diversitate," by observing, "There is a marvellous confusion respecting them, and not a little need of reformation." It is quite clear, that the opinion quoted by Thorne, must have been founded upon tables very different from those generally given; and that his "seventh clyme" must have been much farther north. Jan Janson, referring to the necessarily increasing contraction of the climates as they receded from the equator, when the variance of time is made the basis of the limit, proposed that the northern and southern hemispheres should be divided into ten climates of ten degrees each,—thus rejecting all consideration both of time and of temperature. This would bring the northern limit of the seventh climate to seventy degrees; but this division, which was adopted by Blaeu, was not introduced until more than a century after Thorne wrote.—Janson, *Novus Atlas*, tom. i, cap. 6, Introd. Edit. 1658; Blaeu, *De Globis*, cap. 4, No. 3.

[1] *In* pro *non*, i. e., *not* habitable.

ation or desire of this discouerie I inherited of my father, which with another merchant of Bristowe, named Hugh Eliot, were the discouerers of the newe found lāds, of the which there is no doubt, as now plainly appeareth, if the marriners woulde then haue been ruled, and folowed their pilots mind, the lands of the west Indies, from whence all the gold commeth, had been ours. For all is one coaste, as by the carde appeareth, and is aforesaide. Also in this carde, by the coastes where you see C, your Lordship shall vnderstand it is set for Cape or head land; where I, for Iland; where P, for Port; where R, for Riuer. Also in al this little carde, I thinke nothing be erred touching the situation of the land, saue onely in these Ilands of spicery: which for that as afore is sayd, euery one setteth them after his minde, there can be no certification how they stand. I doe not denie that there lacke many things that a consūmate carde should haue, or that a right good demonstration desireth. For there should be expressed all the mountaines and riuers that are principall of name in the earth, with the names of Portes of the sea, the names of all principall cities, whiche all I might haue set, but not in this Carde, for the little space would not consent.

The cause why the west Indees were not ours: which also Sebastian Gabot writeth in an epistle to Baptist Ramusius. [1]

Your Lordship may see that setting only the names almost of euery region and yet not of all, the roome is occupied. Many Ilands are also left out for the saide lacke of roome: the names almost of all portes put to silence, with the roses of the windes or pointes of the compasse: For that this is not for Pilots to sayle by, but a summarie declaration of that which your Lordship commaunded. And if by this your Lordshippe cannot well perceiue the meaning of this carde, of the which I woulde not maruell, by reason of the rude composition of it, will it please your Lordship to aduise mee to make a bigger and a better mappe, or els that I may cause one to bee made. For I knowe my selfe in this and all

---

[1] Ramusio, *Navigationi*, vol. iii, p. 6, Preface. Edit. 1565.

other nothing perfect but *Licet semper discens, nunquam tamen ad perfectam scientiam peruenient*. Also I knowe to set the forme Sphericall of the worlde in *Plano* after the true rule of Cosmographie, it would haue been made otherwise then this is: howbeit the demonstration shoulde not haue beene so plaine. And also these degrees of longitude, that I set in the lower part of this Card, shold haue been set along by the line equinoctiall, and so then must bee imagined. For the degrees of longitude neare either of the poles are nothing equal in bignes to them in the equinoctiall. But these are set so, for that setting them a long the Equinoctiall, it would haue made obscure a great parte of the mappe. Many other curiosities may be required, which for the nonce I did not set downe, as well for that the intent I had principally was to satisfie your doubt touching the spicerie, as for that I lacke leysure and time. I trust your Lordshippe, correcting that which is erred, will accept my good will, which is to do any thing that I maye in your Lordshippes seruice. But from henceforth, I knowe your Lordshippe wil rather commande me to keepe silence then to be large, when you shalbe weeried with the reading of this discourse. Iesus prosper your estate and health.

Your Lordshippes Robert
Thorne, 1527.

Also this Carde, and that which I write touching the variaunce betweene the Emperour and the king of Portingale, is not to bee shewed or communicated there with many of that Courte. For though there is nothing in it preiudiciall to the Emperour, yet it may bee a cause of paine to the maker: as well for that none may make these Cardes but certaine appointed and allowed for masters, as for that peraduenture it woulde not sounde well to them, that a stranger shoulde knowe or discouer their secretes: and wolde appeare worst of all, if they vnderstand that I write touching y\ short way to the spicerie by our Seas. Though, peraduenture, of troth, it is not to bee looked too, as a thing that by all opinions is vnpossible, and I thinke neuer will come to effect: and, therefore, neither heere nor elswhere is it to bee spoken of. For to moue it amongest wise men it shoulde bee had in derision. And, therefore, to none I woulde haue written nor spoken of such things but to your Lordship, to whome boldly I commit in this all my foolish fantasie as to my selfe. But if it please God that into Englande I may come with your Lordship, I will shewe some coniectures of reason, though against the generall opinion of Cosmographers, by which shall appeare this that I say not to lacke some foundation. And tyll that time, I beseeche your Lordship let it bee put to silence: and in the meane season it may please God to sende our two Englishmen, that are gone to the spicerie, which may also bring more plaine declaration of y^t which in this case might bee desired.[1] Also I knowe, it needed not to haue beene so prolixe in the declaration of this Carde to your Lordship, if the saide Carde had beene very well made after the rules of Cosmographie. For your Lordship woulde soone vnderstande it better then I, or any other that coulde haue made it: and so it shoulde appeare that I shewed *Delphinum natare*. But for that I haue made it after my rude maner, it is necessarie that I be the declarer or gloser of mine owne work, or els your Lordship should haue had much labour to vnderstande it, which nowe with it also cannot bee excused it is so grossely done. But I knewe you looked for no curious things of mee, and therefore I trust your Lordshippe will accept this and holde mee for excused. In other mens letters that they write, they craue pardon that at this present

---

[1] See *ante*, p. 35, where Thorne informs us, that he and his partner had ventured 1400 ducats in a certain fleet of Spanish merchantmen, principally that he might have an opportunity of sending two Englishmen with them, who might thereby haye an opportunity of observing the navigation to the Spice Islands.

they write no larger : but I must finish, asking pardon, that at this present I write so largely. Iesus preserue your Lordship with augmentation of dignities.

Your seruant Robert Thorne. 1527.

This Exhortation to king Henrie the eight, with the discourse to Doctor Ley, his Ambassadour in Spaine, was preserued by one master Emmanuel Lucar, executour to master Robert Thorne, and was friendly imparted vnto mee by master Cyprian Lucar, his sonne, an honest Gentleman, and very forwarde to further any good and laudable action. And that it may bee knowne that this motion tooke present effect with the king, I thought it good herewithall to put downe the testimonie of our Chronicle that the king set our shippes for this discouerie in his lifetime. Master Hall[1] and master Grafton[2] in their Chronicles write both thus : This same moneth king Henry the eight sente two faire ships well manned and victualed, hauing in them diuers cunning men, to seeke strange regions : and so they set foorth out of the Thames the xx day of May, in the xix yeere of his raigne. In the yeere of our Lorde 1527.[3]

[1] Vol. ii, fol. 158, b. Edit. 1550.   [2] Page 1149. Edit. 1569.

[3] These two ships were the Mary of Guildford and the Sampson, which sailed from Plymouth on the 10th of June 1527. The Mary of Guildford arrived at Newfoundland on the 21st of July; but the Sampson had been separated from her consort in a storm about the 1st of July, and was never heard of afterwards. The fullest account of the voyage, and that extremely meagre, is given by John Rut, the master of the Mary of Guildford, in a letter addressed by him to King Henry VIII, from St. John's Bay, Newfoundland, and dated August 3rd, 1527. Purchas, *Pilgrimes*, vol. iii, p. 809. See also Hakluyt (vol. iii, p. 129), who evidently had not seen Rut's letter, and was very imperfectly acquainted with the particulars of this voyage ; and *Memoirs of Cabot*, p. 272, *et seqq.*

FINIS.

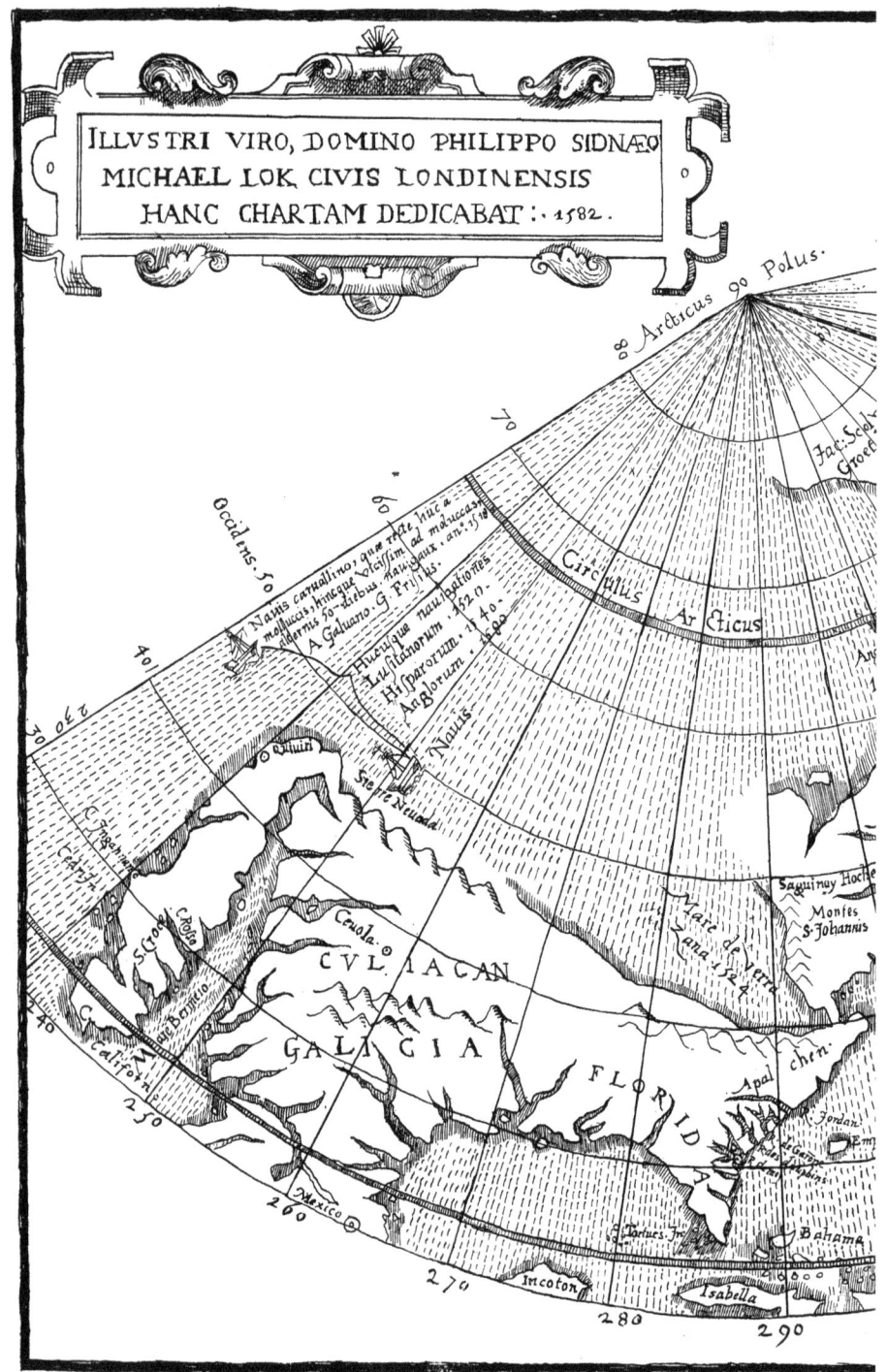

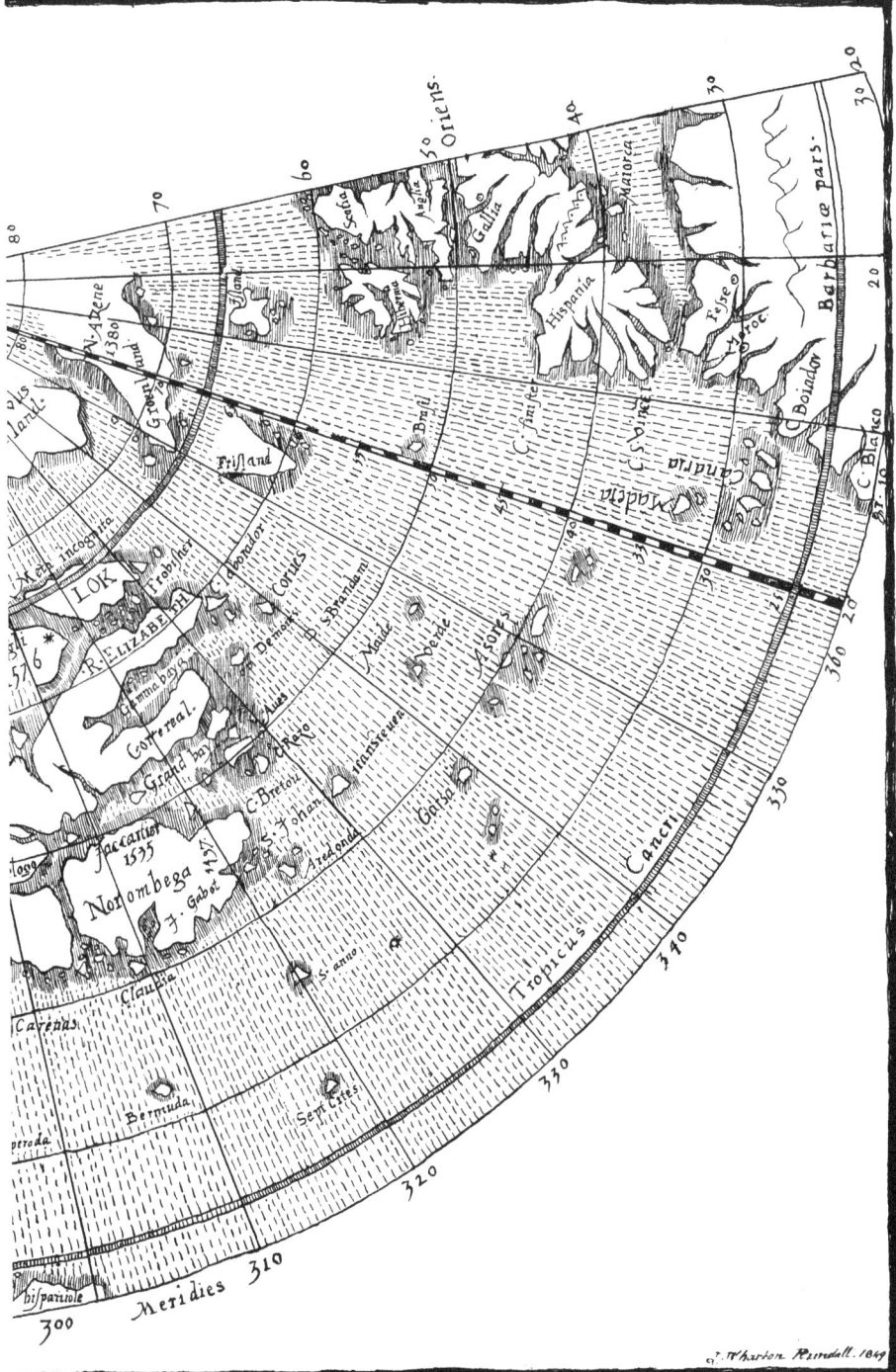

TO THE MOST CHRISTIAN KING OF FRAUNCE, FRAUNCES THE FIRST.

THE RELATION OF JOHN VERARZANUS, A
Florentine, of the lande by him discouered in
the name of his Maiestie, written in Diepe
the eight of July 1524.

I WROTE not to your Maiestie (most Christian king) since the time wee suffered the tempest in the North partes, of the successe of the foure Ships which your Maiestie sent forth to discouer new lands by the Ocean, thinking your Maiestie had been alreadie duly enformed thereof. Nowe by these presents I will giue your Maiestie to vnderstand howe by the violence of the windes wee were forced with ye two ships, the Norman and the Dolphin, in such euill case as they were, to lande in Britaine.[1] Whereafter wee had repaired them in all pointes as was needefull, and armed them very well, wee tooke our course a long by the coast of Spaine. Afterwardes, with the Dolphin alone, wee determined to make discouerie of newe Countries, to prosecute the nauigation wee had alreadie begun, which I purpose at this present to recount vnto your Maiestie, to make manifest the whole proceeding of the matter. The 17 of Ianuarie, the yeere 1524, by the grace of God, wee departed from the dishabited Rocke,[2] by the Isle of Madera, appertaining to the king of Portingall, with fiftie men, with victuals, weapon, and other ship munition very well prouided and furnished

---

[1] Brittany.   [2] One of the Dezertas.

for 8 monethes: And sayling westwards with a faire Easterly winde, in 25 dayes wee ranne 500 leagues, and the 20 of Februarie wee were ouertaken with as sharpe and terrible a tempest as euer any saylers suffered: whereof with ye diuine helpe and mercifull assistaunce of Almightie God, and the goodnesse of our ship, accompanied with the good hap of her fortunate name, wee were deliuered, and with a prosperous wind followed our course West and by North, and in other 25 dayes wee made aboue 400 leagues more: where wee discouered a newe land,[1] neuer before seene of any man, either auncient or moderne, and at the first sight it seemed somewhat lowe, but beeing within a quarter of a league of it, wee perceiued by the great fiers that wee sawe by the Sea coaste that it was inhabited: and saw that the lande stretched to the Southwards: in seeking some conuenient harborough whereby to come a lande and haue knowledge of the place, wee sayled fiftie leagues in vaine, and seeing the lande to runn still to the Southwards, wee resolued to returne backe againe towardes the North, where we found our selues troubled with the like difficulty: at length, beeing in despaire to finde any port, wee caste anker upon the coast, and sent our Boate to shore, where we sawe great store of people, which came to the Sea side, and seeing vs to approche they fled away, and sometimes would stande still and looke backe, beholding vs with great admiration: but afterwardes, beeing animated and assured with signes that wee made them, some of them came harde to the Sea side, seeming to reioyce very much at the sight of vs, and marueiling greatly at our apparell, shape, and whitenes, shewed vs by sundry signes where wee might most commodiously come a land with our Boat, offering vs also of their victuals to eate. Nowe I will briefly declare to your Maiestie their life and manners, as farre as wee coulde haue notice thereof: These people goe altogea-

---

[1] Probably in the neighbourhood of Charleston, in South Carolina, or of the Savannah.

ther naked, except only that they couer their priuie partes with certaine skinnes of beastes like vnto Marterns, which they fasten vnto a narrowe girdle made of grasse, verye artificially wrought, hanged about with tailes of diuers other beastes, which rounde about their bodies hang dangling downe to their knees. Some of them weare garlandes of byrdes feathers. The people are of colour russet, and not much vnlike the Saracens, their hayre blacke, thicke, and not very long, which they tye togeather in a knot behinde, and weare it like a taile. They are wel featured in their limbs, of meane stature,[2] and commonly somewhat bigger then we, brode breasted, strong armes, their legges and other partes of their bodies well fashioned, and they are disfigured in nothing, sauing that they haue somewhat brode visages, and yet not all of them: for wee sawe many of them well fauoured, hauing blacke and great eyes, with a cheerefull and stedie looke, not strong of body, yet sharpe witted, nymble and great runners, as farre as we coulde learne by experience; and in those two last qualities they are like to the people of the East partes of the worlde, and especially to them of the vttermost partes of China, wee coulde not learne of this people their manner of liuing, nor their particular customes, by reason of ye short abode we made on the shore,

---

[1] This should be Norumbega, or Nurumbega, as appears by the following passages, from a piece entitled "*Discorso d'un gran Capitano di Mare Francese*", inserted by Ramusio in his Collection, vol. iii, p. 425. Edit. 1565:—"Della terra di *Norumbega.*"......"La terra è detta da paesani suoi *Nurumbega*", etc. According to Michael Lok's map, and also that of Ortelius and some other geographers, Nurumbega comprised the district between the river and Gulph of St. Lawrence and the Hudson river. Cluverius, however, in his *Introductio ad Universam Geographiam*, p. 552, Amstel. 1697, says: "Pars tamen ejus [Nova Francia], *quæ ad mare accedit* Norumbega ab urbe cognomine dicta." And this corresponds with the map in Ramusio (vol. iii, page 424. Edit. 1565), where Nurumbega appears to comprise the southern portion of that district, from Long Island Sound to the Bay of Fundy.

[2] *i.e.*, middle or medium stature.

our companie being but small, and our ship ryding farre of in the Sea. And not farre from these we founde an other people, whose liuing wee thinke to bee like vnto theirs (as heereafter I will declare vnto your Maiestie), shewing at this present the situation and nature of the foresaide lande: The shore is all couered with small sande, and so ascendeth vpwardes for the space of fifteene foote, rising in forme of little hilles about fiftie paces broade. And sayling forwards, wee founde certaine small Riuers and armes of the Sea, that enter at certain creekes, washing the shore on both sides as the coast lyeth.[1] And beyonde this wee sawe the open Countrie rising in height aboue the sandie shore, with many fayre fieldes and plaines, full of mightie great woods, some verie thicke and some thinne, replenished with diuers sortes of trees, as pleasaunt and delectable to beholde as is possible to imagine. And your Maiestie may not thinke that these are like the woodes of Hercinia,[2] or the wilde Desertes of Tartary, and the Northerne Coastes full of fruitlesse trees : But full of Palme trees, Bay trees, and high Cypresse trees, and many other sortes of trees vnknowne in Europe, which yeeld most sweete sauours, farre from the shore; the propertie whereof wee coulde not learne for the cause aforesaide, and not for any difficultie to passe through the woods : Seeing they are not so thicke but that a man may passe through them. Neither doe wee thinke that they part taking of the East worlde rounde about them are all to geather voide of drugs or spicerie and other richesse of gold, seeing the colour of the lande doth so much argue it. And the lande is full of many beastes, as Stags, Deare, and Hares, and likewise of Lakes and Pooles of Fresh water, with great plentie of foules, conuenient for all kinde of pleasant game. This lande is in

[1] This description corresponds with the character of the shore and country about George Town and Long Bay.

[2] A vast forest in antient Germany, remarkable for its wild character in the time of Cæsar. The Black Forest in Suabia is a portion of it, and attests by its name the character of its gloomy parent.

latitude 34 D, with good and holsome ayre, temperate be- Gr. 34. tweene hot and colde, no vehement windes doe blowe in those Regions, and those that doe commonly raigne in those Coastes, are the North West and West windes in the Sommer season (in the beginning whereof wee were there), the skie cleere and faire, with very little raine: and if at any time the ayre bee cloudie and mistie with the Sowtherne winde, immediately it is dissolued, and waxeth cleare and fayre agayne. The Sea is caulme, not boysterous, the waues gentle, and although all the shore bee somewhat lowe and with out harborough: yet it is not daungerous to the saylers, beeing free from rockes and deepe, so that within foure or fiue foote of the shore, there is twentie foote deepe of water without ebbe or flood, the depth still increasing in such vniforme proportion. There is very good ryding at Sea: for any Ship beeing shaken in a tempest, can neuer perishe there by breaking of her cables, which wee haue proued by experience. For in the beginning of March (as is vsual in all Regions), beeing in the Sea oppressed with Northerne windes, and riding there, wee founde our anker broken before the earth fayled or mooued at all. Wee departed from this place, still running a long the coaste, which we found to trende towarde the East,[1] and wee saw euerie where verie great fiers by reason of the multitude of the inhabitants. While we rode on that Coaste, partlie because it had no harborough, and for that wee wanted water, wee sent our Boat a shore with 25 men:[2] where, by reason of great and continual waues that beate against the shore, being an open coast, without succour, none of our men coulde possible goe a shore without loosing our boate. We sawe there many people, which came vnto the shore, making diuers signes of friendship, and shewing that they were content wee shoulde come a lande, and by trial we Courteous found thē to be very courteous and gentle, as your maiestie and gentle people.

---

[1] Probably Onslow Bay. [2] Probably about Raleigh Bay.

shal vnderstand by the successe. To the intent we might sende them of our thinges, which the Indians commonly desier and esteeme, as sheetes of Paper, glasses, belles, and such like trifles : Wee sent a young man, one of our Marriners, a shore, who swimming towards them, and being within 3 or 4 yeards off the shore, not trusting them, cast the thinges vpon the shore, seeking afterwardes to returne, hee was with such violence of the waues beaten vpon the shore, that he was so bruised that hee lay there almost dead, whiche the Indians perceiuing, ranne to catche him, and drawing him out, they carried him a little way of from the sea : The young man perceiuing they caried him, beeing at the first dismaide, began then greatly to feare, and cried out pitiously, likewise did the Indians, which did accompanie him, going about to cheere him and giue him courage, and then setting him on the grounde at the focte of a little hill against the sunne, beganne to beholde him with great admiration, marueiling at the whitenesse of his fleshe : and putting off his clothes, they made him warme at a great fire, not without our great feare which remained in the boate that they would haue rosted him at that fire and haue eaten him. The young man hauing recouered his strength, and hauing stayed a while with them, shewed them by signes that hee was desirous to returne to the shippe : And they with great loue clapping him fast about with many embracings, accompanying him vnto the sea, and to put him in more assurance, leauing him alone, they went vnto a high grounde and stoode there, beholding him, vntil he was entred into the boate. This yong man obserued, as we did also, that these are of colour enclining to Blacke, as the other were, with their fleshe verie shining, of meane stature, handsome visag, and delicate limmes, and of verie little strength : but of prompt witte, farther wee obserued not.

Departing from hence, following the shore, which trended somewhat towarde the North, in 50 leagues space, wee came to another lande,[1] which shewed much more faire and full of woods, being very great, where we rode at Ancker, and that wee might haue some knowledge thereof, wee sent 20 men a lande, which entred into the countrey about two leagues, and they founde that the people were fledde to the woods for feare, they sawe onely one olde woman with a young maide of 18 or 20 yeeres olde, which, seeing our companie, hid themselues in the grasse for feare, the olde woman caried two Infantes on her shoulders, and behinde her necke a childe of 8 yeeres olde : the yong woman was laden likewise with as many : but when our men came vnto them, the women cryed out, the olde woman made signes that the men were fled vnto the woods as soone as they sawe vs : to quiet them and to winne their fauour, our men gaue them suche victuals as they had with them to eate, which the old woman receiued thankfully : but the yong woman disdained them al, and threwe them disdainefully on the grounde, they tooke a childe from the olde woman to bring into Fraunce, and going about to take the young woman, which was verye beawtifull, and of tal stature, they could not possibly, for ye great outcries that shee made, bring her to the sea, and especially hauing great woods to passe through, and being farre from the shippe, wee purposed to leaue her behinde, bearing away the childe onely. We found those folkes to bee more white than those that we founde before, being clad with certaine leaues y^t hang on boughes of trees, which they sowe together with thredes of wilde hempe, their heads were trussed vp after the same manner as the former were, their ordinarie foode is of pulse, whereof they haue great store, differing in colour and taste frō ours, of good and pleasant taste. Moreouer, they liue by fishing and fouling, which they take with ginnes, and bowes made of hard wood, the arrowes of Canes, being headed with the bones of fishe and other beastes. The beastes in these parts are much wilder

[1] About latitude 38 north.

thē in our Europe, by reason they are continually chased and hunted. Wee sawe many of their boates, made of one tree, 20 foote long, and 4 foote broade, which are not made with Iron, or stone, or any other kinde of metal (because that in all this countrie, for the space of 200 leagues whiche we ranne, wee neuer sawe one stone of any sort) : they help themselues with fyre, burning so much of the tree as is sufficient for the hollownesse of the boate, the like they doe in making the sterne and the foreparte, vntill it be fitte to saile vpon the sea. The lande is, in situation, goodnesse, and fairenes, like the other : it hath woods like the other, thinne and full of diuers sortes of trees: but not so sweete, because the countrey is more northerly and cold.

Wee sawe in this Countrey many Vines growing naturally, which growing vp take hold of the trees, as they do in Lombardie, w^c if by husbandmen they were dressed in good order, without all doubte they woulde yeelde excellent wines: for wee hauing oftentymes seene the fruite thereof dried, whiche was sweete and pleasaunt, and not differing from ours. Wee doe thinke that they doe esteeme the same, because that in euery place where they growe, they take away the vnder braunches growing rounde about, that the fruite thereof may ripen the better.

We found also roses, violettes, lillies, and many sorts of herbes, and sweete and odoriferous flowers, different from ours. We knewe not their dwellinges, because they were farre vp in the lande, and we iudge by manye signes that wee sawe, that they are of wood and of trees framed together.

Wee doe beleeue also, by many coniectures and signes, that many of them sleeping in the fieldes, haue no other couer then the open skye. Further knowledge haue wee not of them, we thinke y^t all the rest whose countreys we passed liue all after one manner. Hauing our aboade three dayes in this cuntrey, riding on the coast for want of harboroughs, we concluded to departe from thence, trending along the shore betweene the North and the East, sayling onely in the daytime, and riding at ancker by night. In the space of 100 leagues sayling, wee founde a very pleasant place, situated amongst certaine litle steepe hilles: from amiddest the which hilles there ran down into the sea a great streame of water, which within the mouth was very deep, and from ye sea to ye mouth of same, with the tyde, which wee found to rise 8 foot, any great vessell laden may passe vp.[1]

But because wee rode at Ancker in a place well fensed from the winde, wee woulde not venture our selues without knowledge of the place, and wee passed vp with our boate onely into the sayde Riuer, and sawe the Countrey very wel peopled. The people are almost like vnto the others, and clad with the fethers of foules of diuers colours, they came towardes vs very cherefully, making great showtes of admiration, shewing vs where we might come to lande most safely with our boate. We entred vp the said riuer into the lande about halfe a league, where it made a most pleasant lake about 3 leagues in compasse: on the which they rowed from the one side to the other, to the number of 30 of their small boates: wherein were many people, whiche passed from one shore to the other to come and see vs. And beholde, vpon the sodaine (as it is wont to fall out in sayling), a contrarie flawe of winde comming from the sea, wee were enforced to returne to our Shippe, leauing this lande to our great discontentment, for the great commoditie and pleasantnesse thereof, whiche wee suppose is not without some riches, all the hills shewing minerall matters in thē. We weied Ancker, and sayled towarde the East, for so the coast trended, and so alwayes for 50 leagues, being in the sight thereof, wee discouered an Ilande in the forme of a triangle, distant from the

_{The pleasantnes and riches of the lande.}

_{The descriptio' of Claudia Ilande.}

---

[1] The mouth of the Hudson River answers to this description. The Hudson is, most probably, the river known in this locality to the geographers of the sixteenth century as the Rio Grande.

maine lande 3 leagues, about the bignesse of the Ilande of the Rodes, it was full of hilles, couered with trees, well peopled, for we sawe fires all along the coaste, wee gaue the name of it of your Maiesties mother,[1] not staying there by reason of the weather being contrarie.

Claudia was wife of King Francis.

And wee came to another lande, being 15 leagues distant from the Ilande, where wee founde a passing good hauen, wherein being entred we founde about 20 small boates of the people, which with diuers cries and wondrings came about our shippe, comming no nerer then 50 paces towards vs, they stayed and behelde the artificialnesse of our ship, our shape, and apparel, thā they al made a loud showte together, declaring that they reioyced : when we had something animated them, vsing their geastes, they came so neere vs, that wee cast them certaine bells and glasses and many toyes, whiche when they had receiued, they lookte on them with laughing, and came without feare aborde our ship. There were amongst these people 2 kings, of so goodly stature and shape as is possible to declare, the eldest was about 40 yeares of ag, the second was a yong man of 20 yeeres old. Their apparell was

The Countrey of Sir H. G. Uoyage.

[1] Or rather his first wife, Claudia. Generally supposed to be the island now called Martha's Vineyard. If this supposition be correct (and it would be difficult to substitute any more plausible conjecture), it becomes impossible to make the subsequent account of Verazzani's course correspond with the present character of the coast, unless we admit, that at this point he sailed back a few leagues. He says : " Wee came to another land, being 15 leagues distant from the Ilande, where we founde a passing good haven":—and, subsequently, describes the land as lying east and west, and the mouth of the haven as open to the south. Sailing from Martha's Vineyard eastward, and following the coast, no haven would be found corresponding in any particular with that described in the text, nearer than Boston, which, however, is much more than fifteen leagues from Martha's Vineyard, which opens to the east and not to the south, and where the land runs north and south, and not east and west ; not to mention other points of difference. If, on the other hand, we suppose that on leaving Claudia, he approached the main land to the north-west, the fifteen leagues would bring him to Narraganset Bay, which in all its main features corresponds with the "passing good haven", as described in the text.

on this maner: the elder had upō his naked body a harts skin, wrought artificialie with diuers braunches like Damaske, his head was bare, with the haire tyed vp behinde with diuers knottes: About his necke he had a large chaine, garnished with diuers stones of sundrie colours, the young man was almost appareled after the same manner. This is the goodliest people, and of the fairest conditions, that wee haue found in this our voyage. They exceed vs in bignes, they are of the colour of brasse, some of thē encline more to whitness: others are of yellowe colour, of comely visage, with long and blacke heire, which they are very carefull to trim and decke vp, they are blacke and quicke eyed. I write not to your Maiestie of the other parte of their bodie, hauing all suche proportion as appertayneth to anye handsome man. The women are of the like conformitie and Beawtie, verie handsome and well-fauored, they are as well mannered and continente as anye women of good education, they are all naked, saue their priuie partes, whiche they couer with a Deares skinne, braunched or embrodered, as the men vse: there are also of them whiche weare on their armes verie riche skinnes of leopardes, they adorne their heades with diuers ornamentes made of their owne heire, whiche hange downe before on both sides their brestes, others vse other kinde of dressing them selues, like vnto the women of Egypt and Syria, these are of the elder sorte: and when they are married, they weare diuers toyes, according to the vsage of the people of the East, as well men as women.

Among whom wee sawe many plates of wrought coper, which they esteeme more then golde, whiche for the colour they make no accompt of, for that among all other it is counted the basest, they make most accompt of Azure and red. The things that they esteemed most of al those which we gaue them, were bels, cristall of Azure colour, and other toies, to hang at their eares or about their necke. They did not desire cloth of silke or of golde, much lesse of any other

sorte, neither cared they for thinges made of steele and
Iron, which wee often shewed them in our armour, whiche
they made no wonder at, and in beholding them they onely
asked the arte of making them : the like they did at our
glasses, which whē they behelde, they sodainely laught and
gaue them vs againe. They are very liberal, for they giue
that which they haue; we became great friendes with these,
and one day wee entred into the hauen with our shippe,
where as before wee rode a league of at sea by reason of the
contrary weather. They came in great companies of their
small boates vnto the ship with their faces all bepainted with
diuers colours, shewing vs y^t it was a signe of ioy, bringing
vs of their victuals; they made signes vnto vs where wee
might safest ride in the hauen for the safegarde of our shippe,
keeping still our companie : and after we were come to an
Ancker, we bestowed fifteene dayes in prouiding our selues
many necessary things, whether euery day the people repayred to see our ship, bringing their wiues with them,
whereof they are very ielous : and they themselues entring
abrode the shippe, and stayinge there a good space, caused
their wiues to stay in their boates, and for al the intreatie
we could make, offering to giue them diuers things, we could
neuer obtaine that they would suffer them to come aborde
our ship. And oftentimes one of the two kings comming
with his queene, and many gentlemen for their pleasure, to
see vs, they all stayed on ye shore, two hundred paces frō
vs, sending a small boate to giue vs intelligēce of their comming, saying they would come to see our shippe, this they
did in token of safetye ; and assoone as they had answere
from vs, they came immediately, and hauing stayed a while
to beholde it, they wondered at hearing the cryes and noyes
of the marriners. The queene and her maids stayed in a
very light boate, at an Iland a quarter of a leage off, while
the king abode a long space in our ship, vttering diuers
conceites with geastures, viewing with great admiration all

the furniture of the shippe, demaunding the propertie of euerie thing perticularly. He tooke likewise great pleasure in beholding our apparell, and in tasting our meates, and so courteously taking his leaue departed. And sometimes our men staying for two or three dayes on a little Ilande nere the ship for diuers necessaries (as it is ye vse of seamen), he returned with 7 or 8 of his gentlemen to see what we did, and asked of vs oft times if wee meant to make any long aboade there, offering vs of their prouision : then the king drawing his bowe, and running vp and downe with his gentlemen, made much sporte to gratifie our men; wee were oftentimes within the lande 5 or 6 leagues, which we found as pleasant as is possible to declare, very apt for any kinde of husbandry, of corne, wine, and oyle : for that there are plaines 25 or 30 leagues broad, open and without any impediment of trees of such fruitfulnesse, that any seede being sowne therein, will bring forth most excellent fruite. We entred afterwards into the woods, which wee found so great and thicke, that any armie, were it neuer so great, might haue hid it selfe therein, the trees whereof are okes, cipres trees, and other sortes, vnknowen in Europe. We found Pomi appii,[1] Damson trees, and Nutte trees, and many other sorts of fruits, differing frō ours : there are beasts in great abundance, as hartes, deares, leopardes, and other kinds, which they take with their nets and bowes, which are their

[1] A particular kind of apple; but this term is not in use at the present day, and probably never extended beyond Italy. Pliny (*Historia Naturalis*, b. 15, c. 14) says : " Ab Appio e Claudiana gente Appiana sunt cognominata"; from which we may infer, either that Appius introduced them into Italy from some foreign country, or that he produced them from some particular graft. Matthioli, in his *Discorsi nelli sei Libri di Dioscoride* (tom. i, p. 260), observes : " In Tuscany, those [apples] called ' appie' and ' mele rose', are prized before all others, because in these two species an aromatic and pleasing odour is found combined with a very agreeable taste. Wherefore, I think that those would not err much who should call the ' appie ' the *honey apple*, and the ' mele rose' the *Epirus apple* of Dioscorides."

chiefe weapons; the arrowes whiche they vse are made with great cunning, and in steade of iron they head them with smeriglio,[1] w^t iasper stone, and hard marble, and other sharp stones, which they vse in stead of iron to cut trees, and make their boates of one whole piece of wood, making it hollowe with great and wonderfull art, wherein 10 or 12 men may bee cōmodiously; their oares are shorte, and broad at the ende, and they vse them in the sea without anye daunger, and by maine force of armes, with as great speedinesse as they liste them selues. We sawe their houses, made in circuler or rounde fourme, 10 or 12 foote in compasse, made with halfe circles of timber, seperate one from another, without any order of building, couered with mattes of strawe wrought cunningly together, which saue them from the winde and raine, and if they had the order of building, and perfect skil of workmāship as we haue, there were no doubt but y^t they would also make eftsoones great and stately buildings. For all the sea coastes are full of cleare and glistering stones, and alablaster, and therefore it is full of good hauens and harbarours for ships. They mooue the foresaide houses from one place to another, according to the comm0ditie of the place and season, wherein they will make their aboade, and only taking of the couer they haue other houses builded incontinent. The father and the whole familie dwell together in one house in great number: in some of them we sawe 25 or 30 persons. They feede as the other doe aforesaide, of pulse, whiche doe growe in that countrey with better order of husbandry thē in the others. They obserue in their sowing the course of the Moone, and the rising of certaine starres, and diuers other customes spoken of by antiquitie. Moreouer, they liue by hunting and fishing; they liue long, and are seldome sicke, and if they chaunce to fall sicke at any time, they heale themselues with fire, without any phisition, and they say that they die for very age. They are very pitiful and charitable towardes their neighbours, they make

[1] Emery.

great lamentations in their aduersitie and in their miserie, the kinred recken vp all their felicitie, at their departure out of life, they vse mourning, mixt w^t singing, w^c continueth for a lōg space. This is asmuch as wee coulde learne of them. This lande is situated in the Paralele of Rome, in 41 degrees and 2 terces : but somewhat more colde by accidentall cause and not of nature (as I will declare vnto your highnesse els where), describing at this present the situation of the foresaide countrie, which lyeth East and West, I say that the mouth of the hauen lyeth open to the South halfe a league broade, and being entred within it, betweene the East and the North, it stretcheth twelue leagues : where it waxeth broder and broder, and maketh a gulfe aboute 20 leagues in compasse, wherein are fiue small Islandes, very fruitfull and pleasant, full of hie and broade trees, among the which Ilandes any great Nauie may ryde safe without any feare of tempest or other daunger. Afterwardes, turning towards the South, and in the entring into the Hauen, on both sides there are most pleasant hilles, with many riuers of most cleere water falling into the Sea.[1]

In the middest of this entraunce there is a rock of freestone growing by nature, apt to builde any Castle or Fortresse there, for ye keeping of the hauen. The fift of May, being furnished with all thinges necessarie, we departed from ye said Coast, keeping along in the sight thereof, and we sayled 150 leagues, finding it all wayes after one manner : but the lande somewhat higher with certaine mountaines, all which beare a shewe of minerall matter ; wee sought not to lande there in any place, because the weather serued our turne for sayling : but wee suppose that it was like to the

---

[1] After a very careful examination of the best printed maps,—American and English, and many MSS.,—we have come to the conclusion, that this haven is Narraganset Bay. In following a route like this of Verazzani, it must be borne in mind, that many of the statements as to distance will be merely rough estimates ; and that even on the point of degrees of latitude, it will not be safe to give writers of this early period credit for strict accuracy.

former; the Coast ranne Eastward for the space of fiftie leagues. And trending afterwardes the North, wee founde another lande[1] high, full of thicke woods, the trees whereof were firres, Cipresses, and such like, as are wont to growe in colde Countries. The people differ much from the other, and looke how much the former seemed to be courteous and gentle, so much were these full of rudenesse and ill manners, and so barbarous, that by no signes that euer wee coulde make, wee could haue any kinde of trafficke with them. They cloth thēselues with Beares skinnes, and Leopardes, and sealles, and other beastes skinnes. Their foode, as farre as wee coulde perceiue, repayring often vnto their dwellings, wee suppose to bee by hunting and fishing, and of certaine fruites, which are a kinde of rootes which the earth yeeldeth of her owne accord. They haue no graine, neither sawe wee any kinde or signe of tyllage, neither is the lande, for the barrennes therof, apt to beare frute or seed. If at any time we desired by exchaunge to haue any of their commodities, they vsed to come to the Sea shore vpon certaine craggie rocks, and wee standing in our Boats, they let downe with a rope what it pleased them to giue vs, crying continually that wee should not approch to the lande, demanding immediately the exchange, taking nothing but kniues, fishookes, and tooles to cut withall, neither did they make any account of our curtesie. And when we had nothing left to exchange with them, when we departed from them, the people shewed all signes of discourtesie and disdaine, as was possible for any creature to inuent. Wee were, in despight of them, two or three leagues within the lande, being in number 25 armed men of vs. And when we went on shore, they shot at vs with their bowes, making great outcries, and afterwardes fled into the woods. Wee founde not in this lande any thing notable, or of importance, sauing very great woods and certaine hilles, they may haue some mynerall matter in them, because wee sawe many of thē haue beadstones of Copper

[1] About Portsmouth, in New Hampshire, or the southern part of Maine.

hanging at their eares. We departed from thence, keeping our course North-East along the coaste, which wee founde more pleasant champion, and without woods, with high mountaines within the lande : continuing directly along the coast for the space of fiftie leagues, wee discouered 32 Ilelandes[1] lying all neare the lande, being small and pleasant to the viewe, high, and hauing many turnings and windings betweene them, making many fayre harboroughes and chanels, as they doe in the goulfe of Venice in Saluonia, and Dalmatia; wee had no knowledge or acquaintance with the people: wee suppose they are of the same maners and nature that the others are. Sayling Northeast for the space of 150 leagues, we approched to the lande that in times past was discouered by the Britons, which is in fiftie degrees.[2] Hauing now spent all our prouision and victuals, and hauing discouered about 700 leagues and more of newe Countries, and being furnished with Water and Wood, wee concluded to returne into Fraunce.

Touching the religion of this people which wee haue founde, for want of their language, we could not vnderstand, neither by signes nor gesture, that they had any religion or lawe at all, or that they did acknowledge any first cause or mouer, neither that they worship the heauen or starres, the Sunne or Moone, or other Planets, and much lesse, whether they bee idolaters; neither coulde wee learne whether that they vsed any kinde of Sacrifices or other adorations, neither in their villages haue they any Temples or houses of prayer. We suppose that they haue no religion at all, and y^t they liue at their owne libertie. And y^t all this proceedeth of ignorance, for that they are very easie to bee persuaded : and all that they see vs Christians doe in our diuine seruice, they did the same, with the like imitation as they sawe vs to doe it.

[1] We conjecture this to be Penobscot Bay. [2] Newfoundland.

THE DISCOUERIE OF THE ILES OF FRISLAND,
Iseland, Engroueland, Estotiland, Drogeo, and Icaria, made by M. Nicolas Zeno, Knight, and M. Antonio his Brother.

IN the yere of our Lord 1200, There was in the Citie of Venice a famous Gentleman, named M. Marino Zeno, who for his great vertue and singular wisedome, was called and elected gouernour in certain common wealthes of Italy, in the administration whereof hee bore himselfe so discreetly, that hee was beloued of all men, and his name greatly reuerenced of those that neuer knewe or sawe his person. And among sundrie his worthie workes, this is recorded of him, that hee pacified certaine greeuous ciuile dissentions that arose among the Cittzens of Verona: whereas otherwise if by his graue aduise and great diligence, they had not beene preuented, the matter was likely to breake out in hot broiles of warre. Hee was the first Agent that the common wealth of Venice kept in Constantinople in the yeere 1205, *quando n'era patrona, conli baroni frācesi.* This Gentleman had a sonne, named M. Pietro, who was the father of the Duke Rinieri, which Duke dying with out issue, made his heyre M. Andrea, the sonne of M. Marco his brother. This M. Andrea was captaine generall and Procurator, a man of great reputation for many rare partes, that were in him. He had a sonne M. Rinieri, a worthie Senatour and prudent councellour: Of whom descende M. Pietro, Generall of the league of the Christians against the Turkes, who was called Dragon, for that in his armes hee bare a Dragon. Hee was father to M. Carlo, the famous Procurator and Generall against the Genowayes in those cruel warres, when as almost all the chiefe princes of

Podesta.

Europe did oppugne and seek to ouerthrow our Empire and libertie, where by his great valiancie and prowesse, like an other Furius Camillus, he delivered his Countrie from the present perill it was in, being readie to become a pray and spoyle vnto the enemie, wherefore hee was afterwarde surnamed the Lion, and for an eternall remembrance of his fortitude and valiant exploits he gaue the Lion in his armes. M. Carlo had two brethren, M. Nicolo the knight and Antonio, the father of M. Dragon, of whom issued M. Caterino, the father of M. Pietro, this M. Pietro had sonnes M. Caterino that dyed the last yeere, M. Francisco, M. Carlo, M. Battista, and M. Vincenzo. That M. Caterino was father to M. Nicolo that is yet liuing. Now M. Nicolo the knight, being a man of great courage and very nobly minded, after this foresaide warre of Genoua, that troubled so our predecessours, entred into a wonderfull great desire and fansie to see the fashions of the world, and to trauaile, and to acquaint himselfe with the manners of sundry nations, and learne their languages, whereby afterwards vpō occasions hee might be ye better able to do seruice to his coūtrie and purchase to himselfe credite and honor. Wherfore hee caused a shippe to bee made, and hauing furnished her at his proper charges (as hee was very wealthie), hee departed out of our Seas, and passing the straites of Gibralterra, he sailed for certaine dayes vpon ye Ocean, keeping his course stil to ye Northwards, w^t intent to see Englaund and Flaunders. Where being assaulted in those Seas by a terrible tempest, was so tossed for the space of many dayes with the Sea and winde, that hee knewe not where hee was, till at length hee discouered lande, and not beeing able any longer to sustaine the violence of the tempest, the ship was cast away vpon the Isle of Friseland. The men were saued and most part of the goods that were in the Ship. And this was in the yeere 1380. The inhabitants of the Iland came running in great multitudes w^t weapons to set vpon M. Nicolo and his men, who beeing sore wether beaten

The ship of M. N. Zeno cast away vpon Frisland in anno 1380.

and ouerlaboured at Sea, and not knowing in what part of
the worlde they were, were not able to make any resistaunce
at all, much lesse to defende them selues couragiously, as it
behooued them in such dangerous case. And they shoulde
haue been doubtlesse very discourteously entreated and
cruelly handeled, if by good hap there had not been hard by
the place a Prince with armed people. Who vnderstanding
that there was euen at that present a great ship cast away
vpon the Iland, came running at the noyse and outcries that
they made against our poore Mariners, and driuing away the
inhabitants, spake in latine, and asked them what they were
and from whence they came, and perceiuing y^t they were
Italians and all of one Countrie, he was surprised with marueilous great ioy. Wherefore promising thē all that they
shoulde receiue no discourtesie, and that they were come into
a place where they shoulde bee well vsed and very welcome,
he tooke them into his protection vpon his faith. This was
a great Lord, and possessed certaine Ilands, called Porland,
lying one the Southside of Frisland, being ye richest and
most populous of all those partes; his name was Zichmni:
and beside the said little Ilands, he was Duke of Sorani,
lying within the land towards Scotland. Of these North
partes I thought good to draw the copie of a Sea carde, which
amongest other antiquities, I haue in my house, which although it be rotten through many yeres, yet it falleth out
indifferent well, and to those that are delighted in these
things, it may serue for some light to the vnderstanding of
that, which without it cannot so easily be conceiued. Zichmni, being Lorde of those Seignories (as is said), was a very
warlike and valiant man, and aboue all things famous in Sea
causes. And hauing this yeere before giuen the ouerthrowe
to the king of Norway, who was Lord of the Ilande, beeing
desirous to winne fame by feates of armes, was come on land
with his mē to giue the attēpt, for ye winning of Frisland,
which is an Iland much bigger then Ireland. Wherefore

A forraine prince happening to be in Frisla'd wt armed men. When M. Zeno suffered shipwrack, there came vnto him and spake latin.

Zichmni prince of Porland or duke of Zorani.

Frisland the king of Norwayes.

seeing that M. Nicolo was a mā of iudgement and discretion, and very expert both in Sea matters and martiall affaires, hee gaue him commission to goe aboord his nauie with all his men, charging the captaine to honour him, and in all things to vse his counsaile. This Nauie of Zichmni was of thirteene vessels, wherof two only were with oares, the rest small barkes, and one ship, with the which they sayled to the Westwardes, and with little paines wonne Ledouo and Ilofe, and diuers other small Ilandes, and turning into a bay called Svdero, in the hauen of the towne named Sanestol, they tooke certaine small Barks laden with salt fish. And heere they founde Zichmni, who came by land with his armie, conquering all the countrie as he went; they staied here but a while, but held on their course to the Westwards, till they came to the other Cape of the goulfe or bay, then turning againe, they found certaine Ilelandes and broken landes, which they reduced all vnto the Seignorie and possession of Zichmni. These Seas for as much as they sayled, were in maner nothing but sholds and rocks, in sort that if M. Nicolo and the Venetian mariners had not beene their Pilots, the whole Fleete, in iudgement of all that were in it, had been cast away, so small was yᵉ skill of Zichmnis men in respect of ours, who had been trained vp in the art and practice of nauigation all the daies of their life. Now the Fleete hauing doone such things (as is declared), yᵉ Captaine, by the counsel of M. Nicolo, determined to goe a lande at a towne called Bondendon, to vnderstande what successe Zichmni had in his warres, where they heard, to their great content, that he had fought a great battaile and put to flight the armie of his enemie: by reason of which victorie they sent Embassadours from all partes of the Ilande to yeeld the countrie vp into his handes, taking down their enseignes in euery towne and castell: They thought good to stay in that place for his comming, being reported for certaine that he would bee there very shortly. At his comming there was great congratulatiō and many

76 THE DISCOUERIE OF

signes of gladnes shewed, as wel for the victorie by lande as for that by Sea, for the which the venetians were honoured and extolled of all men, in such sort y^t there was no talke but of them, and of ye great valour of M. Nicolo. Wherfore, the Prince, who was a great fauourer of valiant men, and especially of those that coulde behaue them selues well at the Sea, caused M. Nicolo to bee brought before him, and hauing commended him with many honourable speeches, and praysed his great industrie and dexterie of wit, by the which he acknowledged himselfe to haue receiued an inestimable benefite, as the sauing of his Fleete and the winning of many places, he made him Knight, and rewarded his men with many riche and bountifull giftes: Then departing from thence, they went in triumphing maner towardes Friseland, the chief Citie of ye Ilande, situate on the Southest side of the Isle within a goulf (as there are very many in that Iland). In this goulfe or bay there is such great abundance of fish taken, that many ships are laden therewith, to serue Flaunders, Britaine, England, Scotland, Norway, and Denmarke, and by this trade they gather great wealth.

<small>M. Zeno made knight by Zichmni.</small>

<small>Ships laden with fish at Frisland; for Flaunders, Britaine, England, Scotland, Norway, and Denmark. But not to bee proued that euer any came the'ce.</small>

And thus much is taken out of a letter that M. Nicolo sent vnto M. Antonio his brother, requesting him that hee woulde seeke some meanes to come to him. Wherefore hee, who had as great desire to trauaile as his brother, bought a Ship, and directing his course that way, after hee had sayled a great while, and escaped many dangers, hee arrived at length in safetie with M. Nicolo, who receiued him very ioyfully, for that hee was his brother not only in fleshe and blood, but also in valour and good qualities. M. Antonio remained in Friselande, and dwelt there for the space of fourteene yeeres, foure yeeres with M. Nicolo, and ten yeeres alone. Where they came into such grace and favour with the Prince, that hee made M. Nicolo Captaine of his Nauie, and with great preparation of warre, they were sent foorth for the enterprise of Estlande, which lyeth upon the coaste between Friseland

<small>A letter sent by Master N. Zeno from Friseland to his brother M. Antonio in Venice. End of the first letter.</small>

and Norway, where they did many dōmages, but hearing that the king of Norway was comming towardes them with a great Fleet, they departed w^t such a terrible flaw of wind y^t they were driuē vpō certain sholdes. Where a great part of their ships were cast away, ye rest were saued upō Grisland, a great Iland, but dishabited. The king of Norway his fleete being taken with the same storme, did vtterly perishe in those seas. Whereof Zichmni hauing notice, by a shippe of his enemies, that was cast by chaunce upon Grisland, hauing repayred his fleete, and perceyuing him selfe northerly neere vnto the Islandes, determined to set vpon Islande, which together with the rest was subiect to the king of Norway: but he founde the countrey so well fortified and defended, that his fleete being so small, and very ill appointed both of weapons and men, hee was gladde to retire. And so hee left that enterprise without perfourming any thing at all, and in the same chanelles he assaulted ye other Iles, called the Islands, which are seven: Talas, Broas, Iscant, Trans, Minant, Dambere, and Bres, and hauing spoyled them all, hee built a fort in Bres, where he left M. Nicolo, with certaine small barkes and men and munition. And nowe thinking he had done well for this voyage, with those fewe shippes which were left hee returned into Frieslande. M. Nicolo remayning nowe in Bres, determined vpon a time to goe forth and discouer lande, wherefore arming out their small barkes in the moneth of July, he sayled to the Northwardes, and arriued in Engrouelande. Where he founde a monastery of Fryers of the order of the *Predicators*, and a church dedicated to S. Thomas, harde by a hill that casteth forth fire like Vesuuius and Ætna.

Engrouelande.

Preaching Friers of S. Thomas.

There is a fountayne of hot burning water, with the whiche they heate the Churche of the monasterie and the Fryers chambers; it commeth also into the kitchen so boyling hotte, that they vse no other fire to dresse their meate, and putting their bread into brasse pottes without any water, it

doeth bake, as it were in a hot ouen. They haue also small
gardens couered ouer in the winter time, which being watered
with this water, are defended from the force of the snowe and
colde, which in those parts being situate farre vnder the
pole, is very extreeme, and by this meanes they produce
flowers and fruites and herbes of sundrie sortes, euen as in
other temperate countreys in their seasons, in suche sorte that
the rude and sauage people of those partes seeing these
supernaturall effectes, doe take those Friers for Gods, and
bring them many presentes as chickens, fleshe, and diuers
other thinges, and haue them all in great reuerence as
Lords. When the frost and snowe is great, they heate their
houses in maner before said, and will, by letting in the water
or opening the windowes, temper the heate and colde at
their pleasure. In ye buildings of the monastery, they vse
no other matter but that which is ministred vnto them by
the fire, for they take the burning stones that are cast out as
it were sparkles or ceindres at the firie mouth of the hill,
and when they are most enflamed, cast water vpon them,
wherby they are dissolued and become excellēt white lime,
and so tough, that being contriued in building, it lasteth for
euer. And the very sparkles after the fire is out of them do
serue in steede of stones to make walles and vautes: for being
once colde, they will neuer dissolue or breake except they be
cut with some irō toole, and the vautes that are made of them
are so light, that they need no sustentacle or proppe to holde
them vp, and they wil endure continually very fayre and
whole. By reason of these great commodities, the friers
haue made there so many buildings and walles that it is a
wonder to see. The couerts or roofes of their houses for the
most part are made in this maner; first they rayse the wall
vp to his full height, then they make it enclining or bowing
in by litle and litle in forme of a vaute. But they are not
greatly troubled with raine in those partes, for that, by reason
of the pole or colde climate, the first snowe being falne, it

A notable lye.

thaweth no more for the space of nine moneths, for so long dureth their winter. They feede of the fleshe of wilde beastes and of fish, for where as the warme water falleth into the sea, there is a large and wide hauen which by reason of the heate of the water, doeth neuer freeze all the winter, by meanes whereof there is suche concourse and flocks of sea foule and such aboundance of fishe, that they take thereof infinite multitudes, whereby they maintayne a great number of people rounde about, whiche they keepe in continuale worke, both in building and taking of foules and fishe, and in a thousande other necessarie affaires and busines about the monasterie.

Their houses are builte about the hill on euery side, in fourme rounde, and 25 foote broade, and in mounting vpwardes they goe narower and narower, leauing at the toppe a litle hole, whereat the ayre commeth in to giue light to the house, and the flore of the house is so hot, that being within they feele no colde at all. Hither in the sommer time come many barkes from the Ilands there about, and from the Cape aboue Norway, and from Trondon. And bring to the Friers al maner things that may be desired, taking in change thereof fishe, which they drie in the sunne, or in the colde, and skins of diuers kindes of beastes. For the which they haue wood to burne, and timber verie artificially carued, and corne and cloth to make them apparell. For in change of the two foresayde commodities, all the nations bordering rounde about them couet to trafficke with them, and so they without any trauell or expences haue that which they desire. To this monasterie resort Friers of Norway, of Suetia, and of other countreys, but the most part are of the Islandes. There are continually in that part many barkes, whiche are kept in there by reason of the sea being frozen, wayting for the season of the yeere to dissolue the Ice. The fishers boates are made like vnto a weauers shuttle; taking the skins of fishes, they fashiō them with the bones of the same fishes, and sowing thē together in many doubles, they make

Trade in sommer time from Trondon to S. Thomas friers in Ingrouela'd.

Resort of friers from Norway and Sueden to the monasterie in Ingrouelande called S. Tho'.

them so sure and substanciall, that it is miraculous to see how in tempests they will shut theselues close within, and let the sea and winde carrie them, they care not whether, without any feare eyther of breaking or drowning. And if they chance to be driuen vpō any rocks they remaine sounde, without the least bruse in the worlde : And they haue, as it were, a sleeue in the bottome, which is tied fast in ye middle, and when there cōmeth any water into their boat, they put it into the one halfe of ye sleeue, thē fastning ye ende of it w^t two peeces of wood, and loosing ye band beneath, they conuey the water forth of the boate : and this they doe as often as they haue occasion, without any perill or impediment at all.

Moreouer, the water of the monasterie, being of sulphurious or brimstone nature, is conueyed into the lodginges of the principall Friers by certaine vessels of brasse, tinne, or stone, so hotte, that it heateth the place as it were a stowe, not carrying with it any stinke or other noysome smell.

Besides this, they haue another conueyance to bring hot water, with a wall vnder the ground, to the ende it should not freese, vnto the middle of the court, where it falleth into a great vessel of brasse, that standeth in the middle of a boyling fountayne, and this is to heate their water to drinke, and to water their gardens, and thus they haue from the hill the greatest commodities that may be wished; and so these Fryers employ all their trauaile and studie for the most part in trimming their gardins, and in making faire and beawtifull buildings, and especially handsome and commodious; neyther are they destitute of ingenious and painefull artificers for the purpose, for they giue very large payment, and to them that bring them fruites and seedes they are very bountifull, and giue they care not what. So that there is great resort of workmen and maisters in diuers faculties, by reason of the good gaines and large allowance that is there.

The most of them speake the Latin tongue, and especially

the superiours and principalls of the monasterie. And this is *In the monasterie S.* as muche as is knowen of Engrouelande, which is all by the *Thomas most of them* relation of M. Nicolo, who maketh also particular description *speake the latin tongue. End* of a riuer that he discouered, as is to be seene in the carde *of the two letter.* that I drewe. And in the ende, N. Nicolo, not being vsed and acquainted with these cruell coldes, fell sicke, and a little while after returned into Frislande, where he dyed. He left behinde him in Venice two sonnes, M. Giouanni and M. Toma, who had two sonnes, M. Nicolo, the father of the famous Cardinal Zeno and M. Pietro, of whom descended the other Zenos that are liuing at this day.

Now M. Nicolo being dead, M. Antonio succeeded him, *N. Zeno died in Frislande.* both in his goods and in his dignities and honour, and albeit he attempted diuers wayes, and made greate supplication, hee coulde neuer obtaine licence to returne into his Countrey, for Zichmni had determined to make himselfe Lorde of the sea. Wherefore, vsing alwayes the counsaile and seruice of M. Antonio, hee sent hym with some small barkes to the Westwardes, for that towardes those partes some of his fishermen had discouered certaine Ilandes verye rich and populous; which discouerie, M. Antonio, in a letter to his brother M. Carlo, recounteth from point to point in this manner, sauing that wee haue chaunged some olde woordes, leauing the matter entire as it was. *3 letter beginneth from the*

Sixe and twentie yeeres agoe there departed foure Fisher *second brother M. Antonio, out of* boates, the whiche a mightie tempest arising, were tossed for *Frislande,* the space of manye dayes verye desperately vpon the Sea, *to his other brother in Venice,* when at length the tempeste ceassying, and the weather *named Master Carlo.* waxing fayre, they discouered an Ilande called Estotilande, *Estotitand.* lying to the Westwardes aboue 1000 Miles from Frislande, vpon the whiche one of the boates was caste awaye, and sixe *6 Fisher men taken.* men that were in it were taken of the inhabitauntes, and brought vnto a verye fayre and populous Citie, where the kyng of the place sent for manye interpreters, but there was none coulde bee founde that vnderstoode the language of the fishermen, excepte one that spake Latin, who was also cast by chaunce vpon the same Ilande, who in the behalfe of the kyng asked them what Countreymen they were, and so vnderstanding theyr case, rehearsed it vnto the King, who willed that they shoulde tarrie in the Countrey, wherefore, they obeyinge his commaundement, for that they coulde not otherwise doe, dwelte fiue yeeres in the Ilande, and learned the language, and one of them was in diuers partes of the Ilande, and reporteth that it is a verye riche Countrey, abounding with all the commodities of the worlde, and that it is little lesse than Islande, but farre more fruitefull, hauing in the middle thereof a verye hyghe mountayne, from the whiche there riseth foure Riuers, that passe throughe the whole Countrey.

The inhabitantes are very wittie people, and haue all the artes and faculties as wee haue : and it is credible, that in time past they haue had trafficke with our men, for he sayde that he sawe latin bookes in the Kings library, whiche they at this present doe not vnderstande, they haue a peculiar language, and letters, or caracters, to themselues. They haue mines of all manner of mettals, but especially they abounde with golde. They haue their trade in Engroueland, from whence they bring skins, and brimstone, and pitch : And he saith, that to ye southwards there is a great populous coūtrey, very rich of gold. They sowe corne, and make bere or ale, which is a kind of drinke that the north people doe vse, as we do wine. They haue mightie great woods; they make their buildings with wals, and there are many cities and castles. They build smal barkes, and haue sayling, but they haue not the lodestone, nor know not the vse of the cōpasse. Wherefore these fishers were had in great estimatiō, insomuch that the king sent them with 12 barkes to the southwardes, to a countrey whiche they call Drogio : but in their voyage they had suche countrary weather, that they thought all to haue perished in the sea, but yet escaping that cruell death, they fel into another more cruel. For they were takē in the countrey, and the most parte of them eaten by the Sauage people, which fecde vpon mans fleshe, as the sweetest meate in their iudgementes that is.

But that fisher, with his fellowes, shewyng them the maner of taking fishe with nettes, saued their liues: and woulde goe euery day a fishing to the sea and in fresh riuers, and take great aboundance of fish, and giue it to the chiefe men of the countrey, whereby hee got himselfe so great fauour, that hee was very well beloued and honoured of euery one. The 6 fisherme' of frisland only saued by shewing the maner to take fishe.
The chiefest of the 6 fishers specified before his co'panions.

The fame of this man being spred abroad in the countrey, there was a Lorde thereby that was verie desirous to haue him with him, and to see how hee vsed his miraculous arte of catching fishe, in so muche that he made warre with the other Lorde, with whom hee was before, and in the ende preuayling, for that hee was more mightie and a better warriour, the fisherman was sent vnto him, with the rest of his company. And for the space of thirteene yeeres that hee dwelt in those partes, he saith that he was sent in this order to more than 25 Lordes, for they had continuall warre amongest them selues, this Lorde with that Lord, and he with another, onely to haue him to dwell with them; so that wandring vp and downe the Countrey, without any certayne abode in one place, hee knewe almost all those partes. He saith that it is a very great countrey, and, as it were, a newe world, the people very rude and voyde of all goodnesse; they goe all naked, so that they are miserablie vexed with colde; neyther haue they the wit to couer their bodies w^t beasts skins, w^t they take in huntinge; they haue no kind of metal; they liue by hūting; they carie certain lances of wood, made sharp at ye point; they haue bowes, the stringes whereof are made of beastes skinnes: They are a very fierce people, they make cruell warres one with another, and eate one an other, they haue gouernours and certayne lawes verye diuers amongest themselues. But the farther to the Southwestwardes, the more ciuility there is, the ayre being somewhat temperat, so that there they haue Cities and temples to Idolls, wherein they sacrifice men, and afterwardes eate them; they haue there some knowledge and vse of gold and siluer.

Nowe this fisher hauing dwelt so many yeeres in those countreys, purposed, if it were possible, to returne home into his countrey, but his companions dispayring euer to see it agayne, let him goe in Gods name, they kept them selues where they were. Wherefore hee bidding them farewel, fledde through the woods towards Drogio, and was verie well receiued of the Lorde that dwelt next to that place, who knewe him, and was a great enemie of the other Lorde, and so running from one Lorde to an other, being those by whō hee had passed before, after long time and many trauelles, he came at length to Drogio, where hee dwelt three yeeres. When as by good fortune he heard by ye inhabitants y^t there were certaine boates arriued upon ye coast, wherefore, entring into good hope to accōplish his intent, he went to ye sea side, and asking thē of what countrey they were, they answered of Estotiland, whereat he was exceeding glad, and requested that they woulde take him into them, whiche they did verye willingly, and for that hee had the language of the Countrey, and there was none of them that coulde speake it, they vsed him for their interpreter.

And after that, hee frequented that trade with them, in such sorte, that hee became verye riche, and so furnishing out a barke of his owne, hee returned into Frislande, where hee made reporte vnto this Lorde of that welthie Countrey.

And hee is throughly credited, because of the Mariners who approoue many straunge thinges that hee reporteth to bee true. Wherefore, this Lorde is resolued to sende me foorth with a fleete towards those partes, and there are so manye that desire to goe in the voyage for the noueltie and strangenesse of the thing, that I thinke we shall be very strongly appointed, without any publike expence at all. And

3 yeres in Drogio.

Where by happ arriued certaine boates from Estotiland.

He became interpreter for ye men that ariued at drogeo in the boates of Estotilande.

Afterwards hee frequented that trade with them in such sort that he became very rich. And so furnished a bark of his owne, and returned to Frislande, where hee reported the story to his Lorde Zichmni.

Zichmni minded to send M. Antonio Zeno

this is the tenor of the letter, before mentioned, which I haue heere set downe to giue intelligence of an other voyage, that M. Antonio made, being set out with many Barkes and men, notwithstanding hee was not captaine as hee had thought at the first hee shoulde, for Zichmni went in his owne person: and concerning this matter, I haue a letter in forme, as followeth. Our great preparation for the voyag of Estotiland, was begun in an vnluckie houre, for three dayes before our departure, the fisherman died that shoulde haue been our guid: notwithstanding, this Lorde woulde not giue ouer the enterprize, but in steade of the fisherman, tooke certayne Marriners that returned out of the Ilande with him, and so making our nauigation to the Westwards, we discouered certayne Ilandes subiect to Frislande, and hauing passed certayne shelues, we stayed at Ledouo for the space of 7 dayes to refreshe our selues, and furnish the fleete with necessarie prouision. Departing from hence, we arriued the first of July at the Ile of Ilofe, and for that the winde made for vs wee stayed not there, but passed forth, and being vpon the maine sea there arose immediatly a cruell tempest, wherewith for eight dayes space wee were miserably vexed, not knowing where wee were, and a great part of the Barkes were cast away; afterwarde waxing faire wether, we gathered vp the broken peeces of the Barkes that were lost, and sayling with a prosperous winde, wee discouered lande at West. Wherefore, keeping our course directly vpon it, wee arriued in a very good and safe harborough, where wee sawe an infinite companie of people readie in armes, come running very furiously to the water side, as it were for defence of the Ilande. Wherefore, Zichmni causing his men to make signes of peace vnto them, they sent tenne men vnto vs that coulde speake tenne languages, but wee coulde vnderstande none of them, except one that was of Island. He being brought before our Prince and asked what was the name of the Iland, and what people inhabited it, and who gouerned it, answered,

86   THE DISCOUERIE OF

Icaria Ilande. All that the Iland was called Icaria, and that all the kinges that
the kings yt had raigned in that Ila'd were called Icari, after had raigned there, were called Icari, after the name of the
first king of that place, which, as they say, was the sonne of
the name of the first king of yt place: which they say was the sonne of Dedalus, king of Scots. Dedalus, king of Scotland, who conquering that Iland, left
his sonne there for king, and left thē those lawes that they
retain to this present, and after this, he desiring to sayle further, in a great tempest that arose, was drowned; wherefore,
Icarius drowned. for a memoriall of his death, they call those Seas yet the
Icarian Sea. Icarian Sea, and the kings of the Iland, Icari; and for that
they were contented with that state which God had giuē
them, neither whold they alter one iote of their lawes and
customes, they would not receiue any straunger, wherefore
they requested our Prince that hee woulde not seeke to violate
their lawes, which they had receiued from that king of worthie memorie, and obserued very duly to that present : which
if hee did attempt, it woulde redounde to his manifest destruction, they being all resolutely bent rather to leaue their life,
than to loose in any respect the vse of their lawes. Notwithstanding, that wee should not thinke they did altogether
refuse the conuersation and trafficke with other men, they
tolde vs for conclusion, that they would willingly receiue one
The people of Icaria de- sirous of the Italian tongue. of our men, and preferre him to be one of ye chiefe amongest
them, only to learne my language the Italian tongue, and to
bee enformed of our maners and customes, as they had
Hauing in that Iland 10 men of ten sundry nations. alreadie receiued those other tenne of tenne sundrie nations,
that came vnto their Iland. To these things our Prince
answered nothing at all, but causing his men to seeke some
good harborough, hee made signes as though he would come
on lande, and sayling round about the Iland, hee espied at
length a harborough on the East side of the Ilande, where
he put in with all his Fleet, the mariners went on land to
take in wood and water, which they did with as great speede
as they coulde, doubting, least they shoulde be assaulted by
the inhabitants, as it fell out in deed, for those that dwelt
there abouts, making signes vnto the other with fire and

smoke, put them selues presently in armes, and the other comming to them, they came all running downe to the Sea side vpon our men with bowes and arrowes and other weapons, that many were slaine and diuers sore wounded. And we made signes of peace vnto them, but it was to no purpose, for their rage encreased more and more, as though they had fought for life and liuing. Wherefore, wee were forced to depart, and to sayle along in a great circuite about the Iland, being alwaies accompanied vpon the hil tops and the Sea coast with an infinite multitude of armed men, and so doubling the Cape of the Iland towardes the North, wee found many great sholdes, amongst the which for the space of ten daies we were in continual danger of loosing our whole Fleete, but that it pleased God all that while to send vs very faire weather. Wherefore, proceeding on till we came to ye East cape, we sawe the inhabitaunts still on the hill tops and by the Sea coast keepe with vs, and in making great outcries, and shooting at vs a farre of, they vttered their olde spitefull affection towards vs. Wherefore we determined to stay in some safe harborough, and see if we might speak once againe with the Islander, but our determination was frustrate, for the people, more like vnto beastes than men, stood continually in armes, w^t intent to beat vs backe if we should come on lande. Wherefore, Zichmni seeing hee coulde not preuaile, and thought if hee shoulde haue perseuered and followed obstinately his purpose, their victuals would haue failed them, hee departed with a faire winde, and sailed sixe dayes to the Westwards, but the winde chaunging to the Southwest, and the Sea waxing rough, wee sayled 4 dayes with the wind in the powpe, and at length discouering land, wee were afraide to approch neere vnto it, being the Sea growen, and we not knowing what lande it was, but God prouided for vs, that the winde ceasing, there came a greate calme. Wherefore, some of our companie rowing to land with oares, returned and brought vs word to our great com-

Infinite multitude of armed men in Icaria.

Zichmni departed from Icaria Westwards.

Sight of land.

forte, that they had founde a very good Countrie, and a better harborough, vpon which newes wee towed our ships and smal Barkes to lande, and being entred into the harborough, wee sawe a farre of a great mountaine y^t cast forth smoke, which gaue vs good hope that we shoulde finde some inhabitantes in ye Iland, neither would Zichmni rest, although it were a great way of, but send a 100 good souldiers to search the Countrie, and bring report what people they were that inhabited it; and in the meane time they tooke in wood and water for the prouision of the Fleete, and catcht great store of fishe and Sea foule, and founde such abundance of birdes egges, that our men that were halfe famished were filled withall. Whiles we were riding here, began the moneth of June, at which time the ayre in the Iland was so temperate and pleasant as is impossible to expresse; but when we coulde see no people at all, wee suspected greatly that this pleasant place was desolate and dishabited. We gaue name to the hauen, calling it Trim, and the point that stretched out into ye sea we called Capo di Trim. The 100 souldiers that were sent foorth, eight dayes after returned, and brought worde that they had been through the Ilande, and at the mountaine, and that the smoke was a naturall thing, proceeding from a great fire that was in the bottome of the hill, and that there was a spring, from which issued a certaine matter like pitch, which ran into the Sea, and that there aboutes dwelt greate multitudes of people half wilde, hiding thēselues in caues of the grounde, of small stature, and very fearefull, for as soone as they sawe them, they fled into their holes; and that there was a great riuer and very good harborough. Zichimni being thus informed, and seeing that it had a holsome and pure ayre, and a very fruitefull soyle, and fayre riuers, with sundrie other commodities, fell into such liking of the place, that he determined to inhabite it, and build there a Citie. But his people being weary and faint with their long and tedious trauaile, began to tumult and mur-

mure, saying, that they would returne into their Countrie, for that the winter was at hand, and if they entred into the harborough, they should not be able to come out againe before the next Sommer. Wherefore, hee retaining only the Barkes with Oares, and such as were willing to stay with him, sent all the rest with the shippes backe againe, and willed that I (though vnwilling) should bee their Captaine. I therefore departing, sayled for the space of twentie dayes to the Estwards without sight of any land, then turning my course towardes Southeast, in fiue dayes I discouered lande, and founde my selfe vpon the Ile of Neome, and knowing the Countrie, I perceiued I was past Islande: Wherefore, taking in some fresh victuals of the inhabitants, being subiect to Zichmni, I sayled with a faire winde in three dayes to Frisland, where the people, who thought they had lost their Prince, because of his long absence, in this our voyage, receiued vs very ioyfully.

<small>Zichmni determining to remaine in the new discouered land kept with him his barkes with oares, and me' that were willing, and sent the rest away homewards: Appointing Antonio Zeno chiefe captaine of them.</small>

<small>Antonio Zeno has sight of Neome, and knewe himselfe past Island. Ende of the 4 letter.</small>

What followed after this letter, I know not but by coniecture, which I gather out of a peece of an other letter, which I will set downe heere vnderneath: That Zichmni builte a towne in the porte of the Iland that hee discouered, and that hee searched the Countrie very diligently and discouered it all, and also the riuers on both sides of Engroueland, for that I see it particularly described in the Sea card, but the discourse or narration is lost. The beginning of the letter is thus. Concerning those things that you desire to knowe of mee, as of the men and their manners and customes, of the beastes, and the Countries adioyning, I haue made thereof a particular booke, which, by God's helpe, I will bring with mee: Wherein I haue described the countrie, the monstrous fishes, ye customes and lawes of Frisland, Island, Estland, the kingdome of Norway, Estotiland, Drogio, and in the end, the life of Master Nicolo, the knight our brother, with the discouerie which he made, and of Groland. I haue also written the life and acts of Zichmni, a Prince as worthie of

<small>A peece of a 5 letter.</small>

<small>Beginning of the letter.</small>

*

immortall memory as any that euer liued, for his great valiancie and singuler humanitie, wherein I haue described the discouerie of Engroueland on both sides, and the Citie that hee builded. Therefore, I will speeke no further hereof in this letter, hoping to be with you very shortly, and to satisfie you in sundrie other thinges by worde of mouth. All these letters were written by master Antonio to master Carlo, his brother. And it greeueth me, that the booke and diuers other writinges concerning these purposes, are miserably lost: For I beeing but a child when they came to my hands, and not knowing what they were (as the manner of children is), I tore them, and rent them in peeces, which now I cannot call to remembrance but to my greef. Notwithstanding that the memory of so many good thinges shoulde not bee lost; whatsoeuer I could get of this matter, I haue disposed and put in order, in the former discourse, to the ende that this age might bee partly satisfied, to ye which we are more beholden for the great discoueries made in those partes, then to any other of the time past, beeing most studious of the relations of the discoueries of strange Countries made by the great mindes and industry of our auncetours.

This discourse was collected by Ramusio, Secretarie to the state of Venice (or by the Printer, Tho. Giunti).

John Baptista Ramusio died in Padua, in July 1557.[1]

---

[1] The first time that this account appears in Ramusio's Collection, is in the edition of the second volume published in 1574, seventeen years after the death of Ramusio: and it is not probable that he would himself have selected for publication a "discourse" like that of the Zeni, which bears upon it the evident impress of fabrication. What share Tommaso Giunti had in this edition, beyond printing it, and prefixing a preface, is not known.

The object of the Hakluyt Society is to extend the knowledge of the bold and energetic and successful efforts of early discoverers, not to bring prominently forward clumsy compilations and absurd fictions. For this reason, no attempt has been made to distinguish by annotation the probably true from the certainly false in the above narrative.

THE TRUE AND LAST DISCOUERIE OF FLORIDA,

made by Captain John Ribault in the yeere 1562.
Dedicated to a great noble man of Fraunce,[1] and
translated into Englishe by one Thomas Hackit.

WHERE as in the yeere of our Lorde God 1562, it pleased God to moue your honour to choose and appoint vs to discouer and view a certaine long coast of the West India, from the head of the lande called Laflorida, drawing towarde the North part, vnto the head of Britons,[2] distant from the saide head of Laflorida 900 leagues or there about: to the ende wee might certifie you and make true report of the temperature, fertilitie, Portes, Hauens, Riuers, and generally of all the commodities that bee seene and found in that lande, and also to learne what people were there dwelling, which thing you haue long time agoe desired, beeing stirred therevnto by this zeale: That Fraunce might one day through newe discoueries haue knowledge of strange Countries, and also thereof to receiue (by meanes of continuall trafficke) riche and inestimable commodities, as other nations haue done, by taking in hand such farre nauigations, both to the honor and prowes of their kings and princes, and also to the encrease of great profite and vse to their common wealthes, countries, and dominions, which is most of all, w't out cōparisō, to be considered and esteemed. It seemeth well y't yee haue been stirred hereunto euen of God aboue, and led to it by the hope and desire you haue that a number of brutishe people and igno-

---

[1] Gaspard de Coligny, admiral of France, an earnest promoter of the attempts made to establish colonies in America, which he regarded as the future asylum for the French Protestants.

[2] Cape Breton, in lat. 46 N.

rant of Jesus Christe, may by his grace come to some knowledge of his holy Lawes and Ordinaunces. So therefore it seemeth that it hath pleased God by his godly prouidence to reserue the care which hee hath had of their saluation vntill this time, and will bring them to our faith at the time by himselfe alone foreseene and ordeined. For if it were needfull to shewe howe many from time to time haue gone about to finde out this great lande and to inhabite there, who neuerthelesse haue alwaies failed, and beene put by from their intention and purpose: some by feare of shipwrackes, and some by great windes and tempestes, that droue them backe, to their merueilous griefe. Of the which there was one, a very famous stranger named Sebastian Gabota, an excellent Pylot, sent thither by king Henry the yeere 1498, and many others, who neuer could attaine to any habitation, nor take possession thereof one only foote of grounde, nor yet approche or enter into these parties and faire riuers, into the which God hath brought vs. Wherefore (my Lorde) it may bee well saide, that the liuing God hath reserued this great lande for your poore seruantes and subiectes, as well to the ende they might bee made great ouer this poore people and rude nation, as also to approue the former affection which our kings haue had vnto this discouerie.

For y⁵ late king Frances the first (of happie memorie), a Prince endued with excellent vertues, the yeere 1524 sent a famous and notable man, a Florentine, named Master John Verarzan,[1] to search and discouer the West parts as farre as might be: Who, departing from Deepe[2] with two vessels little differing from the making and burden of these two Pinnaces of the kinges which your honour hath ordeined for this present nauigation. In the which land they haue found the eleuation [of] the Pole, an VIII degrees.[3] The Countrie (as he

---

[1] Giovanni Verazzani.—See *ante*, p. 55.   [2] Dieppe.

[3] We have no account of any of the voyages of Verazzani, but the first in 1524; and it does not appear that on this occasion he penetrated fur-

writeth) goodly, fruitfull, and so good temperature, that it is not possible to haue a better: beeing then as yet of no mā seen nor discerned. But they not being able to bring to passe at this first voyage that which he had intended, nor to arriue in any Port, by reason of sundrie incōueniences (which cōmōly happē) were cōstrained to return into Fraunce: where, after his arriuall, he neuer ceassed to make suite vntill he was sent thither againe, where at last he died.[1] The which occasion gaue small courage to sende thither agayne, and was the cause that this laudable enterprise was left of, vntill the yeere 1534, at which time his Maiestie (desiring alwayes to enlarge his kingdome, countreys, and dominions, and the aduauncing the ease of his subiectes) sent thither a Pilote of S. Mallowes, a Briton named James Cartier, well seene in the art and knowledge of Nauigation, and especially of the North parts, commonly called the new land, led by some hope to find passage that waies to the south seas: Who, being

James Cartier.

ther south than about twenty-eight degrees. The eight degrees mentioned in the text, may be a mistake for twenty-eight: we cannot understand it in any other manner.

[1] The time and manner of Verazzani's death is not known. In the introduction to his voyage in 1524, published in the third volume of *Ramusio* (p. 417 b.), the following passage occurs:—"In the last voyage which he made, having landed together with some of his companions, they were all killed by the natives, and roasted and eaten in the presence of those who remained on board the ships." Mr. Biddle, in the *Memoirs of Cabot*, p. 278, contends, that he was the Piedmontese pilot who accompanied an English vessel on a voyage of discovery to the north in 1527, and having ventured on shore at Newfoundland, was killed by the natives. There are two objections to this theory: one, that Verazzani was a Florentine, and not a Piedmontese; and the other, that Annibale Caro, in a letter dated ten years afterwards,—viz., on the 13th of October 1537,— addresses himself to one "Verrazzano, a seeker of new worlds and of their marvels", and says: "We have passed no lands that have not been discovered either by yourself or by your brother." (*Lettere Familiari*, page 7. Edit. 1610.) We think that it is proper to lay these facts before the reader, but cannot pretend to draw any conclusion from them. —See Tiraboschi, *Storia della Letteratura Italiana*, tom. vii, page 383. Edit. 1824.

not able at his first going to bring any thing to passe that he pretēded to do, was sent thither againe the yeere following, and likewise Le sire Hemerall;[1] and as it is well knowen they did inhabite and builde, and plant the kings armies in the North part, a good way in the lande, as far as Tauadu and Ochisaon.[2] Wherefore (my Lord) trust iustly that a thing so commendable, and worthie to bee with good courage attempted, that God woulde guid and keepe vs, desiring alwayes to fulfill your commaundement. When wee had done your businesse, and made our preparations the xviii day of Februarie 1562, through the fauour of God wee departed with our two vessels out of the hauen of Claue de Grace[3] into the road Caur:[4] and the next day hoysted vp saile (the winde being in ye East), which lasted so fiue daies, that wee coulde not arriue at the nauch,[5] that is from betweene the coast of Briton[6] and Englande and the Iles of Surlinos[7] and Wiskam:[8] So that the Winde blowing with great fury and tempest out of the West and West Southwest, altogether contrary to our way and course, and all that we could doe was to none effecte, besides the great daunger of breaking of our Mastes, as also to be hindered in our other labours. Wherefore as well to shonne many other inconueniences which might follow to the preiudice and breach of our voyage, hauing regard also to the likely daunger of death, y^t some of our gentlemen and

[1] The person here meant must be François de la Roche, sieur de Roberval, who was appointed governor of Canada by Francis I, in 1540, and sailed for America with emigrants in 1542.

[2] The English edition of Ribault's voyage, which Hakluyt has here reproduced, is disfigured by several gross inaccuracies, particularly in the proper names. The French original is not known to exist, and it is doubtful if it was ever printed. Probably, this translation was made from the manuscript, and hence the extraordinary mis-readings we shall have to correct in the course of our remarks upon this voyage. The two names, Tavidu and Ochisaon, must be Canada and Hochelaga, to which latter district Cartier gave the name of Montreal.

[3] Havre de Grace.
[4] Caux.
[5] The Manche, or English Channel.
[6] Brittany.
[7] The Scilly Islands.
[8] Ushant.

souldiers being troubled with feuers and whot sicknesses, might haue fallen into: as also for other considerations wee thought good to fall into the road of Brest, in Britaine, to see there our sick folke on land, and suffer the tempest to passe. From whence (after wee had taried there two dayes) wee returned againe to Seawarde to followe our nauigation; so that (my Lorde) albeit the winde was for a long season very much against vs, and troublesome, yet at the ende (God giuing vs, through his grace and accustomed goodnesse, a meetely fauourable winde), I determined with all diligence to proue a newe course which hath not beene yet attempted: trauersing the Seas of Oction[1] 1800 Leagues at the least, whiche in deed is the true and short course, that hereafter must be kept to the honour of our nation, reiecting the old conserued opinion, which so long time hath beene holden as true.

Which is, as it was thought a thing impossible to haue the winde at East, Northeast, and keepe the race and course wee enterprised, but that we shoulde be driuen towarde the region of Affrica, the Iles of Canaria, Madera, and other landes there aboutes. And the cause why wee haue beene the more prouoked and assured to take this new race, hath bin because that it seemed to euery one that we might not passe nor goe in this Nauigation without the sight and touching of the Antillies and Lucaries,[2] and there soiourne and take fresh waters and other necessaries, as the Spaniards doe in their voyage to new spaine: wherof (thanked be God) we haue had no neede, nor entered the chanell of Roham:[3] which hath

[1] Seas of Oction. The first edition of this narrative, printed in 1563, has Octian. We presume that what is here rendered "the seas of Oction", was in the French original either " Les mers *d'occident*", meaning the Western or Atlantic Ocean; or " La mer oceane", the main ocean : and that the translator, being unable to read the manuscript before him, made a word for the occasion.

[2] Antillies—The Caribbee Islands ; Lucaries—The Lucayes, or Bahama Islands.

[3] Roham—This must be a mis-reading for Bahama ; the passage referred to being through the old Bahama Channel and the Gulf of Florida.

bin thought impossible. Foreseeing also that it was not
expedient for vs to passe through the Ilandes, as wel to shune
many inconueniences that might happen in passing that way
(wherof springeth nothing but innumerable quarrels, pleadings, cōfusions, and breach of al worthy enterprises and
goodly nauigations, whereof ensueth complaintes and odious
questions betweene the subiectes of the king and his friends
and alies) as also to the ende they might vnderstand that, in
the time to come (God hauing shewed vs such graces, as these
his wonderfull benefites firste shewed to the poore people of
this so goodly newe framing[1] people, of so gentle a nature,
and a countrey so pleasant and fruitefull, lacking nothing at
all that may seeme necessarie for mans food), we would not
haue to doe with their Ilandes and other landes, which (for
that they first discouered them) they keepe with much ielousie:
trusting that if God will suffer the king (through your perswation) to cause some part of this incomparable countrey to
be peopled and inhabited with such a number of his poore
subiectes as you shall thinke good, there neuer happened in
the memory of man so great and good commoditie to France
as this; and (my Lorde) for many causes, whereof a man is
neuer able to say or write to the ful, as vnder the assured
hope that we haue alwayes had in executing vprightly that
which I had receiued in charge of you, God woulde blesse
our wayes and nauigations. After we had constantly and
with diligence, in time conuenient, determined upon the way,
wee shoulde haue thought it noysome and tedious to all our
companie if it had before bin knowē vnto any without tourning or wauering to or fro from their first ententiō. And notwithstanding that satan did often what he could to sowe
many obstractes, troubles, and lettes, according to his accustomed subtilties, so it is come to passe that God, by his onely
goodnes, hath giuen vs grace to make the furthest arte and

[1] There is, most probably, a mistake here: but we are unable to suggest an explanation of it.

trauars of the seas, that euer was made in our memorie or knowledge, in longitude from the East to the West:[1] and therefore was it commonly sayde both in Fraunce and Spaine, and also among vs, that it was impossible for vs safely to arriue thither, whither the Lord did conduct vs. Al which perswaded but of ignoraunce and lacke of attempting: which wee haue not bin afrayde to giue aduenture to prooue. Albeit that all Mariners Cardes doe set the Coastes with shipwrackes, without portes or Riuers: which wee haue found otherwise, as it followeth.

Thursday the last of Aprill, at the breake of the day, wee discouered and clearely perceyued a fayre Coast, stretchyng of a great length, couered with an infinite number of high and fayre trees, wee being not past 7 or 8 leagues from the shore, the countrey seeming vnto vs plaine, without anye shewe of hils, and approching neerer, within foure or fiue leagues of the land, we cast an ancker at ten fadome water, the bottome of the Sea being plaine with muche Ocias,[2] and fast holde on the South side, as farre as a certaine point or Cape situate vnder that Latitude of nine and twentie degrees and a halfe, which we haue named Cape François.[3]

Wee could espie neither Riuer nor Bay, wherefore wee sent our Boates, furnished with men of experience, to sounde and knowe the coast neere the shore: who returning to vs about one of the clock at after noone, declared that they had founde, among other thinges, VIII fadome of water at the harde bancke of the sea. Wherevpon hauing diligently wayed vp our Anckers, and hoysted vp our sayles with wind at will,

---

[1] See, however, the relation of Giovanni Verazzani (*ante*, page 56), who also crossed the Atlantic without touching at any of the West Indian Islands.

[2] Ocias—Another blunder; perhaps for the word osiers.

[3] The nearest cape to the latitude $29\frac{1}{2}$ is Cape Canaveral, which is situate in latitude 28° 16′ 50″. "Under that latitude", we are inclined to conjecture, means to the south of the latitude of the spot where they cast anchor.

we sayled and vewed the coast all along with vnspeakable pleasure, of the odorous smell and beawtie of the same. And because there appeared vnto vs no signe of any Porte, about the setting of the sunne we cast ancker againe: which done, we did behold to and fro the goodly order of the woods, wherewith God hath decked euery way the sayd land. Then perceiuing towarde the North, a leaping and a breaking of the water, as a streame falling out of the lande into the Sea. For the whiche wee set vp sayles againe, to double the same while it was yet day. And as wee had so done, and passed beyond it, there appeared vnto vs a fayre entrie of a faire riuer, which caused vs to cast Ancker agayne there nerer the land: to the end the next day we might see what it was, and though that the winde blew for a time vehemently to the shoreward: yet the hold and Anckerrage was so good, that one cable and one Ancker helde vs fast with out danger or sliding.

The next day, in the morning, being the first of May, wee assayed to enter this Porte with two newe barges and a boate well trimmed, finding little water barges whiche might haue astonied and caused vs to returne backe to shipborde, if God had not speedily brought vs in. Where finding 36 fadome water, entred into a goodly and great riuer,[1] which as we went founde to encrease still in depth and largenesse, boyling and roaring through the multitude of all kind of fish. This being entred, wee perceiued a great number of ye Indians, inhabitants there, comming along the sandes and Sea bankes, comming neare vnto vs, without any taking of feare or doubt, shewing vnto vs the easiest landing place: and thereupon, we giuing them also on our parts thanks of assurance and friendlinesse. Forthwith, one of appearance out of the best among them, brother vnto one of their kinges or

---

[1] This was, most probably, St. John's river; there is no other near the locality pointed out in the text that corresponds with the author's description.

gouernours, commaunded one of the Indians to enter into the water, and to approach our boats, to show vs the coastes landing place. We seeing this (without any more doubting or difficultie), landed, and the messenger (after we had rewarded him with some looking-glasse, and other pretie things of small value) ran incontinently toward his Lord : who forthwith sent mee his girdle, in token of assurance and friendship, which girdle was made of red leather, as well couered and coloured as was possible : and as I began to go towards him, hee set foorth and came and receiued me gently, and reised after his manner, all his men following with great silence and modestie : yea, more then our men did. And after we had awhile with gentle vsage congratulated with him, we fell to the ground a little way from them, to call upon the name of God, and to beseech Him to cōtinue still His goodnesse towards vs, and bring to the knowledge of our Sauiour Christ this poore people. While wee were thus praying (they sitting vpon the grounde, which was strawed and dressed with Bay bowes), behelde and hearkened vnto vs very attentiuely, without either speaking or mouing : and as I made a signe vnto their king, lifting vp mine arm, and stretching foorth one finger, only to make them looke vp to heauen ward : He likewise lifting vp his arme towards heauen, put foorth two fingers, whereby it seemed that he made vs to vnderstande that they worshippid the Sunne and y$_e$ moone for Gods : as afterwardes wee vnderstoode it so. In the meane time, their numbers increased, and thither came the kings brother that was first with vs, their mother, wiues, sisters, and children, and being thus assembled, they caused a great number of Bay boughes to bee cut, and therewith a place to be dressed for vs, distant from theirs two fadom. For it is their maner to talke and bargaine sitting : and the chiefe of them to bee apart from the meaner sort, with a shewe of great obedience to their kinges, superiours, and elders. They bee all naked,

*

and of a goodly stature, mightie, and as well shapen and proportioned of body, as any people in ye world : very gentle, curteous, and of a good nature.

The most part of them couer their raines and priuities with faire Harts skinnes, painted most commonly with sundrie colours : and the fore part of their body and armes bee painted with pretie deuised workes, of Azure, red and blacke, so well and so properly, as the best Painter of Europe coulde not amende it. The women haue their bodies painted with a certaine Herbe like vnto Mosse, whereof the Cedar trees, and all other trees, bee alwayes couered. The men for pleasure doe alwayes trimme them selues therwith, after sundrie fashions : They bee of tauny colour, hauke nosed, and of a pleasant countenance. The women be well fauoured, and will not suffer one dishonestly to approch too neare them. But wee were not in their houses, for we sawe none at that time.

After we had taried in this North side of the riuer the most part of the day (which riuer wee haue called May for that wee discouered the same the firste day of the Moneth) wee congratulated, made aliaunce, and entred into amitie with them, and presented the king and his brethren with Gownes of blewe cloth garnished with yellowe Flouredeluces. And it seemed that they were sory for our departure : so that the most part of them entred into the water vp to the necke, to set our boates aflote.

Why the riuer of May was so called.

Putting into vs sundry kinde of fishes, which with merueilous speede they ranne to take in their packs made in the water with great Reedes, so well and cunningly set togeather, after the fashion of a Laberinth or Maze with so many turnes and crookes, as it is impossible to do it without much cunning and industrie.

But desiring to imploy the rest of the day on the other side of this riuer, to viewe and know those Indians that wee sawe there, we trauersed thither, and without any difficultie landed amongest them who receiued vs very gently and with great humanitie: putting vs of their fruites, euen into our boates, Mulberies, Raspis, and such other fruites as they founde ready by the way.

Soone after this came thither the king with his brethren, and others with bowes and arrowes in their handes, vsing therewithall a goodly and a graue fashion, with their behauiour right souldierlike, and as warlike boldnes as may be. They were naked and painted as the other, their haire likewise long, and trussed vp (with a lace made of herbes) to the top of their heads: but they had neither their wiues nor children in their companie. After we had a good while louingly enterteined and presented them with like gifts of habersher wares, cutting hookes and hatchets, and clothed the king and his brethren with like robes, as we had giuen to them on the other side: we entred and viewed the countrie thereaboutes, which is the fairest, fruitfullest, and pleasantest of al the world, abounding in hony, venison, wilde foule, forests, woods of all sortes, Palme trees, Cypresse and Cedars, Bayes ye highest and greatest, with also the fayrest vines in all the world, with grapes according, which without natural art and without mans helpe or trimming will grow to toppes of Okes and other trees that be of a wonderfull greatnesse and height. And the sight of the faire medowes is a pleasure not able to be expressed with tongue: full of Hernes, Curlues, Bitters, Mallards, Egrepths,[1] woodcocks and all other kinde of small birds: with Harts, Hindes, Buckes, wilde Swine, and all other kindes of wilde beastes, as we perceiued well, both by their footing there, and also afterwardes in other places, by their crie and roaring in the night.

Also, there be Conies and Hares: Silke wormes in merueilous number, a great deale fairer and better then be our silk wormes. To bee short, it is a thing vnspeakable to

---

[1] Egrets: beautiful birds, like herons, but white.

consider the thinges that bee seene there, and shalbe founde more and more in this incomperable lande, which neuer yet broken with plough yrons, bringeth forth al things according to his first nature, wherewith the eternall God indued it. About their houses they labour and till the grounde, sowing their fieldes with a graine called Mahis, whereof they make their meale: and in their Gardens they plant beanes, gourdes, cucumbers, Citrons, peason, and many other fruits and rootes vnknowen vnto vs. Their spades and mattocks be made of Wood, so well and fitly as is possible: which they make with certaine stones, oyster shelles, and muscles, wherewith also they make their bowes and smal launces: and cut and polish all sortes of wood that they imploye about their buildings and necessarie vse : There groweth also many Walnut trees, Hasell trees, Cheritrees, very faire and great.

And generally wee haue seene thereof the same simples and herbes that wee haue in Fraunce, and of the like goodnesse, sauour, and taste. The people be very good archers, and of great strength: Their bowe stringes are made of Leather, and their arrowes of Reedes, which they doe head with the teeth of fishes. As we now demaunded of them concerning ye land called Seuola,[1] whereof some haue written

[1] The correct form of this name appears to be Sibola, or Cibola. Sibola is the name of an Indian district, or province, situate on the river Gila, and about one thousand miles north-west from Mexico. The attention of the Spaniards was first directed towards it by a missionary named Marcos de Niça, who, in the year 1539, penetrated into this at that time unconquered region. On his return to Mexico, he gave such a glowing description of the wealth and populousness of Sibola and its seven cities, that an expedition was fitted out for the conquest of the country, under the command of Rodrigo del Rio, the governor of New Biscay. The result of this enterprise was far from justifying the representations of the friar. The Spaniards became masters of the district at the expense of considerable loss in men and horses, and of great suffering from cold and starvation ; but the gold and precious stones they had been taught to expect were nowhere to be found.— Lopez de Gomara, *Hist. Gen. de las Indias* (Anvers, 1554; fol. 272) ; Herrera, *Hist. de las Indias* (Dec. VI, lib. vii, viii). See also the Maps of America by Ortelius and Mercator.

not to bee farre from thence, and to bee situate within the lande, and toward the Sea called the South Sea. They shewed vs by signes that which we vnderstood well enough, that they might goe thither with their Boates (by riuers) in twentie dayes.[1] They that haue written of this kingdome and towne of Seuola, and other townes and kingdomes thereaboutes, say, that there is great aboundance of golde and siluer, precious stones, and other great riches: and that the people had their arrowes headed (in steede of yron) with sharpe pointed Turquesses. Thus the night approching, it was conuenient for vs to returne by day a ship-boorde. Wee tooke leaue of them muche to their griefe, but more to ours without comparison, for that wee had no meane to enter the riuers with our shippe. And albeit, it was not their custome eyther to eate or drinke from the Sunne rising till his going downe: yet the king openly woulde needes drinke with vs, praying vs verie gently to giue him the cuppe whereout we had drunke: and so making him to vnderstande that wee woulde see him againe the next day, we retired to our shippes, which lay about sixe leagues from the hauen to the sea.

Seuola within xx daies trauailing by boate of the riuer of May.

The next day in the morning we returned to land againe, accompanied with the Captaines, Gentlemen, and Souldiers, and other of our small trope: carrying with vs a Pillour or columne of harde stone, our kings armes graued therein, to plant and set the same in the enterie of the Porte in some high place, where it might bee easely seene, and being come thither before the Indians were assembled, we espied on the south syde of the Riuer a place very fitte for that purpose vpon a little hill, compassed with Cypres, Bayes, Paulmes, and other trees, with sweete smelling and pleasant shrubbes.

---

[1] From the eastern shore of Florida to Sibola is about two thousand miles in a direct line. There was, therefore, as little possibility of the journey, if practicable at all, being accomplished in twenty days, as there was probability that the Indians of Florida knew anything of the country in question.

104   THE DISCOUERIE OF

In the middle whereof we planted the first bound or limit of his Maiestie. This done, perceiuing our first Indians assembled, not without some misliking of those on the South parte, where we had set the limitte, who taried for vs in the same place where they met with vs the day before, seeming vnto vs that there is some enimitie betweene them and the others. But when they perceyued our long tarying on this side, they ran to see what we had done in that place, where we landed first, and had set our limitte : which they vewed a great while without touching it any way, or abassing, or euer speaking to vs thereof at any time after. Howebeit, we could skāt depart, but as it were w^t griefe of minde, frō this our first alliance, they rowing vnto vs all along the riuer from all parts, and presenting vs with some of their hartsskins, painted and vnpainted, meale, litle cakes, freshe water, rootes like vnto Rinbabe,[1] which they haue in great estimation, and make therof a potion of medicine: also they brought little bagges of redde colours, and some small spices like vnto Vire, perceyuing among them selues fayre thinges painted as it had bin with graine of scarlet, showing vnto vs by signes that they had in the lande golde and siluer and copper : whereof wee haue brought some. Also lead, like vnto ours, which we shewed. Also turquesses and great aboundance of pearles, whiche, as they declared vnto vs, they tooke out of oysters, whereof there is taken euer along the riuer side, and among the reedes, and in the marshes : and so merueylous aboundance as is skant credible : and we haue perceiued that there be as many and as faire pearles found there as in any countrey of the worlde. For we sawe a man of theirs, as we entered into our boates, that had a pearle hanging at a coller of golde and siluer about his necke, as great as an Acorne at ye least. This man, as he had taken fishe in one of their fishing packs, thereby brought that same to our boates, and our men perceiuing the great-

Golde, silver, and copper, in Florida.

Turquesses and aboundance of pearles.

Marshes.

Pearles as big as acornes.

---

[1] Most probably rhubarb.

nesse therof, one of them putting his finger toward it, the man drewe backe, and woulde no more come neare the boate: not for any feare that he had that they woulde haue taken his Coller and Pearle from him, for he would haue giuen it them for a looking glasse or a knife:

But that hee doubted lest they woulde haue pulled him into the boate, and so by force haue caried him away. He was one of the goodliest men of all the company. But for that we had no leasure to tary any longer with them, the day being well passed, whiche greeued vs, for the commoditie and great riches, whiche as wee vnderstoode and sawe, might bee gotten there, desiring also to employ the rest of the day with our seconde aliance, the Indians on the south side, as we perceiued them the day before, which still taried looking for vs: Wee passed the riuer to their shore, where as wee founde them tarying for vs, quietly and in good order, with newe paintings vpon their face, and feathers vpon their heads: the King, with his Bowe and Arrowes lying by him, sate on the grounde, strawed with boughes, betweene his two brethren, whiche were goodly men and well shapen, and of a wonderfull show of actiuities, hauing vpon their heades, one haire trussed vpright of heyght, of some kinde of wild beast, gathered and wrought together with great cunning, wrethed and fasted after the forme of a Diademe. One of them had hanging about his necke a rounde plate of redde copper well polished, with one other lesser of Siluer in the middest of it, and at his eare a litle plate of Copper, wherewith they vse to stripe the sweat from their bodies. They shewed vs that there was great store of this mettell within the countrey, about fiue or sixe daies iourney from thence, both in the southside and northside of the same riuers, and that they went thither in their Boates.[1] Which Boates they make but

[1] Copper is no longer named among the mineral productions of the country. The statement in the text was most probably either an exaggeration on the part of the natives, or a misconception on the part of the French.

of one piece of a tree, woorking it whole so cunningly and featly, that they put in one of these boates fifteene or twentie persons, and go their wayes very safely. They that rowe stande vpright, hauing their ores short, after the fashion of a Peele. Thus being among them, they presented vs with meale dressed and baked, very good and wel tasted, and of good nourishmēt, also beanes and fish, as crabbes, lobstars, creuises,[1] and many other kinde of good fishes, shewing vs by signes y^t their dwellings were farre off, and if their prouision had been neere hande, they woulde haue presented vs with manye other refreshinges.

The night nowe approaching, we were faine to returne to our Shippe, very much to our griefe : for that we durste not hazarde to enter with our Shippe, by reason of a barre of sande, that was at the enterie of the Porte, howe be it, at a full Sea there is two fadome and a halfe of water at the least, and it is but a leape ouer a surge to passe this Barre, not passing the length of two cables, and then forthwith euery where within sixe or seuen fadome water. So that it maketh a very fayre hauen, and Shippes of a meane burden, from fourescore to a hundred tunnes, may enter therein at all floodes, yea, of a farre greater burthen, if there were French men dwelling there that might skoure the enterye, as they doe in Fraunce : for there is nothing lacking for the lyfe of man. The situation is vnder the eleuation of xxx degrees, a good climate, healthfull, and of a good temperature, merueilous pleasāt, ye people good and of a good and amiable nature, which willingly will obay : yea, be content to serue those that shall with gentlenes and humanitie goe about to allure them, as it is needfull for those that be sent thither hereafter so to doe, and as I haue charged those that be left there to do, to the ende they may aske and learne of thē where they take their gold, copper, and turquesses, and other things yet vnknowen vnto vs ; by reason of the time we soiourned

Gentlenes must be vsed towards them.

[1] Ecrévisses : cray-fish, or lobsters.

there. For if any rude or rigorous meanes should be vsed towards this people, they woulde flie hither and thither through the Woods and Forests, and abandon their habitations and countreys.

The next day being the thirde day of May, desiring alwaies to finde out harbours to rest in, we set vp saile againe : And after we had raunged the coast as neere the shore as we could, there appeared vnto vs, about seuen leagues of on this side of ye riuer of May, a great opening or Bay of some riuer, whither with one of our boates we rowed, and there found one entrie almost like y^t of the riuer of May, and within the same as great a depth, and as large a diuiding it selfe into many great streames, great and broade stretchinges towardes the high lande, with many other lesse, that diuide the countrey into faire and great landes, and great number of small and fayre Medowes. Being entred into them about three leagues, wee found in a place very commodious, strong, and pleasant of situation, certayne Indians, who receiued vs very gently : Howe be it, we being somewhat neare their houses, it seemed it was somewhat against their good willes that we went thither, for at their cries and noyses they made their wiues and children and hoshoulde stuffe to be caried into the Woods : Howe be it they suffered vs to goe into their houses, but they themselues woulde not accompany vs thither. Their houses bee made of Wood, fitly and close, set vpright and couered with Reedes : the most part of them after the fashion of a pauilion. But there was one house amongest the rest verie long and broade, with settles rounde about made of Reedes, trimly couched together, which serue them both for beddes and seates, they be of height two foote from the grounde, set vpon great rounde pillers, painted with red, yelowe, and blewe, well and trimlie polished : some sorte of this people perceiuing that we had in no maner wise hurted their dwellings nor gardens, which they dressed very diligently, they returned all vnto vs before our inbarking, seeming very well contented by their giuing vnto vs water, fruites, and Hart skinnes. It is a place wonderfull fertill, and of strong situatiō, the ground fat, so that it is likely that it would bring forth Wheate and all other corne twise a yeere, and the commodities for liuelihood and the hope of more riches, bee like vnto those we found and considered vpon the riuer of May : without comming into the sea, this arme doth diuide, and maketh many other Iles of May, as also many other great Ilandes : by the which wee trauell from one Ilande to another, betweene lande and land. And it seemeth that men may sayle without danger through al the countrey, and neuer enter into the great sea, which were a wonderfull aduantage.

This is the lande of Checere[1] whereof some haue written, and which many haue gone about to find out, for ye great riches they perceiued by some Indians to be founde there. It is set vnder so good a climate, that none of our men, (though wee were there in the hotest time of the yeere, the sunne entring into Cancer), were troubled with any sicknesses. The people there liue long and in great health and strength, so that the aged men goe without staues, and are able to goe and runne like the youngest of them, who onely are knowen to be olde by the wrinckles in their face, and decay of sight. Wee departed from them verie friendly, and with their contentation. But the night ouertaking vs, we were constrayned to lye in our ships all that night, till it was day, floting vpon this riuer, which we have called Sene,[2] because that the en-

---

[1] Checere, Chicora, or Chicoria, a province in Florida, probably the locality afterwards called St. Helens, in South Carolina.—See Garcilasso de la Vega, *La Florida del Inca* (page 4 ; Madrid, 1723 ; fol.) ; Cardenas, *Ensayo Cronologico para la Historia General de la Florida* (pages 4, 5, etc. ; Madrid, 1723 ; fol.).

[2] This bay and river may be either Nassau Inlet and River, or Cumberland Sound and St. Mary's River ; most probably the latter, the inland connexion between that and the St. John's River, which we conjecture to be the river May, corresponding very closely with the description in the text.

TERRA FLORIDA. 109

tery of it is as broade as from hauer degrace vnto Honesleue.[1] The riuer of Sene.
At the breake of the day wee espied out of the South syde
one of the fayrest, pleasauntest, and greatest medowe grounde
that might be seene, into the which wee went, finding at the
very entrie a long, faire, and great Lake, and an innumerable
number of footesteps of great Hartes and Hindes of a wonder- Heardes of tame hartes
full greatnesse, the steppes being all fresh and new, and it
seemeth that the people doe nourish them like tame Cattell,
in great heards: for we saw the steppes of an Indian that
folowed them.

The Chanell and depth of this riuer of Seyne is one y^t side
of the medowe that is in the Ile of May. Being returned to
our ships, we sayled to knowe more and more of this coast,
goying as neere the shore as we coulde. And as wee had
sayled about six or seuen leagues, there appeared vnto vs
another Bay, where we cast anker, and tarrying so all the
night, in the morning wee went thither, and finding (by our
sounding) at the entrie many banks and beatings, we durst
not enter there with our great ship, hauing named the riuer
Somme,[2] which is 8, 9, 10, 11 fadome depth, diuiding itselfe
into many great Ilands, and small goodly medow grounds and
pastures, and euery where such abundance of fish as is incredible, and on the Weast Northwest side, there is a great
riuer that commeth frō the countrie of a great length ouer:
and another on the Northeast side, which returne into the
Sea. So that (my Lord) it is a countrie full of hauens, riuers, Good hauens and riuers.
and Ilands of such fruitfulnes, as cannot with tongue be ex-
pressed: and where in short time great and precious cōmodities might bee found. And besides this wee discouered
and found also VII riuers more, as great and as good, cutting 7 great and good riuers.
and diuiding the land into faire and great Ilands. The In-
dians inhabitants there be like in manners, and the countrie

[1] Honfleur.
[2] The river Somme appears to correspond most nearly with the river St. Illa and Jykill, or St. Andrew's Sound.

in fertillitie apt and commodious throughout, to beare and bring foorth plentifully all that men would plant or sowe vpon it. There bee euery where the highest and greatest Firtrees y^t can be seene, very well smelling, and where out might bee gathered (with cutting the only bark) as much Rosen, Turpentine, and Frākēsence, as men would desire. And to be short there lacketh nothing. Wherefore being not able to enter and lie with our great vessels there, we could make no long abiding, nor enter so farre into the riuers and countries as wee would faine haue done : for it is well knowne how many inconueniences haue happened vnto men, not only in attempting of newe discoueries, but also in all places by leauing their great vessels in the Sea, farre from the land, vnfurnished of the heads and best men. As for ye other riuers we haue giuen them names as followeth : and vnto the Ilandes ioyning vnto them the same name that the next riuer vnto it hath, as you shall see by the portratures or Cardes y^t I haue made thereof. As to the fourth name of Loire, to ye fift Charnet, to ye sixt Carō, to the 7 riuer Belle, to ye 8 riuer Graūde, to the 9 port Royall, and to the tenth Belle Virrir.[1]

Maps and Sea Cardes.

Upon Whitsunday the xxvii day of May, after wee had perceiued and considered that there was no remedie, but to assay to find the meanes to harber our ships, as wel to amend and trimme them, as to get vs fresh water, wood, and other necessaries, whereof wee hauing opinion that there was no fayrer or fitter place for the purpose then port Royall, and

[1] The names of these rivers, as given by Laudonniere (*L'Histoire Notable de la Floride*, edited by Basanier, Paris, 1586, fol. 10, 11), are Loire, Charente, Garonne, Gironde, Belle, Grande, and the last, Belle à Veoir. No indications are given in the text by which these seven rivers can be distinguished at the present day. More than one writer has offered *conjectures* on this point; but as proof is impossible, we have thought it unadvisable to follow their example. The same remark will apply to the two rivers named respectively, by Ribault, Libourne and Chenonceau.—See Holmes, *Annals of America*, page 566, and the authorities there cited.

TERRA FLORIDA.

when wee had sounded the entrie of the Chanell, (thanked be God), wee entered safely therein with our shippes, against the opinion of many, finding the same one of the fayrest and greatest Hauens of the worlde. Port Royall, a most excellent hauen.

Howe be it, it must be remembred, least men approaching neare it within seuen leagues of the lande, bee abashed and afraide on the Eastside, drawing towarde the Southeast, the grounde to be flatte, for neuerthelesse at a full sea, there is euery where foure fadome water keeping the right Chanel. Note.

In this part there are many riuers of meane bignesse and large, where without daunger the greatest shippes of the worlde might bee harboured, which wee founde no Indian inhabiting there aboutes. The Porte and Riuers side is neerer then tenne or twelue leages vpwardes into the countreys, although it bee one of the goodliest, best, and fruitefullest countreys that euer was seene, and where nothing lacketh, and also where as good and likely commodities bee founde as in other places thereby.

For we founde there a great number of Pepertrees, the Pepper yet greene and not ready to bee gathered : Also the best water of the world, and so many sortes of fishes that yee may take them without net or angle so many as ye will. Also an innumerable sort of wilde foule of all sortes, and in little Ilandes at the entrie of this hauen, on the East Northeast side, there is so great number of Egrepes that the bushes bee all white and couered with them, so that one may take of the young ones with his hande as many as hee will carry away. There bee also a number of other foules, as Hernes, Bitters, Curlues. And to bee short, there is so many small byrdes, that it is a strange thing to bee seene. Wee founde the Indians there more doubtfull and fearefull then the others before : Yet after we had been in their houses and congregated with them, and shewed curtesie to those that we founde to haue abandoned there through boats meale, victuall, and small houssholde stuffe, and both in not taking awaye or Pepper.

touching any part thereof, and in leauing in that place where they dressed their meate, Kniues, Looking glasses, little Beades of glasse, which they loue and esteeme aboue golde and pearles, for to hang them at their eares and neck, and to giue them to their wiues and children : they were somewhat emboldened.

A special note.

For some of them came to our boates, of the which wee carried two goodly and strong aboorde our shippes, clothing and vsing them as gently as it was possible. But they ceased not day nor nyght to lament, and at length they escaped away. Wherefore albeit I was willing (according to your commaundement and memoriall) to bring away some of them with vs, on the Princes behalfe and yours, I forbare to doe so for many considerations and reasons that they told mee, and for that we were in doubt that (leauing some of our men there to inhabite) all the Countrie, men, women, and children, woulde not haue ceased to pursue them for to haue theirs againe : seeing they bee not able to consider and way to what entent wee shoulde haue carried them away : and this may bee better doone to their contentation, when they haue better acquaintance of vs, and know that there is no suche crueltie in vs as in other people and nations, of whom they haue beene beguiled vnder colour of good faith : whiche doing in the ende turned to the doers no good. This is the riuer of Jordain[1] in mine opinion, whereof so much hath beene

A commandement.

The riuer Iordan.

[1] It appears by a passage in Garcilasso de la Vega's *Florida del Inca*, pages 3-4, that Lucas Vasquez de Ayllon and six others, fitted out two vessels in San Domingo, about the year 1520, and sailed to the coast of Florida, for the purpose of obtaining Indians to work in their gold mines. The ships were driven by bad weather to a cape, " which they named Saint Elena, because it was on that saint's day that they arrived there, and into a river which they called Jordan, because the seamen who first saw it so named it." The Jordan is, most probably, the Broad River in South Carolina, as we find from Cardenas, *Ensayo Cronologico*, pages 4-5, and 44, that the province of Chicora, in which the Jordan is said to be situated, was afterwards called Saint Elena : " El reino de Chicora que despues se llamó Santa Elena," etc.

spokē, which is very faire, and the coūtrie good both for yᵉ easie habitation, and also for many other things which should bee long to write.

The twentie of May wee planted another columne or pillor grauen with the kinges armes on the South side, in a high place of the entrie of a great riuer, which wee called Libourne: where there is a lake of fresh water very good, and on the same side, a little lower towards the entrie of the Hauen, is one of the fayrest fountaines that a man may drink of, which falleth by violence down to the riuer from an high place out of a red and sandy ground, and yet for all that fruitefull and of good ayre, where it shoulde seeme that the Indians haue had some faire habitation.

There we sawe the fayrest and the greatest vines with grapes according and young trees, and smal woods, very wel smelling, that euer were seen: whereby it appeareth to be the pleasantest and most commodious dwelling of al yᵉ world. Wherefore (my Lorde) trusting you will not thinke it amisse (considering the commodities that may be brought thence) if we leaue a number of men there, which may fortifie and prouide themselues of things necessary: for in all new discoueries it is the chiefest thing that may be done, at the beginning to fortifie and people the countrey. I had not so soone set forth this to our companie, but many of them affraid[1] to tary there, yet with such a good will and ioly corage, that such a number did thus offer themselues as we had much to do to stay their importunitie. *Exceeding faire and great vines.* *Fortification most necessarie in all newe discoueries.*

And namely of our shipmaisters and principall pilotes, and such as we could not spare. How bee it, wee lefte there but to the number of thirtie in all, Gentlemen, souldiers, and marriners, and that at their own suit and prayer, and of their owne free willes, and by the aduice and deliberation of the Gentlemen sent on the behalfe of the Prince and yours.[2] *30 lefte behind at their owne suite.*

[1] Affraid. This must be a misprint for *offered.*

[2] The state of affairs in France at the time of Ribault's return, pre-

And haue left vnto the forehead and rulers (following therein your good will) Captaine Albert de la Pierria, a souldier of long experience, and the first that from the beginning did offer to tarry. And further by theyr aduice, choyce, and will inskaled and fortified them in an Iland on the north side, a place of strong situation and commodious, vpon a riuer which wee named Chenonceau, and the habitation and Fortresse Charlefote.[1]

<small>They fortified in an Iland.</small>

After we had instructed and duly admonished them of that they shoulde doe (as well for their maner of proceeding, as for the good and louing behauior of them) the xi day of the moneth of June last past, we departed from port Royal: minding yet to range and view the coast vntill the xL degrees of the eleuation: But for as much as there came vpon vs troublesome and cloudie weather, very incommodious for our purpose, and considering also amongst many other thinges, that we had spent our cables and furniture thereof, which is the most principall thing that longeth to them that go to discouer countreys, where continually both night and day they must lie at ancker: also our victualls beeing perished and spilte, our lacke of Boateswaines to set forth our rowe barges and leaue our vessels furnished. The declaration made vnto vs of our Pilots and some others that had before been at some of those places, where we purposed to sayle, and haue been already found by some of the kings subjects, the daunger also and inconueniences that might thereof happen vnto vs: and by reason of the great mystes and fogges wherof the seasō was already come, we perceiued very well wheras we

<small>Fortie degrees of eleuation.</small>

<small>Mistes and fogs when they come.</small>

---

vented any attention being directed towards this colony until 1564. The colonists in the mean time had been obliged to abandon the country: the circumstances which led to this resolution on their part, will be found stated in the Introduction.

[1] It is generally supposed, that Charlesfort was constructed near the site of the present town of Beaufort. Charlesfort must not be confounded with Fort Carolin, erected by Laudonniere two years afterwards, about two leagues from the mouth of the River May.

were, y^t we could do no good, and that it was to late, and ye good and fit season for to vndertake this thing already past. All these thinges thus well considered and wayed, and also for that we thought it meet and necessarie that your honour should with diligence be aduertised (through the help of God) to returne homewards to make relatiō vnto you of the effect of our nauigation. Praying God that it may please him to keepe you in long health and prosperitie.

NOTES IN WRITING BESIDES MORE PRIUIE BY

Mouth that were giuen by a Gentleman, Anno 1580, to
M. Arthure Pette and to M. Charles Jackman, sent by
the Marchants of the Muscouie Companie for the
discouerie of the northeast strayte, not altogether
vnfit for some other enterprises of discouerie,
hereafter to bee taken in hande.

What respect of Ilandes is to be had, and why.

WHEREAS the Portingales haue in their course to their Indies in the Southeast, certaine portes and fortificatiōs to thrust into by the way, to diuers great purposes: So you are to see what Ilands and what portes you had neede to haue by the way in your course, to the Northeast. For which cause I wish you to enter into consideration of the matter, and to note all the Ilands, and to set them downe in plat,[1] to two endes, that is to say, That wee may deuise to take the benefite by them. And also foresee how by thē the Sauages or ciuill Princes may in any sort anoy vs in our purposed trade that way.

And for that the people to the which wee purpose in this voyage to goe, be no Christians, it were good that the masse of our commodities were always in our owne disposition and not at the will of others. Therefore it were good that we did seeke out some small Iland in the Scithian Sea,[2] where we might plant, Fortifie,and Staple safely, frō whēce (as time shoulde serue) wee might feede those heathen nations with

---

[1] Plat; *i.e.*, a map or chart.
[2] That part of the Arctic Ocean which lies to the east of Nova Zembla.

our commodities without cloying them, or without venturing our hole masse in the bowels of their countrey.

And to whiche Ilande if neede were (and if we shoulde thinke so good) we might allure the Northeast navie, the nauie of Cambalu[1] to resort with their commodities to vs there planted, and stapling there.

And if such an Iland might be found so standing as might shorten our course, and so standing as that the Nauie of Cābulu, or other those parties might cōueniently saile vnto w'out their dislike in respect of distāce : thē would it fal out wel. For so besides lesse daūger, and more safetie, our ships might there vnlade and lade againe, and returne the selfsame sommer to the ports of England or of Norway.

And if such an Iland may be found for the stabling of our commodities, to the which they of Cambalu would not saile, yet we might, hauing shippes there, imploy them in passing betweene Cambalu and that stapling place.

Respect of hauens and harbarowes.

And if no such Ilandes may be found in the Scithiā sea toward the firme of Asia, then you are to search out the ports that be about Noua Sembla, all along the tract of that land, to the end you may winter there the first yeere, if you be let by contrarie winds, and to the ende that if wee may in short time come vnto Cābalu, and vnlade and set saile

---

[1] Cathay, as we have already explained (page 24), is the name which was formerly given to the northern part of China, and Cambalu, Kanbalu, or Khan-balik, or Khan-baligh, the name given to its capital, is the modern Pekin. It is an old Mongolian form, and means "the city of the Lord"; or, in other words, the residence of the Khan. The name was in use in the time of Marco Polo, who describes the city as situated towards the north-eastern extremity of the province of Kataia, and says, that it was the winter residence of the Khan : it also occurs as late as 1653, in an account of the Russian embassy to China in that year.—*Travels of Marco Polo.* Translated with notes, by W. Marsden. London, 1818, 4to, page 300.

againe for returne without ventering,[1] there at Cābalu, that you may on your way come as farre in returne as a port about Nouasēbla: That the Sommer following, you may the sooner be in England for the more speedy vent of your East cōmodities, and for the speedier discharge of your Mariners: if you can not goe forward and backe in one selfe same sommer.

And touching the tract of the land of Noua sembla, toward the East, out of the circle Artick, in the more temperate zone, you are to haue regard, for if you finde the soyle planted with people, it is like y^t in time an ample vēt of our warm wollē clothes may be founde. And if there be no people at al there to be found, then you shall specially note what plentie of whales and of other fish is to be found there, to the end wee may turne our newfoūd land fishing, or Island fishing, or our whalefishing, y^t way, for the ayde and cōfort of our new trades to the Northeast to the coasts of Asia.

Respect of fishe and certayne other thinges.

And if the ayre may be found vpon that tract temperate, and the soyle yeelding wood, water, land, and grasse, and the seas fish, then we may plant on the mayne the offals of our people, as the Portingals doe in Brasil, and so they may in our fishing in our passage, and diuers wayes yeelde commoditie to England, by harbouring and vitelling of vs.

And it may be, that the inland there may yeelde mastes, pitch, tarre, hempe, and all thinges for the Nauie, as plentifully as Eastland[2] doth.

The ilandes to be noted with their commodities and wantes.

To note the Ilands, whether they be hie lande or lowe land, moūtanie or flat, sandy, grauelly, clay, chalchy, or of

---

[1] *i.e.*, wintering. [2] Esthonia.

what soyle, wooddy or not wooddy, with springs and riuers, or not, and what wyld beasts they haue in the same.

And whether there seeme to be in the same apt matter to build withall, as stone, free or rough, and stone to make lime withall, and wood or coale to burne the same withall.

To note the goodnes or the badnes of the hauens and harborowes in the Ilandes.

If a straite be founde, what is to bee done, and what greate importance it may bee of.

And if there be a strayte in the passage into the Scithian Seas, the same is specially and with great regard to bee noted, especially if the same straite be narrow and to be kept, I say it is to be noted as a thing that doeth much importe, for what Prince soeuer shall be Lorde of the same, and shall possesse the same, as the king of Denmarke doth possesse the straite of Denmarke, he onely shall haue the trade out of these regions into the Northeast partes of the world for himselfe, and for his priuate profit, or for his subiectes only, or to enioy wonderfull benefite of the toll of the same, like as the king of Dēmarke doth enioy of his straites, by suffering the Merchantes of other Princes to passe that way. If any such straite be found, the eleuation, the hie or lowe lande, the hauens neere, the length of the straites, and all other such circūstaunces, are to be set downe for many purposes: And all the Mariners in ye voyage are to be sworne to keepe close al such thinges, that other Princes preuent vs not of the same, after our returne, vpon the disclosing of the mariners, if any suche thing should happe.

Which way the Sauage may be made able to purchase our cloth, and other their wantes.

If you finde any Iland or mayne lande populous, and that the same people hath neede of cloth: Then are you to deuise what commodities they haue to purchase the same withall.

If they be poore, then you are to consider of the soyle, and how by any possibilitie the same may be made to enrich thē, that hereafter they may haue somthing to purchase the cloth withall.

If you enter into any mayne by portable riuer, and shall finde any great woods, you are to note what kynd of timber they be of: That we may know whether they are for pitche, tarre, mastes, deleborde, clapborde, or for buylding of ships or houses, for so if the people haue no vse of them, they maye be brought perhaps to vse.

Not to venture the losse of any one man.

You must haue great care to preserue your people, since your number is so small, and not to venture any one man in any wise.

To bring home besides marchandize certaine trifles.

Bring home with you (if you may) from Cambalu, or other ciuill place, one or other young man, although you leaue one for him.

Also the fruites of the countries, if they will not of thē-selues dure, drie them, and so preserue them.

And bring with you the Curnelles of peres and apples, and the stones of such stone fruites as you shall find there.

Also the seedes of all strange herbes and flowres, for such seedes of fruites and hearbes comming from another part of the world and so farre off, wil delite the fancie of many, for the strangenes, and for that the same may growe and continue the delite long time.

If you arriue at Cambalu or Quinsay,[1] to bring thence the

---

[1] The proper name of this city is Hang-cheu-feu: it stands on the

Mappe of that Countrey, for so shall you haue the perfecte description, which is to great purpose.

To bring thence some old printed booke, to see whether they haue had print there before it was deuised in Europe, as some write.[1]

To note their force by sea and by lande.

If you arriue in Cambalu or Quinsay, to take a speciall viewe of their Nauie, and to note the force, greatnesse, maner

river Tsien-tang-kiang; was the ancient capital of Southern China, and is now the capital of the province of Che-kiang. Quinsai, Kin-sai, Kin-tsay, or according to Morrison, King-sze, appears to have been no more than a descriptive appellation, signifying, says Marco Polo, "the celestial city", "and which it merits, from its preeminence to all others in the world in point of grandeur and beauty." The literal signification is— "The residence of the Imperial Court".—*Travels of Marco Polo :* Edited by W. Marsden. London, 1818, 4to., p. 508 et seqq.; Morrison's *Chinese Dictionary*, p. 794.

[1] There is much reason to believe, that the art of printing books, as exercised by the Chinese at the present day, was known to them as early as the first half of the tenth century.—See Medhurst, *China, its State and Prospects*, p. 573. London, 1838. The earliest work, however, of which we have been able to obtain an account, from one having had the opportunity of personally inspecting it, bears date the eighth year of the last period of the reign of Shun Te, or A.D. 1348. Mr. Prevost, our informant, who is at present engaged in cataloguing the splendid collection of Chinese books in the British Museum, has favoured us with the following description of the book. "The title is Chin Tsaou Tsëen Wan, or The Thousand Character Classic. It is one of the most popular works in China, and consists of exactly one thousand different characters, not one being repeated. It is composed in octosyllabic verses, which rhyme in couplets; each verse presenting to the student some useful Chinese notion, either in morals or in general knowledge. The object of this work is to teach the written character, both in its semi-cursive and in its stenographic form, termed Tsaou, or grass-writing: the text is, therefore, printed in parallel columns, alternately in the Chin, or correct, and the Tsaou, or cursive character. The author lived in the first half of the sixth century." This work, when seen by Mr. Prevost, was in the possession of Colonel Tynte.

of building of them, the sayles, the tackels, the anckers, the furniture of them, with ordinaunce, armour, and munition.

Also, to note the force of the walles and bulwarkes of their cities, their ordinaunce, and whether they haue any caliuers, and what powder and shot.

To note what armour they haue.

What swordes.

What pikes, halbertes, and billes.

What horses of force, and what light horses they haue.

And so throughout to note the force of the countrey, both by sea and by lande.

Things to be marked to make coniectures by.

To take speciall note of their buildings, and of the ornaments of their houses within.

Take a speciall note of their apparell and furniture, and of the substance that the same is made of, of which a marchant may make a gesse, as well of their commodities as also of their wantes.

To note their shoppes and warehouses, and with what commodities they abounde, the price also.

To see their shambles, and to viewe all such thinges as are brought into the markets, for so you shall sone see the commodities, and the maner of the people of the inlande, and so giue a gesse of many things.

To note their fieldes of grayne, and their trees of fruite, and howe they abounde or not abounde in one and other, and what plentie or scarcetie of fishe they haue.

Thinges to be carried with you, whereof more or lesse is to be caried for a shewe of our commodities to bee made.

Kersies of all orient coulours, specially of stamel,[1] brode cloth of orient colours also.

---

[1] Stamel—Fine worsted.

Frisadoes,[1] motleys,[2] bristowe frices, spanish blankettes, bayes of all colloures, specially with stamell, wosteds, carels,[3] sayes,[4] wedmoles,[5] flanelles, rashe,[6] etc.

Feltes of diuers colours.

Taffeta hats.

Deepe cappes for mariners coloured in stamell, whereof if ample vent may be found, it woulde turne to an infinite commoditie of the common poore people by knitting.

Quilted Cappes of leuant Taffeta of diuers colours, for the night.

Knit stockes of silke of orient colours.

Knit stockes of Jersey yerne, of orient colours, whereof if ample vent might followe, the poore multitude shoulde be set in worke.

Stocks of kersey, of diuers colours, for men and for women.

Garters of Silke, of seuerall kindes, and of colours diuers.

Girdels of Buffe, and all other leather, with gilt and ungilt Buckles, specially wast girdels, wast girdles of veluet.

Gloues of all sortes, knit and of leather.

Gloues perfumed.

---

[1] Frisadoes. This appears to have been a Spanish term, applied to friezed cloths.

[2] Motleys—Cloth of mixed colours.

[3] Carels—Cloths made of fustian.

[4] Sayes—Thin woollen stuff, or serge.

[5] Wedmole. This stuff, as also the name, is of northern origin. Molbech, in his *Danish Dictionary*, describes it, under the word Vadmel, as "A kind of coarse home-made stuff, universally worn by the common people." It was also in use in Iceland, Sweden, Norway, and the Zetland Islands. Kennett, in the Glossary to his Parochial Antiquities (Oxford, 1818, 4to.), has the following entry : " Waddemole, now called Woadmel, and in Oxfordshire, Woddenell, a coarse sort of stuff used for the covering of the collars of cart-horses. Mr. Ray, in his collection of east and south country words, describes it to be a hairy coarse stuff made of Iceland wool, and brought thence by our seamen to Norfolk, Suffolk, etc."

[6] Rashe—A species of inferior silk, or silk and stuff manufacture.

Poyntes of all sortes of silke, threed, and lether, of all maner of colours.

Shooes of spanishe leather, of diuers colours, of diuers lengthes, cut and vncut.

Shooes of other leather.

Veluet shooes and pantoples.[1]

These shooes and pantoples to be sent this time, rather for a showe then for any other cause.

Purses knit, and of leather.

Night cappes knit and other.

A Garnishe of Pewter, for a showe of a vent of that Englishe commoditie, Bottelles, flagons, spoones, etc., of that metall.

Glasses of Englishe making.

Venice glasses.

Looking glasses for women, great and fayre.

Small dials, a few for proofe, although there they wil not hold the order they do heere.

Spectacles of the common sort.

Others of Cristall, trymmed with siluer and otherwise.

Owre glasses.

Commes of Iuorie.

Commes of Boxe.

Commes of Horne.

Linen of diuers sorts.

Handkerchewes, with silke of seuerall colours, wrought.

Glasen eyes to ride with against dust.

Kniues in sheathes, both single and double, of good edge.

Needles, great and small, of euery kinde.

Buttons, greater and smaller, with mouldes of leather and not of wood, and such as be durable of double silke, and that of sundrie colours.

Boxes with weightes of golde, and of euery kinde of the coyne of golde, good and badde, to shewe that the people

---

[1] Pantoples—Pantables, slippers with high soles.

here vse weight and measure, which is a certayne showe of wisedome, and of a certayne gouernment setled here.

All the seuerall siluer Coynes of our Englishe moneys to bee caried with you, to bee showed to the gouernours at Cambalu, which is a thing that shal in silence speake to wise men more then you imagine.

Lockes and keyes, hinges, boltes, haspes, etc., great and small, of excellent workemanshippe, whereof if vent may bee hereafter, wee shall set our subiectes in worke, whiche you must haue in great regarde. For in finding ample vente of any thing that is to be wrought in this realme, is more worth to our people besides the gaine of the marchant, then Christchurch, Bridewel, the Sauoy, and all the Hospitals of Englande.

For banketing on shipborde persons of credite.

First, the sweetest perfumes to set vnder hatches to make the place sweete against their comming aborde, if you arriue at Cambalu, Quinsey, or in such great cities, and not among sauages.

Marmelade.
Sucket.[1]
Figges barelled.
Reysings of the sunne.
Comfets of diuers kindes made of purpose, that shall not dissolue, by him that is most excellent.
Prunes damaske.
Dried peres.
Walnuttes.
Almondes.
Smalnuttes.
Oliues, to make them taste their wine.

---

[1] Sucket—A sweetmeat.

The Apple Iohn, that dureth two yeeres, to make showe of our fruites.

Hullocke.[1]

Sacke.

Vials of good sweet waters, and casting bottels of glasses, to besprinckel the gests withall, after their comming aborde.

Suger, to vse with their wine, if they will.

The sweete oyle of Santie,[2] and excellent Frenche vineger, and a fine kinde of Bisket, stiped in the same, doe make a banketting dishe, and a little Suger cast in it cooleth and comforteth, and refresheth the spirites of man.

Synomome water ⎫ is to be had with you to make a shew
Imperiall water ⎬ of by taste, and also to comfort your
⎭ sicke in the voyage.

With these and such like, you may banket where you arriue the greater and best persons.

Or with the gift of these Marmelades in small boxes, or small violles of sweete waters, you may gratifie by way of gift, or you may make a merchandise of them.

The mappe of England [3] and of London.

Take with you the mappe of Englande set out in faire colours, one of the biggest sort I meane, to make shewe of your Countrie from whence you come.

And also the large mappe of London, to make shewe of your Citie, and let the riuer be drawne full of shippes of all sortes, to make the more shewe of your greate trade and trafficke in trade of merchandise.[4]

---

[1] Hullocke—Hollock, a kind of sweet wine.

[2] Santie—Zante.

[3] The map here recommended to be taken, was either that by Humphrey Lluyd, or Lloyd, published by Ortelius, in his *Theatrum Orbis Terrarum* (Antwerp, 1573); or Saxton's, published in his Atlas, at London, in 1579.

[4] This must be the large plan of London, made by Ralph Aggas, the

Ortelius booke of mappes.[1]

If you take Ortelius booke of mappes with you to marke all these regions, it were not amisse, and if neede were to present the same to the great Cam, for it would bec to a Prince of merueilous account.

The booke of the attyre of all nations.[2]

Such a booke carried with you and bestowed in gift, woulde be much esteemed, as I persuade my selfe.

Bookes.

If any man will lende you the newe Herball,[3] and suche bookes as make shewe of Herbes, Plantes, Trees, Fishes, Foules, and Beastes, of these regions, it may much delight the great Cam, and the nobilitie, and also their merchants, to haue the viewe of them : for all things in these parties so

---

surveyor, about the year 1560, and entitled "Civitas Londinum". It is of extreme rarity in its original state, but has been frequently re-published, with alterations and additions, showing the altered state of the city.

[1] The title of this work is *Theatrum Orbis Terrarum*.

[2] There are two works, either of which may be here alluded to, viz.—*Omnium pœne Gentium Imagines ubi Oris totiusque Corporis et Vestium Habitus diligentissime exprimuntur*, by H. Damman and A. Bruyn, (Cologne, 1577, fol.) ; and *Habitus Variarum Orbis Gentium*, by J. J. Boissard (fol. 1581). The first is most probably the work alluded to.

[3] The book which bests corresponds with this description is "A New Herball, wherein are conteyned the names of Herbes, in Greke, Latin, Englysh, Duch, Frenche, and in the Poticaries and Herbaries Latin, with the properties, degrees, and naturall places of the same, gathered and made by Wylliam Turner, phisicion unto the Duke of Somersettes Grace. Imprinted at London, by Steven Mierdman," 1551, fol. It was enlarged by the addition of a second and third part ; and a new edition of the entire work was published in 1568. At the time Hakluyt wrote, it had most probably quite superseded "The Grete Herbal", first printed by Peter Treveris, in 1516, fol.

much differing from the thinges of those regions, since they may not be here to see thē, by meane of the distance, yet to see those things in a shadowe, by this meane will delight them.

The booke of Rates.

Take with you the booke of Rates, to the ende you may pricke all those commodities there specified that you shall chaunce to find in Cambalu, in Quinsey, or in any part of the East, where you shall chaunce to bee.

Parchment.

Rowles of Parchment, for that we may vent much without hurt to the Realme, and it lyes in small roome.

Glewe.

To carrye Glewe, for that wee haue plentie, and want vent.

Red-Oker for Painters.

To seeke vent, because wee haue great mines of it, and haue no vent.

Sope of both kindes.

To trie what vent it may haue, for that we make of both kindes, and may perhaps make more.

Saffron.

To trie what vent you may haue of Saffron, because this Realme yeeldes the best of the worlde, and for the tillage and other labours, may set the poore greatly in work to their reliefe.

Aquauitæ.

By newe deuise wonderfull quantities may bee made heere, and therefore to secke the vent.

Blacke Conie skinnes.

To trie the vent at Cambalue, for that it lyes towardes the North, and for that wee abounde with the commoditie, and may spare it.

Threade of all colours.

The vent thereof may set our people in worke.

Copper Spurres, and haukes belles.

To see the vent, for it may set our people in worke.

A note and a caueat for the merchant.

That before you offer your commodities to sale, that you indeuour to learne what commodities the Countrie there hath. For if you bring thither veluet, taffeta, spice, or any such commoditie, that you your selfe desire to lade your selfe home with, you must not sell yours deare, least hereafter you purchase theirs not so cheape as you woulde.

Seedes for sale.

Carrie with you for that purpose all sortes of Garden seedes, as well of sweete strawing herbes and of flowers, as also of pot herbes, and all sorts for rootes, etc.

Leadde of the first melting.
Leadde of the second melting of the slagges.

To make triall of the vent of Leadde of all kindes.

English yron, and wyer of yron and copper.

To trye the sale of the same.

Brymstone.

To trie the vent of the same, because wee abounde of it, made in the Realme.

Anthimoney, a minerall.

To see whether they haue any ample vse there for it, for that wee may lade whole nauies of it, and haue no vse of it, vnlesse it bee for some small portion in founding of belles, or a lithel that the Alcumistes vse, of this you may haue two sortes at the Appoticaries.

Tinder boxes, with Steele, flint, and matches and tinder, the matches to be made of Gineper,[1] to auoide the offence of brimstone.

To trie and to make the better sale of Brimstone by shewing the vse.

Candles of waxe to light.

A painted Bellowes.

For that perhaps they haue not the vse of them.

A pot of cast yron.

To trie the sale, for that it is a naturall commoditie of this Realme.

All maner of edge tooles.

To bee sold there, or to the lesse ciuill people, by the way where you shall twich.[2]

What I woulde haue you there to remember.

To note specially what excellent dying they vse in these regions, and therefore to note their garments and ornaments of houses: and to see their die houses, and the materialles and simples that they vse about the same: and to bring

---

[1] Gineper—Juniper, used for matches, in order that the strong smell of the wood might overpower that of the brimstone.

[2] Touch.

Musters[1] and shewes of the colours and of the materials, for that it may serue this clothing realme to great purpose.

To take with you for your owne vse.

All maner of Engyns to take fishe and foule.

To take with you those thinges that bee in perfection of goodnesse.

For as the goodnesse nowe at the first may make your commodities in credit in time to come: So false and sophisticate commodities shall drawe you and all your commodities into contempt and ill opinion.

[1] Samples or patterns.

NOTES FRAMED BY A GENTLEMAN HERETOFORE

to bee giuen to one that prepared for a discouerie, and went not: and not vnfitt to be committed to print, considering the same may stirre vp considerations of these and of such other thinges, not vnmeete in such new voyages as may be attempted hereafter.

THAT the first Seate be chosen on ye seaside, so as (if it may be) you may haue your owne Nauie within Bay, riuer, or lake, within your seat safe from the enemie. And so as the enemie shalbe forced to lie in opē rode abroade without, to be dispersed with all windes and tempests that shall arise. Thus seated you shall bee least subiecte to annoy of the enemie, so may you by your Nauie within, passe out to all partes of the worlde, and so may the shippes of Englande haue accesse to you to supply all wantes, so may your commodities be caried away also. This seate is to bee chosen in temperate Climat, in sweete ayre, where you may possesse alwayes sweete water, wood, seacoles, or turfe, with fish, flesh, grayne, fruits, herbes, and rootes, or so many of those, as may suffice very[1] necessitie for the life of such as shall plant there. And for the possessing of mines of golde, of siluer, copper, quicksiluer, or of any suche precious thing, the wantes of diuers of those needfull thinges may be supplied from some other place by sea, etc.

[1] Every.

Stone to make Lyme of.
Slate stone to tile withall, or such clay as maketh tyle.
Stone to wall withal, if Brycke may not bee made.
Timber for building easely to be conueied to the place.
Reede to couer houses, or such like, if tile or slate be not.

Are to be looked for as thinges without which no Citie may bee made, nor people in ciuill sorte be kept together.

The people there to plant and to continue, are eyther to liue without trafficke, or by trafficke and by trade of marchandize. If they shall liue without sea trafficke, at the first they become naked by want of linen and wollen, and very miserable by infinite wantes that will otherwise ensue, and so will they be forced of them selues to depart, or els easely they will bee consumed by the Sp.[1] by the Fr.[2] or by the naturall inhabithantes of the countrey, and so the interprice becomes reprochfull to our nation, and a lett to many other good purposes that may be taken in hande.

And by trade of marchandize they can not liue, excepte the sea or the lande there may yeelde commoditie for commoditie. And therefore you ought to haue most speciall regarde of that point, and so to plant, that the naturall commodities of the place and seate may drawe to you accesse of Nauigation for the same, or that by your owne Nauigation you may carie the same out, and fetche home the supplye of the wantes of the seate.

Such nauigation so to bee employed, shall, besides the supply of wantes, bee able to encounter with forreyne force.

And for that in the ample vente of suche thinges as are brought to you out of engl. by sea, standeth a matter of great consequence, it behoueth that all humanitie and curtesie, and much forbearing of reuenge to the inland people, be vsed, so shall you haue firme amitie with your neyghbours,

---

[1] Spaniards.   [2] French.

so shall you have their inland commodities to maintayne trafficke, and so shall you waxe rich and strong in force. Diuers and seuerall commodities of the inland are not in great plentie to be brought to your handes, without the ayde of some portable or Nauigable ryuer, or ample lacke, and therefore to haue the helpe of suche a one is most requisite: And so is it of effecte for the dispersing of your owne commodities in exchange into the inlandes.

Nothing is more to be indeuoured with the Inland people then familiaritie. For so may you best discouer al the naturall commodities of their countrey, and also all their wantes, all their strengthes, all their weakenesse, and with whome they are in warre, and with whome considerate in peace and amitie, etc., whiche knowen, you may woorke many great effectes of greatest consequence.

And in your planting, the consideration of the climate and of the soyle bee matters that are to bee respected. For if it be so that you may let in the salt sea water, not mixed with the fresh, into flattes, where the sunne is of the heate that it is at Rochell, in the Bay of portingall, or in Spaine, then may you procure a man of skill, and so you haue wonne one noble commoditie for the fishing, and for trade of marchandize, by making of Salt.

Or if the soyle and clymate bee such as may yeelde you the Grape as good as that at Burdeus,[1] as that in Portingale, or as that about Siui[2] in Spaine, or that in the Ilands of the Canaries, then there resteth but a woorkeman to put in execution to make wines, and to dresse Resings of the sunne and other, etc.

Or if you finde a soyle of the temperature of the South part of Spaine or Barbarie, in whiche you finde the Olif tree to growe: Then you may bee assured of a noble marchandize for this realme, considering that our great trade of clothing doth require oyle, and weying howe deere of late it

[1] Bourdeaux.   [2] Seville.

is become by the vent they haue of that commoditie in the West Indies, and if you finde the wilde olif there it may be graffed.

Or if you can finde the berrie of Cochenile, with whiche wee colour Stammelles, or any Roote, Berrie, Fruite, wood, or earth, fitte for dying, you winne a notable thing fitt for our state of clothing. This Cochenile is naturall in the west Indies on that firme.

Or if you haue hides of beastes fit for sole Lether, etc., It wilbe a marchandize right good, and the sauages there yet can not tanne Lether after our kinde, yet excellently after their owne maner.

Or if the soyle shall yeelde Figges, Almondes, Sugar Canes, Quinces, Orenges, Lemons, Potatos, etc., there may arise some trade and trafficke, by figges, almonds, sugar, marmelade, Sucket, etc.

Or if great woods bee founde, if they be of Cypres, chests may bee made, if they bee of some kinde of trees, pitche and tarre may be made, if they bee of some other, then they may yeelde Rosin, Turpentine, etc., and al for trade and trafficke, and Caskes for wine and oyle may be made: likewise, ships and houses, etc.

And because trafficke is a thing so materiall, I wish that great obseruation be taken what euery soyle yeeldeth naturally, in what commoditie soeuer, and what it may be made to yeeld by indeuour, and to send vs notice home, that therevppon wee may deuise what meanes may be thought of to rayse trades.

Nowe admit that we might not be suffered by the sauages to enioy any whole countrey, or any more thē the scope of a Citie, yet if wee might enioy trafficke, and be assured of the same, wee might bee much inriched, our Nauie might be increased, and a place of safetie might there be found, if change of religion or ciuill warres shoulde happen in this realme, which are thinges of great benefite. But if we may inioy any large Territorie of apt soyle, we might so vse the matter, as we should not depende vpon Spaine for oyles, sacks, resinges, orenges, lemons, Spanish skinnes, etc. Nor vppon Fraunce for woad, baysalt, and Gascoyne wines, nor on Estlande for flaxe, pitch, tarre, mastes, etc. So we shoulde not so exhaust our treasure, and so exceedingly inriche our doubtfull friendes, as we doe, but shoulde purchasse the commodities that we want for halfe the treasure that now we do : but should by our own industries and the benefits of the soile there, cheapely purches oyles, wines, salt, fruits, pitch, tarre, flaxe, hempe, mastes, boordes, fishe, gold, siluer, copper, tallowe, hides, and many commodities : besides, if there be no flatts to make salt on, if you haue plentie of wood you may make it in sufficient quantitie for common vses at home there.

If you can keepe a safe hauen, although you haue not the friendship of the neere neyghbours, yet you may haue trafficke by sea vpon one shore or other, vpon that firme in time to come, if not present.

If you finde great plenty of tymber on the shore side, or vpon any portable riuer, you were best to cut downe of the same the first wynter, to bee seasoned for shippes, barkes, botes, and houses.

And if neere such wood there be any riuer or brooke, vpon the which a sawing mill may be placed, it woulde doe great seruice, and therefore consideration woulde bee had of suche place.

And if such port and chosē place of setling were in possessiō, and after fortified by art, although by ye land side our Englishmē were kept in, and might not inioy any traffick with the next neighbours, nor any vittel : yet might they vittel themselues of fishe to serue verie necessitie, and enter into amitie with the enemies of their next neighbours, and so haue vent of their marchandize of England, and also haue vittel, or by meanes herevpon to be vsed, to force the next neighbours to amitie. And keeping a nauie at the setling place, they shoulde finde out along the tracte of the lande to haue trafficke, and at diuers Ilandes also. And so this first seate might in time become a stapling place of the commodities of many countreys and territories, and in tyme this place myght become of all the prouinces round about the only gouernour. And if the place first chosē should not so wel please our people, as some other more lately founde out: There might bee an easie remoue, and that might be rased, or rather kept, for others of our nation to auoyde an ill neyghbour, etc.

If the soyles adioyning to such conuenient hauen and setling places be founde marshie and boggie, then men skilful in draining are to be caried thither. For arte may worke wonderfull effectes therein, and make the soyle rich for many vses.

To plante vppon an Ilande in the mouth of some notable riuer, or vpon the poynt of the lande entring into the riuer, if no such Iland be, were to great ende. For if such riuer were nauigable or portable farre into the lande, then would arise great hope of planting in fertill soyles, and trafficke on the one or on thother side of the riuer, or on both, or the linking in amitie with one or other petie king contēding there for dominion.

Such riuers founde, both barges and boates may bee made for the safe passage of such as shal perce ye same. These to bee couered with doubles of course linnen, artificially wrought, to defend the arrow or the dart of the sauage from the rower.

Since euery soyle of the world by arte may be made to yeelde things to feede and to cloth man, bring in your returne a perfect note of the soyle without and within, and we shall deuise if neede require to amende the same, and to draw it to more perfectiō. And if you finde not fruits in

T

your planting place to your liking, we shal in v drifats[1] furnish you w^t such kinds of plants to be caried thither ye winter after your planting, as shall the very next summer folowing, yeeld you some fruite, and the yere next folowing, as much as shal suffice a towne as big as Callice, and that shortly after shall be able to yeeld you great store of strong durable good sider to drinke, and these trees shalbe able to increase you within lesse then VII yeres as many trees presently to beare as may suffice the people of diuers parishes, which at the first setling may stand you in great steade, if the soyle haue not the commoditie of fruites of goodnesse already. And because you ought greedily to hunt after thinges that yeelde present reliefe, without trouble of cariage thither, therefore I make mencion of these thus specially, to the ende you may haue it specially in mynde.

[1] Boxes, or packing-cases.

FINIS.

THE NAMES OF CERTAINE COMMODITIES GROW-
ing in part of America, not presently inhabited by
any Christians, frō Florida northward, gathered out of
the discourses of Verarzanus, Thorne, Cartier,
Ribalt, Theuet, and Best, which haue bin personally in those Countreys, and haue seene these
things amongst many others.

Beastes.

Leopardes
Stagges
Hartes
Deare
Beares
Hares
Wildeswine
Connyes
White beares
A beast farre bigger then an oxe[1]
Wolues
Dogges
A kinde of beast like a Conny[2]
Beuers
Marterns
Foxes
Bagers
Otters
Weesels
A beast called Su, being like a Bull.[3]

Birdes.

Haukes
Bitters
Curlewes
Herons
Woodcockes
Partridges
Small birdes
Plentie of foule for al pleasant game

Aporates
Blackbirdes
Cranes
Crowes, like Cornish Choughes
Duckes
Godetes[4]
Geese
Pigions
Margaues[5]
Feasants
Swannes
Thrushes
Turtles
Fintches
Nightingales, etc.

Fishes.

Coddes
Salmons
Seales
Makerels
Tortoyses
Whales
Horsefishes[6]
A fish like a grayhound good meate
Lampreys
Crabbes
Crefishes
Lobsters
Eeles
The riuers full of incredible store of all good fishe.

---

[1] This may be the elk.
[2] Most probably the marmot.
[3] The bison.
[4] Probably the godwit.
[5] Perhaps the muckawis; caprimulgus rufus.
[6] The hippocampus.

NAMES OF CERTAINE COMMODITIES

Wormes.

Silke wormes fayre and great.

Trees.

Bay
Cypres
Damson
Palme
Many trees yeelding sweet sauour
Okes
Nut trees
Firre
Vines
Cahene, good against poyson
Cedars   } Hasell trees
Cheritrees   } Walnut trees
Pepper trees
Ameda, which healeth many diseases
Ashe   ⎧ Elmes
Boxe   ⎨ Whitelmes
Cidron ⎬ Pynes
Yewe   ⎩ Willowes
Filbird trees, better than ours
Whitethornes, bearing a berrie as big as a Damson
Vines, bearing a great grape.

Fruites.

Cowcumbers ⎧ Guordes
Cytrons   ⎨ Mulberries
Raspis   ⎬ Almonds
Apples   ⎨ Melons
Damsons   ⎩ Figges
Reasons, great and small
Muske melons { Lemons
Orenges   { Dates, very great
Strawberries
Gooseberries, red and white.

Gummes.

Rosen   ⎧ Pitche. Tarre
Turpentine ⎨ Honnie
Frankencense⎩ Waxe

Spices and Drugges.

Pepper
Small spices, like to vire
Reubarbe in Florida: diuerse other kindes.

Hearbes and Floures.

Many sortes of herbes, differing from ours
Many simples, like those of Fraunce
Hempe
Parseley
Roses ⎧ Redde
      ⎨ White
      ⎩ Damaske.

Grayne and Pulse.

Corne, like Rie ⎧ Myllet
Oates   ⎨ Beanes of diuers
Peason   ⎩ coulers
Another strãge corne, of good nourishment
Maiz.

Metalles.

Gold, in good quantitie
Siluer
Coper
Leade
Many hills shew mineral matter.

Precious Stones.

Turqueses
Rubies
Pearles, great and faire
Precious stones, of diuers colours
Esurgni, a stone much estemed there
Kiph, a kind of stone shining bright.

Other Stones.

Marble, very hard { Jasper
Alabaster   { Freestone
Quarries of glistring stones.

Colours.

Yelowe ⎧ Redde
Blewe ⎨ Scarlet
       ⎩ Roane colour

Deare skinnes, wrought like branch-
  ed Damaske
Harts skinnes, paynted and died,
  of diuers colours
Bagges of red colours
A roote called Auaty, that they
  dye red withall in Florida.

*So as the commodities already
knowen, besides many yet vnknowen, are these, and that
in great quantitie.*

Fleshe   { Fruites
Fish   { Grayne
Beueradges, or drink, of diuers
  sortes
Golde   { Copper
Silver   { Lead

Pearles   { Furres
Spices   { Feathers
Drugges   { Gummes
           { Oyles
Silke
Hides vndressed
Beasts skins, wrought like Damaske
Lether died
Hartes skinnes painted
Stones for fayre building
Precious stones
Colours
All kinde of good wood.

Imprinted at London, at the
*three Cranes, in the Vine-
tree, by Thomas Daw-
son.* 1582.

APPENDIX.

THE WILL OF RICHARD HAKLUYT.—THE CHIEFE PLACES WHERE
SONDRY SORTE OF SPICES DO GROWE, ETC.—NOTES OF
CERTAYNE COMODITIES IN GOOD REQUEST IN
THE EAST INDIES, ETC.

APPENDIX.

THE following pieces have never before been made public. The Will is printed from an official copy in the possession of Bolton Corney, Esq., to whom the editor is indebted for the loan of this very interesting document. The Notes have evidently been drawn up by Hakluyt at the request of some person or persons of consideration, desirous of availing themselves of his intimate acquaintance with all particulars bearing upon maritime enterprise, and were most probably intended for the use of some company of merchants. They are perhaps rather curious than valuable at the present day; but their practical utility at the time they were framed must have been great; and from whatever point of view we may regard them, they will be found to possess considerable interest.

THE WILL OF RICHARD HAKLUYT.
EXTRACTED FROM THE REGISTRY OF THE PREROGATIVE COURT OF CANTERBURY.

In the name of God, Amen. The twente daye of August, in the yeare of Lord God one thowsand six hundreth and twelve, I, Richard Hackluit, person of Wetheringsett, in the countie of Suffolke, beinge of good and pfect memorie thanked be God, revokinge and frustratinge hereby all former willes or testaments whatsoever heretofore by me thought vpon or made, doe make, declare, and ordaine, this my last will or testament hereafter followinge. First, I comend my soule into the handes of God, from whence I receaved the same, trusting thorow the only merits of Jesus Christ and the sanctification of the blessed Spirit, to be both in body and soule a member of His most holy and heavenly kingdome. And as concerninge my body, I yeald it (by course of nature and God his ordinance) vnto the earth to be neverthelesse decentlie buried (in hope of a happie resurrection) by the discretion and charges of my executor. Item, I give vnto Edmond Hackluit, *my* my only sonne, and to his heires for ever, all that my mañour called Bridg-place, wth all royalties, prerogatives, proffitts, and advantages, wth all the landes, meadowes, pastures, woods, underwoods, or other the appurteñances to the said mañour, any waye belonginge or appertayninge, in as full and ample mañer, as I lately purchased the same of Mr. John Scrivener, late of Barbican, in the suburbs of the cittie of London. Also, I geve vnto the said Edmonde Hackluit, and to his heires for ever, all that my tenement, wth the landes theirvnto belonginge, lyinge and beinge in Leominster Oare, now demised by my brother Oliver Hackluit, for sixtene nobles a yeare; further, I give vnto the said Edmond Hackluit, and to his heires for ever, all those my tenements lying in the north-west end of Tuttell-streete, in the cittie of Westminster, wch I lately purchased in fee of one Mr. Line, neere adioyninge to the inn called the White Harte, vpon condition neverthelesse hereafter followinge and not otherwise,—that is to saye, that the said Edmond or his assignes doe paye, or cause to be payed, vnto Mr. Thomas Peters, late of Fleete-streete, in London, to the use of Frañcis Hackluit, the wife of me Richard Hackluit, the full and whole some of three hundreth pounds of lawfull English money, in full contentacon and satisfaction of a certaine bond obligatorie heretofore by me sealed and delivered, for the contentment, reliefe, and maintyñance of the said Frañcis, in such manner and forme as in the said bond is specified.

Howbeit, my meaninge, intent, and will, is, that yf the said Frāncis, or her assignes, doe deliver into the hands of my said sonne Edmond, the said bond obligatorie, whereby it may be lawfully cancelled, and he freed and for ever lawfully discharged from the said dett of three hundreth poundes, and of all penalties or forfaytures therevpon arising or to arise at any tyme hereafter wthin one moneth and imediately ensewinge after my decease, wthout fraud, cooven, or delaye, that then I will, that after the deliverye of the bond aforesaid, that all the said tenements lyinge and beinge in the north-west end of Tuttell-streete aforesaid, devised to my sonne Edmond, shalbe and remain fully and wholye to my said wife Frāncis and to her heires for ever, as fully and whollye as I had before appointed them to my said sonne and his heirs, any gifte or graunt whatsoever to the contrarye in any wise notwthstandinge. Also, I will that the said Frāncis my wife shall have all the plate, jewelles, and houshold stuffe, of what nature soever, wch are in the possession of me, in any place whereof the said Frāncis was possessed in the tyme of her widowhood by administration. Item, I give and bequeath vnto Oliver Hackluit my brother, the some of tenn pounds, to be payd vnto him or his assignes wthin one yeare next ensewing after my decease, to be bestowed amongste his sonnes at his owne discretion. Item, I geve and bequeath to Joane Hackluit, daughter of the said Oliver, other tenn pounds, to bee payed vnto her wthin two monethes nexte and imediatelye ensewinge after the day of her mariage, the same beinge lawfully demaunded. Item, I give vnto my sister Katherine Morer, dwellinge in Holbourne, the some of twentie pounds; tenn pounds whereof I will to be payed vnto her wthin one moneth after my decease, and the other tenn pounds wthin six monethes after my decease. Item, I give and bequeath to John Morer, her sonne, fiftie shillings, to be payed vnto him wthin one yeare after my decease; and likewise other fiftie shillings to

Barbary Moorer, her daughter, to be payed her also w^th^in one yeare after my decease. Item, I give to Mistris Longe, dwellinge in the Tower, twentie shillinges. Also, to Mr. Thomas Peters, and to his wife, to either of them, twentie shillinges, which last three poundes I will shalbe payed w^th^in one yeare after my decease. Item, I give unto Mr. Edward Rigges twentie shillinges and my best cassock, desiringe him to preach a funerall sermon at my buriall. Item, I geve to Mr. Collman, my curate, tenn shillinges and my old gowne. Item, I geve to my sister Bacon tenn shillinges; and to my servānt, Thomas Button, tenn shillinges; and to Lionell Pearson, five shillinges; and to Mary Upson, three shillinges and four-pence. Also, I geve to the townsmen of Wetheringset and Brockford, to be distributed to the poore people, by the discretion of my executor and the churchwardens for the tyme beinge, the som̄e of five markes, to be payed w^th^in one year after my decease. Item, I doe geve to the right worshipfull colledge of Westminster the som̄e of five pounds, to be payed into the handes of the treasurer w^th^in sixe monethes after my decease, towards the repayringe of the north windowe of the said church. Also, whereas I have a table, a bedsted, and certaine furniture of hangings, pictures, and other implements, in a chamber belonging to me in the Savoye, I doe give and bequeath them all vnto the said howse, to the use of the Dorturye their. Also, whereas I have at Bristow sondry implements, hangings, and furniture their, in my lodginge and chambers, I do freely geve all to the only vse and benefitt of the said Colledge, to be disposed at the discretion of the right worshipfull Mr. Deane. Item, I geve to my cosen, Thomas Hackluit, two dublets, two paire of britches, one of my best shirts, and twenty shillinges in money. I geve to Oliver Cogram, my good friend, one of my old cassocks, an old dublett, and a paire of old britches, and a paire of course shetes. Further, I geve to my sister Katherine one of my gownes, wch my sonne Edward thinketh good, and to be delivered before winter. Lastly, I geve to my lovinge cosen, Mistris Dorothe Patrickson, the some of fyve pounds, to be payed vnto her wthin six monthes after my decease. And likewise I geve to the worshipfull Mr. John Davyes, her sonne, the some of other five pounds, to be likewise payed him wthin six monethes after my decease; whom I heartelye intreate and apoint to be the only supravisour of this my last will and testament, that accordingly, in all poynts, it may be truelye and effectually pfourmed; whose counsaile I have vsed heretofore in my two late purchases, of Bridge-place in Suffolke, and my tenements in Tuttell Streete, as is afore remembred. Also, I geve to Mr. Richard Ireland and to Mr. Wilson, now scholemaster of Westminster, to either of them tenn shillinges, as a token of my love and good will towards them; and to Michaell Locke the younger, other tenn shillinges. And I ordayne Edmond Hackluit, my sonne, my sole and only executor of this my last will and testament, vnto whome I geve hereby all my ready money, plate, jewells, billes, bondes, debtts, and dutyes, howsholdstuffe, goods, cattell, corne, implements, chattles, or whatsoever els to me belongeth or appertayneth, to the end he shall paye my debts and legacies, wth all funerall expences, and vndertake the proovinge of this my will, and all other things wch in right belongeth to an executor. In Wettness whereof I have herevnto sett my hand and seale the day and yeare first above written. By me, Richard Hakluyt, person, of Wetheringset. These being witnesses: Edward Rigges, John Colman, David Allshais.

Probatum fuit testamentum suprascriptum apud London, coram venerabili viro Māgro Edmundo Pope, legum Doctore Surrogato venerabilis viri Domini Johannis Benet, militis, legum etiam Doctoris, Curie prerogative Cantuariensis Māgri Custodis sive Comissarij legitime constituti, vicesimo tertio die mensis Novembris, anno Dñi millessimo sexcentesimo decimo sexto, juramento Edmundi Hackluit, filij nr̃alis et ltimi dicti defuncti, et executoris in eodem testamento nominat'cui comĩssa fuit administracõ bonorum, jurium et creditorum dicti defuncti, de bene et fideliter administrando, etc., ad sancta Dei Evangelia jurat'.

Chas. Dyneley } *Deputy*
John Iggulden } *Registers.*
W. F. Gostling }

Bibl. Bodl. MS. Arch. Seld. B. 8.

THE CHIEFE PLACES WHERE SONDRY SORTE of spices do growe in the East Indies, gathered out of sondry the best and latest authours, by R. Hakluyt.

This noat was made in February, 1600.

The places where Peper groweth.

THE greatest parte of the peper browght by the Portugales out of the East Indies unto Lisbon, groweth in the country of Malabar, and is embarqued at the townes of Onor, Barzelor, Mangalor, Cananor, Crangenor, Cochin, and Coulan. All which places are in the Portugalas possession. It groweth also about Calicut; but the kinge of Calicut and they are seldome in amity.

Places yielding Peper out of the Portugales iurisdiction.

First, in the Isle of Zeilon,—*Cæsar Fredrick*,[1] *Cap. de Zeilon*, and *John Huighen van Linschoten*.[2]

---

[1] The title of the English edition of this work is "The Voyage and Travaile of M. Cæsar Frederick, Merchant of Venice, into the East India, the Indies, and beyond the Indies. Wherein are contained very pleasant and rare matters, with the customes and rites of those countries. Also heerein are discovered the merchandises and commodities of those countreyes, as well the aboundaunce of goulde and siluer, as spices, drugges, pearles, and other jewelles. Written at sea in the Hercules of London. Comming from Turkie this 25 of March 1588." London, 1588, 4to. This is a translation from an Italian original, which was published at Venice in 1587, in 8vo., under the title "Viaggio di M. Cesare de i Federici nell' India Orientale e oltra l' India. Nelquale ... si descrivano le spetiarie, droghe, gioie e perle che d'essi si cavano." etc.

[2] "John Huighen van Linschoten, his discours of voyages into ye Easte and West Indies. Devided into foure Bookes. Printed at London by John Wolfe." This work was published originally in Dutch, from which the above translation was made by William Phillip.

APPENDIX.

Out of the first voiage of the Hollanders, in Latin and French, cap. 15 & 20.

Places where Peper groweth in the Isle of Sumatra.

1. Daia	6. Andragiri
2. Achen	7. Jambe
3. Pedir	8. Speriamon
4. Pacem	9. Baros
5. Camper	10. Dampin.

Places where Peper groweth in the Isle of Iaua Maior. *Out of the first voyage of the Hol.,* cap. 15 and 20.[1]

1. Pariban	10. Anier
2. Cheruguin	11. Bantam
3. Buama	12. Punctan
4. Labuan	13. Panarucan; where longe
5. Cherola	peper groweth, as also in
6. Charita	Pegu and Bangala, *Gons.*
7. Meleassari	*de Ouied,*[2] and *Cæs. Fred.,*
8. Cangabaia	in the end of this dis-
9. Chuconin	course.

Peper also groweth in Queda, on the Maine of Malaca, over against Achen. *Linsch.,* cap. 17; and the 1 *Voy. of the Hol.,* cap. 17.

It groweth also in the kingdome of Patané, on the east side of the sayde Maine of Malaca. *Hist. of China,*[3] cap. 22.

---

[1] "Premier livre de l'histoire de la Navigation aux Indes Orientales par les Hollandois, etc. Plus les Monnoyes, Espices, Drogues et Marchandises et le pris d'icelles, etc. Par G. M. A. W. L." Amstelredam, 1598. fol. A very indifferent abridgment of this account was published in English, under the following title: "The description of a voyage made by certaine ships of Holland into the East Indies. With their adventures and successe: together with the description of the countries, townes, and inhabitantes of the same, etc. Translated out of Dutch into English by W. P." The translator is William Phillip.

[2] "Oviedo de la natural hystoria de las Indias." Toledo, 1526, fol.

[3] "The Historie of the great and mightie kingdome of China and the

APPENDIX. 153

It groweth likewise in the kingdome of Siam. *Ibidem.*
Also it groweth in the territories neere Malaca. *Linsch.,* cap. 62.

Item. There groweth excellent peper in the Isles of Nicubar, somewhat to the north of Sumatra. *Hist. China,* cap. 25.

There groweth also longe peper in the Isle of Baratene, as appeareth by the testimony of Sir Frances Drake, *in the 3rd volume of my English Voiages,* pag. 741.

The price of peper may be read in *Linsch.,* pag. 161.

The places where Sinamon groweth.

The best sinamon groweth in the Isle of Zeilon, the kinge whereof is the Portugales mortall enemy; where, neuertheless, they have a small forte, called Colombo. *Cæs. Fred., Cap. de Zeilon.*

Wild sinamon, called by the Portugales Canella de Mato, groweth in the Malabar, on the back side of Cochin, and is browght in greate quantitye into Europe for the best. *Linsch.,* cap. 14.

In the Isles of Nicubar, lying to the north-west of Sumatra, between the latitude of 6 and 10 degrees, are many trees of sinamon, which is the best in all the world, and is sold at a small price. *Hist. China,* cap. 25.

Likewise there groweth in the islande of Java, and on the maine by Malaca. *Linsch.,* cap. 63.

The places where Cloves do growe.

Cloves do growe in the isles of Maluco, namely in Tarenate, Tidore, Motelo, Machian, Bachian, Alatua; on the northwest end of the Isle of Ceiran, and in the isles of Ambonio.

situation thereof. Togither with the great riches, huge citties, politike governement, and rare inventions in the same. Translated out of Spanish by R. Parke. London : Printed by J. Wolfe, 1588," 4to.

The above is a translation from the Spanish of Gonzalez de Mendoza.

In the isles of Tidore and Ambonio the Portugales have two small fortes, as appeareth by the greate Italian map, taken in the Madre di Dios, which I have translated and caused to be drawne for the Company.

Great store of cloves are to be sold in Bantam.

Cloves are also browght from Siam to Malaca. *Hist. Chin.*, cap. 22.

The places where Nuttmegges and Mace do growe.

Nuttmegges and maces grow chiefly in the Isle of Banda and the seven small isles thereto adjoyninge.

They likewise grow in three other islands greater then Banda, lyinge to the north-west thereof, called Ama, Liazer, and Rucellas. As appeereth out of the foresayd greate Italian map.

Nuttmegges also come from the greate Isle of Borneo. *Hist. Chin.*, cap. 22.

Sir Frances Drake found nuttmeggs, ginger, and longe peper, growing in the Isle of Baratave. *Vol. 3 of my Eng. Voi.*, pag. 741.

Nuttmeggs also grow in the isles of Java and Sunda. *Linsch.*, cap. 66.

Places where Camphora groweth.

The best camphora groweth in canes, in the Isle of Borneo.

It groweth also about Chinchen, in a citty of China.

It groweth likewise in the isles of Sumatra and Java. It is much used in medicines, and is one of the richest wares of India. *Linsch.*, cap. 80, and *the* 1 *Voy. of the Hol.*, pag. 14.

Anil, or Indico.

It groweth in Cambaya; but is sold good cheape in Bantam, the chiefe citty of Java. *The* 1 *Voy. of the Hol.*, pag. 20.

Amber.

It is fownd on the coaste of Africa, about Gofala, Mozambique, and Malinde.[1]

Amber is of coulour grey and black: but the black is the best.

It is also fownd necre the isles of Maldivar, as likewise on the coast of China. *Linsch.*, cap. 70.

Much is browght also from the West Indies, and from the coast of Florida, which is of two sorts,—liquid amber, and clare amber.

Muske.

Muske cometh from Tartarie and from China. It is often falsified by the Chinois and Jewes. *Cæs. Fred.*, pag. 38, and *Linsch.*, cap. 70.

Civet.

Civet, called by the Portugales, Algalia, is fownd in Bengala, which the people falsifie; but the best cometh from the Nina, on the coast of Guinie, and from the isles of Cabo verde. *Linsch.*, cap. 70.

Beniamin.

Beniamin groweth much in the kingdome of Siam, and also in the island of Sumatra, and in the isles of Java, and in the country neere unto Malaca. There are two sorts, white and black. The black is best, which groweth out of the youngest trees. *Linsch.*, cap. 71. It is one of the costliest druggs of all the East, because it excelleth all other in sweetenes.

Frankincense.

Frankincense, called in Latin, Thus, groweth in Arabia Felix. The best is white, like drops, and is called the male; the worst is black: both are the gume of a tree. *Linsch.*, cap. 72.

---

[1] Melinda.

Myrrhe.

Myrrhe groweth like beniamin and frankincense, and commeth out of Arabia Felix, and out of the contry of the Abassins.[1] *Ibidem.*

Manna.

Manna commeth out of Arabia and Persia, but most out of the province of Usbeke, lyinge behind Persia, in Tartarie. There be four sorts thereof: 1, whitish; 2, reddish; 3, that which commeth in greate peces, with the leaves among it; the 4th kind is browght in lether bags, and is melted like hony, and is of a white coulor. *Linsch.*, cap. 73.

Rheubarbe.

Rheubarb groweth about Campion, a province and citty lyinge north of China. It is most brought by land through the contry of Usbeke, lyinge to the east of Persia in Tartarie, and adjoyning to Persia on the back side of India, and so commith to Ormus, and thence to Sumatra and Java. The best is browght, for the most parte, over land to Venice. Read *Ramusius,* in the preface of his 2 volume.

Rheubarb also groweth abundantly in the country of Malabar.

It also commeth from Cathaio or China to Malaca, by water. *Ramus.,* vol. ii, cap. 323, and *Linsch.,* cap. 37.

Sandalo, or Sanders.

Sandalo, or sanders, are of three sorts, white, yellow, and red. The white and the yellow, which is the best, come from the islands of Timor and Solor, and another island next adjoyninge on the west, whether the Captaine of Malaca sendeth

---

[1] Abyssinians.

yearly a shippe. *Cæs. Fred.*, fo. 19. The red sanders grow in Coromandel and Tenasseri, on the coast of Pegû. *Linsch.*, cap. 74.

Snakewood, or Palo da cobra.

Snakewood, or Palo da cobra, groweth most in the Isle of Zeilon. One ounce thereof, bruised and mixed with water, is good against all poison and sicknes, and the stinginge of snakes, wherof it hath the name. Wherfore it is now much browght and carryed into all countryes, especially into Portugale, and thence hether. *Linsch.*, cap. 75.

Lignum Aloes, or Calamba.

The lignum aloes, which, in India, is called Calamba, and Palo d'aguilla, is most plentifull in Malaca, in the Isle of Sumatra, Camboya, Siam, and the contries borderinge on the same. The best and finest is called Calamba; and the other, Palo d'aguilla. The Calamba, yf it be good, is sold by weight against sillver and gold. *Linsch.*, cap. 76.

The Root of China.

The roote of China beinge a most sovereigne remidie against the French poxe, is very common, and so good cheape in the Indies, that it is not worth above halfe a pardao the pound, which is a teston and a halfe of Portugale money. The best rootes are the blackest, with few knotts, and white within. They grow in no place but in China. *Linsch.*, cap. 77

Of opium, famarindi, mirabolans, spikenard, aloe zocotrina, anacardi, calamus aromaticus, costus, cubebes, galanga, etc., read *Linsch.*, from the 78 to the 83 chapter, where you shall find their proper names in the Indies, the places where they growe, the several kindes of them, their uses, prices, etc.

OF the severall prices of precious stones and spices, with their weights and measures, as they were accustomed to be sold by the Moores and Gentiles, as also of the places where they growe, I have 3 severall treatises : one of Ramusius, in Italian and English ; the second, of Cæs. Fred., in English ; and the third, in my first volume of English Voyages.

Of the prices of pearles and certeine pretious stones, I delivered your worships a note in Portugese and English, and more may be fownd therof in *Linschot.*, cap. 84 and 91.

Likewise I have delivered you a catalogue of the severall commodities good for the East Indies, wherof sence I have fownd a greater nomber. I have also provided for you two copies of that large Italian intercepted map of the Malucos, the notes wherof, for the better understandinge, are translated into English.

I have also large notes, of 20 yeares observation, concerninge the north-west passage, which your worships shall command, yf you shall have occasion to use the same.

	REAS.
Diamants[1] perfect, of one graine lavardos de toto fundo,[2] are worth 3 milreis[3] - -	3,000
Diamants of 1½ graine are worth - -	4,000
Diamants of 2 graines are worth - -	8,000
Diamants of 2½ graines are worth - -	10,000
Diamants of 3 graines are worth - -	15,000
Diamants of 3½ graines are worth -	18 and 20,000
Diamants of 1 quilate are worth - -	25,000

Dimants of this sorte, perfect in all their grownds, are of

---

[1] The "notes" from this place to the end of the section will be found repeated in substance at p. 162.

[2] See this term explained at p. 162, where it is rendered "wrought throughout". It means, properly, cut the same on the under as on the upper side.

[3] A milreis is worth 5s. 7½d.

APPENDIX. 159

this vallew; yf they be of a greater weight they go by quilates,[1] and rise double in vallew.

Diamants chapas,[2] which are to be bought, and gaine made in workinge them.

Diamants chapas, 3 to a quilate, worth 6,000 reis - - - - - - -	6,000
Diamants of 4 to a quilate, worth - -	5,000
Diamants of 5 to a quilate, worth from	3 to 4,000
Diamants of 1 quilate, worth - - -	10,000
Diamants of 2 to a quilate, worth - -	10,000
Diamants of 15 to a quilate, worth, being pointed, - - - - - -	3,000
Rubies, being perfect, of 5 and 6 in a quilate, worth - - - - - -	6,000
Rubies of 4 to a quilate, worth 20 crusados[3] -	8,000
Rubies of 2 to a quilate, worth 30 crusados -	12,000
Rubies of 1 quilate, worth 30 crusados -	12,000

Towchinge rubies, sometime they be at a high rate, and sometime at a lower, these ought to be perfect in all respects, and to be bought as good cheape as you may.

	REIS.
Pearles of 1 graine are worth 1 vintaine,[4] yf they be perfect - - - - -	20
Pearles of 1½ graine, worth halfe a tostorne -	050
Pearles of 2 graines, worth 2 rialls, beinge perfect - - - - - - -	080
Pearles of 2½ graines, worth 5 rialls - -	200
Pearles of 3 graines, worth 8 rialls - -	320
Pearles of 3½ graines, worth 10 rialls - -	400
Pearles of 1 quilate, beinge 4 graines, worth 12 rialls - - - - - -	480

[1] A quilate is four grains, or one carat.
[2] Table diamonds.
[3] A crusado is worth 2s. 3d.
[4] A vintin is of the value of $1\frac{7}{20}$d. or not quite three halfpence.

APPENDIX.

Pearles of 5 graines, worth 15 rialls - -	600
Pearles of 1½ quilate, beinge 6 graines, worth 20 rialls - - - - - -	800
Pearles of 7 graines, worth 3 crusados - -	1,200
Pearles of 2 quilates, 8 graines, worth 2 milries	2,000
Pearles of 9 graines, worth 7 crusados - -	2,800
Pearles of 2½ quilate, 10 graines, worth 10 crusados - - - - - -	4,000
Pearles of 11 graines, worth - - -	5,000
Pearles of 3 quilates, worth - - -	6,000
Pearles of 13 graines, worth 20 crusados -	8,000
Pearles of 3½ quilates, worth 30 crusados -	12,000
Pearles of 15 graines, worth 40 crusados -	16,000
Pearles of 4 quilates, worth 70 crusados -	28,000
Pearles of 17 graines, worth 90 crusados -	36,000
Pearles of 4 quilates and ½, worth 110 crusados	44,000
Pearles of 19 graines, worth 130 crusados -	54,000
Pearles of 5 quilates, worth 150 crusados -	600,000

These pearles ought to be perfect in all respects. Towchinge the buying of these pearles, it must be accordinge to the time, and they may be bowght at sometime cheaper then at another; for a man may gaine by them according to the vallew and estimation that every person hath of them, for they be things without certeine limits or estimation, and are esteemed accordinge to the time.

A REMEMBRANCE of what is good to bring from the Indyas into Spayne, beinge good marchandize, and bowght by him that is skillfull and trusty.

Small seede pearrell, naturall white, of the first size. Of the same sorte, of the second size. Small sęde pearrell, of the same sorte, of the 3rd size. And of the 4th size, which is called Ane. Of the 5th and 6th sorte, which hath not crosse nor yellow. Small pearrell of the 7th and 8th size.

Small sede pearrell, that is called Ane ervell; let it be of the largest you can gett.

Bringe no sede pearle of the first 2 nor 3 size, but bringe of the 4th sorte, for they yeld more proffitt and gaine then other sizes.

Rubis, perfect of coullor, of 5 or 6 enfanos.[1] Yf you can find any good saphires, well coullored or white, beinge bowght cheape and cleane, they will yeld greate gayne. *Rubies, Saphiers.*

Diamondes bought by him that hath knowledge of the new or old cutt, or poynted, being cleane, from 3 to 6 in mangellin.

Diamondes, poynted, from 1 to 2 mangelins.[2] And rubis, beinge perfect, yf ye find any, buy them accordinge to the state of the contry, for in these things there is no certeine price, but they are things that yeld most proffitt.

Heere follow the prizes.

Small pearle, naturall, of the first size, are worth heere, 8,000 or 10,000 res. per ounce. Small pearle of the seconde size, 6,000 or 7,000 res. The 3rd and 4th size are worth 4,500 res. per ounce. Small pearle of the 5th and 6th size are worth heere, this yeare, 2,200 res. The 7th and 8th size, 1,100 res. Small pearle, called Ane ervell, hath no limitted price, but are esteemed according to the greatnes and goodnes of them, and are of many prizes.

Pearle of the 4th size are sold heere for 30 and 35 ryalls and 40, accordinge to their wayght. Rubis of 5 or 6 infanos, being perfect, are worth heere 5 or 6000 res.

You must vnderstand, that things naturall, and espinellas,[3]

---

[1] For the explanation of this word, see post, p. 165.

[2] The word mangalis, or mangelim, is here the same as the quilate or carat, but it is also used to express five, six, or seven and a half grains.

[3] A kind of ruby.

that are large and good, are to be bowght the best cheape you can gett them, for they have no certeyn prize.

Yf you can find any amatistes or jacincts, buy them in like sorte as you can.

Diamondes of 3 in mangelin rongs, are worth 6,000 res.; of the 4th in mangelin, 5,000 res.

Diamondes of 5 and of 6 in mangelin, are worth 3 and 4,000 res.

Diamondes of 15 in mangellin, pointed, 3,000 res. Diamondes of 1 mangellin, 8 and 10,000 res.

Diamondes of 2 mangellins, 15,000 res. These thinges are worth more or lesse, accordinge to the times; but these are the best marchandize for stones.

Diamondes wrought throughout.

Diamondes wrought of every side, of 1 grayne, are worth 3,000 res; of 1 graine $\frac{1}{2}$, 4,000 res.

Diamondes of 2 graines are worth 8,000 res. Diamondes of $2\frac{1}{2}$ graines are worth 10,000 res.

Diamondes of 3 graines, 15,000 res.

Diamondes of $3\frac{1}{2}$ [graines], 20,000 res.

Diamondes of 1 quartine, which is 4 graines, are worth 25,000 res. Diamondes of this sorte, beinge perfect, and wrought on every side, are the things most esteemed; and the bigger sizes are worth in vallew by waight. Diamondes rough are so to be bought that I may gaine by workinge of them.

Diamondes rough, of 3 quartines, which is 12 graines, 6,000 res.

Diamondes rough, of 4 quartaines, are worth 5,000 res.

Diamondes of 5 quartaines are worth 4,000 res.

Diamondes of 1 quartaine, and of 2 pointed, are worth 10,000 res.

Rubis perfect of 5 or 6 quartines, are worth 6,000 res.

Rubis of 4 quartines, 8,000 res.

APPENDIX.

Rubis of 2 quartaines are worth 30 Ds.[1]

Rubis of 1 quartine, 30 Ds. Towchinge rubis, they are bought cheaper, or deerer, as time serves, but they must be perfect in all perfection.

Prizes of Pearles.

Pearles beinge perfect of 1 graine are worth 20 res.
Pearles of $1\frac{1}{2}$ graines, 50 res.
Pearles of 2 graines are worth 80 res.
Pearles of $2\frac{1}{2}$ graines are worth 200 res.
Pearles of 3 graines, 320 res. Of $3\frac{1}{2}$ graines, 400 res.
Pearles of a quartine, being 4 graines, 480 res.
Pearles of 5 graines are worth 600 res.
Pearles of 6 graines, 800 res. Pearles of 7 graines, 1,200 res.
Pearles of 2 quartines, 2,000 res.
Pearles of 9 graines, 2,800 res.
Pearles of 10 graines, 4,000 res.
Pearles of 11 graines, 5,000 res.
Pearles of 3 quartines, 6,000 res.
Pearles of 13 graines, 8,000 res.
Pearles of 3 quartines $\frac{1}{2}$, 12,000 res.
Pearles of 15 graines, 16,000 res.
Pearles of 4 quartines, 28,000 res.
Pearles of 17 graines, 36,000 res.
Pearles of 4 quartines $\frac{1}{2}$, 44,000 res.
Pearles of 19 graines, 54,000 res.
Pearles of 5 quartines, 600,000 res.

These pearles must be perfect in all perfection; towchinge their prizes, it wilbe accordinge to the time; but they are things much esteemed; buy them as cheape as you can.

NICHOLAS.
SOBRAS.

[1] Ducados.

A REMEMBRANCE of suche things as are good marchandize to bringe from the Est Indies into Spayne, beinge bought by a skyllfull and trusty factor.[1]

Aliofre,[2] or perles of the first sorte or size.

Aliofre of the second sort.

Aliofre of the third sort.

Aliofre of the fourthe sort, which is called Ane.

Aliofre of the 5 and 6 sorte, which have no Calixo, nor is not yellow.

Aliofre of the 7 and 8 sorte.

Aliofre, which is called Ane ervel, which must be of the bigest sort that can be gotten.

Bringe not into Europe any Perles of the first, second, or third sort, but those of the 4th sorte, in which there is more gayne then in the others.

To buy Rubies perfect of hart, of 5 or 6 Enfanon, beinge about 2 caratts of Venice weight.

Saphires good of hart or white, and cleane, and baratas, wherin a marchant may do much good.

Diamondes bought by one that hath skill of the new or old rockes, which have their chapas and pointes cleane, from 3 to 6 in a mangalin, beinge $\frac{2}{3}$ of a carate. Diamondes pointed from one mangali, unto 2 mangalis, and rubies perfect, which must go together with them, which must be bought accordinge to the custome of the country, for heerin there is no certeine price sett downe, and these are the commodities wherein a man may do most good accordinge to the time.

The severall prices of pearles, rubies, saphires, spinels, amatists, jacynthes, or ballasses.

---

[1] This section is substantially the same as the first page and a half of that which precedes it: as there are some variations, however, it has been thought advisable not to omit this part of the manuscript.

[2] A corruption of the Portuguese and Spanish word Aljofar, which is again a corruption of the Arabic word El Jauhar.

Aliofre nataraon, or pearles of the first jueira or size, beinge perfect, are worth 8,000 and 10,000 reyos the ounce.

Aliofre of the second sort are worth from 6,000 to 7,000 reies the ounce.

Aliofre of the 3rd and 4th sorte are woorth 4,500 reies.

Aliofre of the 5th and 6th sorte were sold this yeare at 2,200 reies.

Aliofre of the 7th and 8th sorte is sold, and is worth heere 1,100 reies.

Aliofre Ane Cruel (or seede pearle) hath no certeine price, because it is sold accordinge to the bignes and goodnes therof, and is of many prices.

Pearles of the 4th sorte are sold in the Indies at 30 reies, at 35 reies, and at 40 reies, accordinge to their difference in weight.

Rubies which be perfect, of 5 and 6 to an enfanon (beinge a kind of weight which conteineth about 2 carates of Venice weight), are worth 5,000 or 6,000 reies.

Saphieres are at uncerteine prices, which a man must buy as good cheape as he may.

Good and greate spinells, beinge a kind of base rubies, must be bought as good cheape as you may, for they are not sold at any certeine price.

Amatistes, or jacinthes, and balasses, are bought after the same manner.

Diamants of 3 to a mangalin beinge chapas, are sold at 6,000 reies; of 4 to a mangalin, 5,000 reies; of 5 and 6 to a mangalin, they are worth from 3,000 to 4,000 reies.

Diamondes of 15 to a mangalin, beinge pointed, are sold at 3,000 reies.

Diamantes of one mangalin are worth from 8,000 to 10,000 reies.

Diamantes of 2 mangalins are worth 15,000 reies.

At certeine times the prices of these juells riseth and falleth, but these are the best marchandize of all other juells.

NOTES OF CERTAYNE COMODITIES IN GOOD REQUEST IN the East Indies, the Malucoes, and China, gathered out of the last and best authours which have lived and trafficked in those parts, by Richard Hakluyt.

Out of Cæsar Fredericke, a Venetian, who lived 18 yeres in many parts of the East Indies.

Safron. Velvets, damasks, satins, armesine of Portugal, which is a kind of silke taffata, safron and skarlets.—*fol.* 10, *pag.* 2.

The ships that come from the streight of the Red Sea or Mecca, bring to Pegu and Sivion wollen cloth (made at Venice, of these coullours, to witte, murrey, violet, red-mosine, skarlet, light or grasse greene), skarlets, velvets, opinno or affron, and chekines of gold.—*fol.* 32, *pag.* 1, and *fol.* 36, *p.* 1.

Bracelets of elephants teeth of diverse colours, much esteemed.—*fol.* 6, *pag.* 2.

The money of Pegu called Gansa, is made of copper and lead, which two mettals may therefore prove good marchandize.—*fol.* 32, *pag.* 2.

Notes of Commodities fit for the East Indies. Out of John Huygen Van Linschoten.

Sacks, Canarie wyne, Malmesies, Oyle Olive, Holland cloth, Cambricke.

Wyne, as sacks, canarie wyne, and malmesies.—*pag.* 4.

Oyle of olives.—*pagina* 4.

Holland cloth and cambricke good marchandize in Jaua.—*p.* 54.

Wollen cloth good marchandize in China.—*pag.* 40.

Reals of 8, wyne, both Portugale and Indian, oyles of olive greatly desired, velvet, cloth of skarlet (whereof they have none, nor yet can make any, although they have both sheepe and woll inough), looking glasse, ivorie, al kind of cristal, and glasse, are wel sold in China.—*pagina* 44.

APPENDIX. 167

Emraulds, wrought and unwrought, very gayneful marchandize to bee carried to India, Pegu, and other places, brought thither from Cairo, and the Spanish Indies, which in these oriental parts are much worne and esteemed: So that many Venetians that have travayled thither with emraulds, and bartered them for rubies, are become very rich, because amonge them men had rather have them then rubies.—*pag.* 134.

Costly wares carried from Turkie into India by the Streight of Mecca.—*pag.* 214.

Notes out of *The Historie of China,* in English.

Noe wollen cloth is made in China.—*pag.* 20.
Spanish wollen cloth much esteemed in China.—*pag.* 163.
Helmets of tynne gilded over, worne in China.—*pag.* 188.

Notes out of Mr. Lancaster's Voyage, printed in *the second volume of Richard Hakluyt.*

There were found in the galeon of Malacca, which Mr. Lancaster tooke in the entrance of the Streight of Sincapura, 300 butts of canarie wynes, al kind of haberdash ware, as hats, redde caps knit of Spanish wol, worsted stockings knit, which are worne of the mastizoes, shooes, velvets, taffataes, chamlets, and silks. Aboundance of suckets, Venice glasses of al sorts, certayne papers of counterfeiete stones, which an Italian brought from Venice to deceve the rude Indians withal, abundance of playing cards, 2 or 3 packs of French paper.—*pag.* 107. Hats, red caps, knit stockings, chamlets.

Notes of Commodities carried by the Hollanders in their first voyage, printed in folio in Latine and French.[1]

Hatchets good marchandise aboute the Cape of Bona Sperane. Barres of yron.—*fol.* 4, *pag.* 2. Hatchets.

[1] It was also printed at Amsterdam, in Dutch, in the same year (1598), in which the French and Latin editions appeared.

APPENDIX.

On the cost of Madagascar.

<small>White and red wollen caps.</small> Beades.—*folio* 5, *pag.* 2.
White and redde wollen caps.—*folio* 5 and 6.
<small>Tynne spoones.</small> Little looking glasses, red caps, beads, tynne spoones, much esteemed in the river of St. Augustine on the northwest parte of the Isle of Madagascar.—*folio* 7.
A fayre oxe given for a tynne spoone.—*fol.* 7, *pag.* 2.
Three or 4 sheepe given for one tyn spoone.—*fol.* 7.
A yong girle offred for a tynne spoone.—*fol.* 8, *p.* 2.
<small>Lynen handkerchiefs.</small> Lynen hankerchiefe, beads, and bracelets, good wares in the isle of St. Marie on the coste of Madagascar.—*fol.* 10.
Earings, beads, small looking glasses, drinking glasses.—*fol.* 10, *p.* 2.
Pynnes.—*folio* 11.
Wollen cloth esteemed.—*folio* 11.
<small>Lynen cloth.</small> Lynen cloth straked in use.—*folio* 11.
Beads, chaplets, and bracelets.—*folio* 12.
Spanish wyne greatly desired in the bay of Antengil in Madagascar.—*folio* 12, *pag.* 2.
Fyne lynen cloth.—*folio* 12, *etc.*
Bracelets of brasse.—*folio* 12, *pag.* 1.
Bracelets of tynne or false silver.—*folio* 13, *pag.* 2.
Greene glasse bracelets much esteemed.—*folio* 14.
<small>Jet.</small> Jet bracelets, rings, earings, beads, like to be good marchandise, which are chiefely to bee had in England.

Commodities uttered in Sumatra, Jaua, and Baly.

Lynen cloth in request in Sumatra.—*folio* 16.
<small>Shirts redie made.</small> Shirts redie made.—*folio* 18, *pag.* 2.
<small>Caffa is a silke made in Naples and Florence, called Tabydi Neapolis, like unrased velvet, blacke, greene, and peach color.</small> Knives exchanged for spices.—*folio* 18, *pag.* 2.
Eight elnes of greene caffa, given for a present to the Admiral and Sabandar of Bantan.—*folio* 19, *pag.* 2.
Three small Norumberge looking glasses, exchanged for a great jarre of moyst Indico.—*folio* 20, *pag.* 2.

APPENDIX.   169

The presents given to the viceroy, were christal vessels, a gilded looking glasse, and a piece of skarlet.—*fol.* 20, *p.* 1.

Greene velvet and skarlet given to the viceroy.—*fol.* 20, *p.* 2.

Drinking glasses given to the viceroy.—*fol.* 21, *p.* 2.

Blacke and redde cloth worne by the noblemen.—*fol.* 27, *p.* 1.

Armor some what like shirts of mayle, used in Bantam.—*fol.* 27, *p.* 2.

Waxe sold by weight in Bantam.—*folio* 28.   Waxe.

Tynne and leade.—*folio* 28, *pag.* 2.

Saffron much used by the Javans in their meate and rice.—*fol.* 39.   They mingle their safron with oyle that it dry not.

Yron and lead much desired in the isle Lebock,[1] on the north syde of Jaua.—*folio* 43, *pag.* 2.

The greate desire of yron in other places.—*fol.* 44, *pag.* 1.

Wrought velvet, red coral, christal glasses, looking glasses, sent to the king of the isle of Baly.—*fol.* 47, *pag.* 2.   Red coral.

Greate store of gold in Baly.—*fol.* 48, *pag.* 1.

Notes out of *The Hollanders Second Voyage to Jaua and the isles of the Malucoes, begon* 1598 *and ended* 1600.[2]

There presents to the kinge of Bantan were, A fayre covered cuppe of silver and gilt, certayne velvets and cloth of sylke, very fine drinking glasses, excellent fyne looking glasses.—*pag.* 6.

Pewter and other weres.—*pag.* 7.

Belles.—*pag.* 8.   Belles.

---

[1] Lubock.

[2] "The Journall, or dayly register, contayning a true manifestation and historical declaration of the voyage accomplished by eight shippes of Amsterdam, under the conduct of Jacob Corneliszen Neck, admirall, and Wybrandt van Warwick, vice-admirall, which sayled from Amsterdam the first day of March 1598. London, 1601," 4to. This is a translation from the Dutch, of which we have only been able to see editions printed subsequently to the above version.

Notes out of *The last Voyage of the Hollanders to the Malucoes.*[1]

Yron nayles and spikes good marchandise. — *fol.* 29, *pag.* 2.

[1] This, most probably, refers to the second voyage to the east, by Van Neck, an account of which was published under the title "Kort ende waerachtigh verhael van de tweede Schipvaerd, by de Hollanders op Ost-Indien gedaen, onder den Heer Admirael Jacob van Neck, getogen uyt het Journael van Roelof Roelofsz, vermaender op' t Schip Amsterdam ende doorgaens uyt andere Schryvers vermeerdert."

CERTAYNE NOTES GATHERED OF SUCH AS HAVE HAD much familiaritie with the Portugales that trade in the East Indies, by Richard Hakluyt.

1. Yron wyer.
2. Axes and hatchets heads.
3. Cutting hookes.
4. Ivory combes and boxe combes.
5. Spectacles.
6. Amber of Danske yelowe in greate request.
7. Emraulds wrought.
8. Saphires.
9. Waxe candles used in there mesquitoes and pagodes.
10. False sylver lace and false sylver threed.
11. False gold lace and false gold threed in greate quantitie, to decke there hangings and garments.

12. Cruses or potts of red and white earth, such as they melt gold and sylver in, packed up in bran in pipes and barels.

A jueller, a paynter, and certayne musisians, are very necessarie for the voyage.

But above al others, a trustie interpretour in the Easterne Arabian tongue; for by using the Portugal tonge, you are in greate danger of being betrayed, as the Hollanders were 7 tymes in their first voyage.

<small>Yf you goe without a smal barke or 2, I compte your voyage halfe over-throwne, before you goe foorth.</small>

THE END.

<small>RICHARDS, PRINTER, 100, ST. MARTIN'S LANE.</small>

INDEX.

A.

ABELFADA (Ismael), *see* Abulfeda
Abulfeda (Ismail Ibn Ali), geographical works, xlii ; birth, etc., 3
Adams (Clement), 3
Aithonus, *see* Hayto
Alexander VI, Pope, grant to Spain in 1493 of the Western Hemisphere, 42
America, " Divers voyages touching the discoverie of", description of this work, xxxvi ; futile attempts to colonize America, xcv ; arguments in favour of sending colonies to, from England, 8, 9 ; names of commodities growing in some parts of, 139
Anghiera (Pietro Martire), works, xliv ; birth, etc., 3

B.

Barbosa (Duarte), works, lvii ; birth, etc., 5
Barros (Joaō de), works, lviii ; birth, etc., 5 ; account of, 9 ; said to have caused Brazil to be colonized by the Portuguese, 9 ; this statement doubtful, *ib.*
Belleforest (François), works, 1 ; birth, etc., 4
Benjamin, *Tudelensis*, works, lii ; birth, etc., 5
Best (George), works, li, 4
Brazil, when discovered, 9 ; colonized by the Portuguese, *ib.* ; origin of name and its antiquity, 46
Brigham (Anthony), 6
Burrough (Stephen), works, lxi ; birth, etc., 6 ; account of, on a monumental brass in Chatham church, 15
Burrough (William), works, lxi, 6
Burros (Steven), *see* Burrough
Burros (William), *see* Burrough

C.

Cabot (John), discoverer of America, lxviii ; account of his expedition in 1496, *ib.* ; letters patent granted to him and to his three sons by Henry VII, 19
Cabot (Sebastian), works, lvii ; birth, etc., 5 ; argument in favour of a north-west passage, 11 ; extract from Peter Martyr respecting his voyage along the east coast of North America, lxxxviii ; extract from Gomara on the same subject, lxxix ; note of his voyage, 23 ; extract from Ramusio respecting his voyage to the north, 24 ; maps and discourses in the possession of William Worthington, 26
Cabral (Pedro Alvarez), took possession of Brazil in 1500, 9
Calicut, Vasco da Gama arrives at, by sea in 1498, 42
Cam (Diego), discovers Congo in 1484, 41
Cape Verde islands, discovery of, 45
Cartier (Jacques), lviii, xcv, 5
Cathaia, explanation of, 24
Chancellor (Nicholas), works, lii, 4
Chancellor (Richard), works, lx, 6
Charles V, emperor of Germany, study of navigation promoted by, 14
Chart, by R. Thorne, explanation of, 36
Chaves (Alonso de), account of, 14
Chicoria, described, 108
Claudia island, discovered by Verazzani, 63
Climate, described, 49
Colombo (Cristoforo), works, lvi ; birth, etc., 5
Congo, discovered by Diego Cam, in 1484, 41
Conti (Nicolò di), works, lvi, 5
Contractation House, 14
Coronado (Francis Vasques de), *see* Vasques
Cortereal (Anus), ship sent by him in 1574 to discover a north-west passage, 7

INDEX.

Cortereal (Gaspar), 5
Crantzius (Albertus), *see* Krantz
Cuba, discovered by Columbus in 1492, 43

D.

Diamonds, prices of, 158, 161, 164, 165
Diaz (Bartholomeu), doubles the Cape of Good Hope for the first time in 1487, 42
Dominica, discovered by Columbus in 1493, 43
Drake (Sir Francis), 6 ; makes a voyage of discovery along the western coast of North America as high as the 48th degree, 12 ; offer to found a lectureship in navigation, 16
Drogeo, discovery of, 72

E.

Eleot (Hugh), *see* Elliot
Engroveland, discovery of, 72 ; Franciscan monastery at, described, 77 ; Zichmni arrives there, and builds a city, 87
Erondelle (P.), translation of part of Lescarbot's "Histoire de la Nouvelle France," xxx
Estotiland, discovery of, 72 ; description of, 81

F.

Fenton (Edward), 6
Finæus (Orontius), *see* Finé
Finé (Oronce), works, xlix ; birth, etc., 3
Florida, first French colony in, under Albert de la Pierria, xciv ; mismanagement and sufferings of the first colonists, ci ; second colony under the command of Laudonnière, cv ; destroyed by the Spaniards, cviii ; natives of, their evidence in favour of the north-west passage, 11 ; discovery of, by J. Ribault, 91, 97 ; description of the country, its inhabitants and produce, 98
Fracastoro (Girolamo), works, xlv ; birth, etc., 3
Frisland, discovery of the island of, 72
Frobisher (Sir Martin), 6 ; made three voyages in search of the north-west passage, 12

G.

Gabot, *see* Cabot
Gaetano (Juan), works, lix, 5

Gaeton (John), *see* Gaetano
Galvam (Antonio), works, lxi ; birth, etc., 6 ; his "Tratado", published in English by Hakluyt, xxxi
Galvano (Francis) *see* Galvam
Gama (Vasco da), works, lvii ; birth, etc. 5 ; doubles the Cape of Good Hope in 1497, and arrives at Calicut in 1498, 42
Gemma, *Frisius*, *see* Gemma (R.)
Gemma (Reinerus), works, xlv ; birth, etc. 3
Geography, names of writers on, 3, 4
Gilbert (Sir Humphrey), works, l. ; birth, etc. 4, 6
Giunti (Tommaso), xlviii ; birth, etc. 3
Gonsalva (Gil) said to have sought a passage by the north-west, lxiv, 11
Gonzalez de Mendoza, (——), History of China translated by Parke, xxix
Good Hope, Cape of, doubled for the first time by Bartholomeu Diaz in 1487, 42
Grafton (Richard), extract from his chronicle, relating to the voyage of discovery by two ships in 1527, 54
Guicciardini (Giovanni Batista), works, xlvi ; birth, etc. 3

H.

Haithonus, *see* Hatto
Hakluyt, *Family of* ; account of, ii-iv
Hakluyt (Richard), birth and education, iv ; circumstance which led him to study Geography, v ; his desire to procure the establishment of a lecture on navigation, vii ; addresses the Lord Admiral Howard on the subject, vii ; letter to Sir Francis Walsingham principally upon the same subject, viii ; proposal to him to accompany Sir Humphrey Gilbert in his voyage to Newfoundland in 1583, ix ; second letter to Sir F. Walsingham, xi ; appointed chaplain to Sir Edward Stafford, ambassador to the Court of France, xiii ; made a prebendary of Bristol, xiii ; one of those to whom Sir Walter Raleigh assigned his letters patent for discoveries in heathen lands, xiv ; instituted to the rectory of Wettering-set-cum-Blochford, in Suffolk, xiv ; his marriage, xiv ; chief promoter of a petition to King James for a charter for the colonization of Virginia, xiv ; death, xv ; his anxiety to promote geographical discovery, xvi ; his exertions to procure information, xvii ; encouraged by Sir F. Wal-

INDEX. 3

singham to continue his labours, xvii; his first work, the "Divers Voyages", xviii; induces Basanier to edit the voyages of Ribault and others to Florida, and also publishes an English translation of the work, xix; publishes an edition of Peter Martyr Anghiera's work, De orbe novo, xx; publishes his "Principal Navigations...... of the English Nation", etc. xxii-xxviii; induces Pory to publish a translation of the History of Africa by Leo Africanus, xxix; induces Parke to publish a translation of the History of China, from the Spanish of Gonzalez de Mendoza, xxix; induces P. Erondelle to publish a translation of part of Lescarbot's Histoire de la nouvelle France, xxx; publishes an English translation of a work by A. Galvam, xxxi; translates F. de Souto's Discoveries in Florida, xxxii; a promontory on the continent of Greenland named after him, xxxiv; a river discovered in a voyage to Pechora named after him, *ib*.; description of his "Divers Voyages," xxxvi *et seq.*; Will. 145; note of the chief places where spices grow in the East Indies, 151; of the several prices of precious stones and spices, 158; good merchandize to bring from the East Indies into Spain, 160; note of commodities in good request in the East Indies, the Moluccas, and China, 166

Hall (E.), extract from his chronicle relating to the voyage of discovery by two ships in 1527, 54

Harton, *see* Hatto

Hatto, works, liii; birth, etc. 5

Hayto, *see* Hatto

Henry VII., king of England, letters patent granted by him to John Cabot and his three sons, lxxi, 19; letters patent granted to Richard Warde and others, lxxiii; also to Hugh Elyot and others, lxxxv

Hernandez de Oviedo y Valdez (Gonsalvo), works, xlv; birth, etc. 3

Heyes (Edward), works, lxiii, 6

Hudson's straits, discovered by Gaspar Cortereal, and by the ship said to have been sent out by Anus Cortereal, 7

I. J.

Jackman (Charles), 6
Icaria, discovery of, 72, 85
Iceland, discovery of, 72
Jenkinson (Anthony), works, lxii, 6
Jordan, river, 112

K.

Krantz (Albert), works, xliv; birth, etc. 3

L.

La Pierria (Albert de), remains in Florida at the head of [28] thirty settlers left there by Ribault, c, 114; explores the country and endeavours to conciliate the natives, ci; is put to death by his companions, cii.
Laudonnière (——), sails to Florida in command of three ships, with emigrants, cv; erects a fort named Caroline, on the river St. John, *ib.*; relieved by Ribault when about to abandon the colony in despair, cvii; colony destroyed by the Spaniards, cviii
Lee (Edward), account of, 33
Leo, *Africanus*, History of Africa, translated by J. Pory, xxix
Lescarbot (M.) Histoire de la Nouvelle France, translated by Erondelle, xxx
Letters patent, granted by the sovereigns of England for the discovery and planting of unknown lands, lxxi
Lock (Michael) translation of Hakluyt's edition of Peter Martyr Anghiera's work, De Orbe Novo, xxi; autobiographical account of, xc
Longitude, adopted by Ptolemy, and by different countries, 37
Lucar (Cyprian), 54
Lucar (Emanuel), 54

M.

Magalhaens (Fernando de), works, lviii, 5
Magalianes (Fernandus), *see* Magalhaens
Mandeville (Sir John), works, xliii; birth, etc. 3
Martyr (Peter), *see* Anghiera
Mary of Guildford, voyage of discovery to the north, 54
May, river, discovered, 98
Medina (Pedro de), works, 14
Mendoza (Antonio de), works, xlvi; birth, etc. 3
Mercator (Gerard), works, xlvi; birth, etc. 3; opinion in favour of the existence of the north-west passage, 13
Meridian, *see* Longitude
Münster (Sebastian), works, xlviii; birth, etc. 3

N.

Navigation, study of, recommended, 14 ; Reader in the art of, appointed by the Emperor Charles V, *ib.* ; Importance of founding a lectureship on, in London, 16 ; mariners ignorant of navigation in the sixteenth century and at the present day, *ib.*

Niça (Marcos de), discovers Sibola, 102

Nolle (Antonio), discovers the Cape Verde Islands, 45

North-west passage, probability and advantages of, 7, 11, 24, 29, 35, 48.

Norumbega, origin of the name, 57

Notes given to Pette and Jackman, sent out by the Muscovy Company for the discovery of the north-east passage, 116 ; notes to be given to one that prepared for a discovery, 132 ; notes of certain commodities in good request in the East Indies, the Moluccas, and China, 166

O.

Ortel (Abram), works, xlix ; birth, etc., 4

Osorio (Jeronimo), works, xlix ; birth, etc., 4

Oviedo y Valdez (Gonsalvo Hernandez de), *see* Hernandez

P.

Parke (R.), Translation of the History of China from the Spanish of Gonzalez de Mendoza, xxix

Paulus (Marcus), *see* Polo

Pearls, prices of, 159, 161, 163, 164, 165

Pet (Arthur), 6

Philippine Islands, discovery of, 33 ; precious stones and metals, etc., found there, *ib.*

Pierria (Albert de la), *see* La Pierria

Pinzon (Vicente Yañez), discovered Brazil in 1499, 9

Polo (Marco), works, lii ; birth, etc., 5

Pomi Appii, description of, 67

Portugal, grants to, by different popes, of all discoveries from Cape Bojador to the East Indies, 42 ; the world divided between Portugal and Spain, 44 ; all discoveries within 370 leagues west from the Cape Verde Islands secured to Portugal, *ib.* ; commissioners appointed by Spain and Portugal to settle the line of demarcation for these 370 leagues, 47

Pory (John), Translation of the History of Africa, written by Leo Africanus, xxix

R.

Ramusio (Giovanni Batista), works, xlvii ; birth, etc., *ib.* ; extract from, respecting S. Cabot, 24

Ribault (Jean), 6 ; title of first edition of his work in English, 17 ; speech to the first settlers in Florida, xcvii ; second voyage to Florida in 1565, cvii. Sails against the Spaniards who had arrived on the coast, cvii ; is shipwrecked, cix ; he and 350 of his men surrender, and are murdered by the Spaniards, cix ; voyage of discovery to the east coast of North America, 91 ; arrives on the coast of Florida, 97 ; enters the River May, or St. John's River, and communicates with the inhabitants on both banks, 98, 101 ; inhabitants described, 100 ; productions of the country, 101, 104, 109 ; examines the coast northwards, 107 ; discovers several rivers, 108 ; builds a fort named Charlesfort, on a river called Chenoncean, and leaves thirty men there under the command of Captain Albert de la Pierria, 113

Rochester, twenty men hung in, at one time, 8

Rubies, prices of, 159, 161, 162, 164, 165

S.

Saguinay, natives of, their evidence as to the existence of the north-west passage, 11

Sampson, voyage of discovery of the ship Sampson to the north, 54

Savage men, three brought home, 23

Sclavonia, district formerly comprised within this term, 40

Settle (Dionysius), works, li, 4

Seyne, river, discovered, 108

Sibola, described, 102

Sidney (Sir Philip), interest taken by him in maritime discovery, lxvi ; takes an assignment of part of the interest of Sir Humphrey Gilbert under the letters patent granted to him in 1578, lxvii

Somme, river, discovered, 109

Souto (Fernando de), discoveries in Florida, translated by Hakluyt, xxxii

Spain, grant to, by Pope Alexander VI, in 1493, of the western hemisphere, 42 ; the world divided be-

INDEX. 5

tween Portugal and Spain, 44 ; good merchandize to bring from the East Indies into, 160

Spice Islands, placed in different degrees of longitude by the Spaniards and Portuguese, 41 ; dispute between Spain and Portugal respecting, 41, 44 ; may be reached by the north-west passage, 35, 48

Spices, chief places where they grow in the East Indies, 151

Stowe (John), extracts from his Annals, 23

T.

Thevet (André), works, 1 ; birth, etc., 4, 6

Thorne (M.), 5

Thorne (Robert), Declaration of the Indies, 27 ; reasons for attempting the north-west passage, 29 ; book to Dr. Ley, 33 ; explanation of his map, 36

Tordesillas, capitulation of, securing to Portugal all discoveries within three hundred and seventy leagues west from the Cape Verde Islands, 44 ; efforts to carry the capitulation into effect, 47

Transportation, first adopted, in modern times, by the Portuguese and Spaniards, 10 ; when introduced into the penal code of England, *ib.*

Travellers, names of, 5, 6

V.

Valdez (Gonsalvo Hernandez de Oviedo y), *see* Hernandez.

Vasques de Coronado (Francis), works, lix, 5

Verazzani (Giovanni), observations on his voyage, lxxxviii ; manuscript account of his voyage, xcii ; sets out a north-west passage in his map, 11 ; relation of his voyage of discovery, 55 ; departs from one of the Dezertas, *ib.* ; discovers land, in the neighbourhood of Charleston, or of the Savannah, 56 ; manners and customs of the natives, *ib.* ; description of the country and its animals, 58 ; sails northward to what is supposed to be George Town and Long Bay, 58 ; sends a young man on shore, probably about Raleigh Bay, with presents, who is thrown on the beach by the violence of the surf, and stunned, but kindly treated by the natives, 60 ; sends twenty men ashore, about lat. 38 degrees, who examine the country, and endeavour to bring off a young woman and child, but are obliged to content themselves with the child, 61 ; description of the boats of the natives, and mode of construction, 62 ; vines grow naturally here, *ib.* ; sails one hundred leagues further, and arrives at what is supposed to be the mouth of the Hudson, 63 ; enters the river, *ib.* ; sails fifty leagues further, and discovers Claudia Island, *ib.* ; this island supposed to be Martha's Vineyard, 64 ; sails fifteen leagues further, and arrives at what is supposed to be Narraganset Bay, 64 ; associates with the natives, *ib.*; description of them, and of their manners and customs, 65, 68 ; have copper, which they esteem more than gold, 65 ; would not allow their women to go on board the ship, 66 ; description of the country and its productions, 67 ; leaves this coast, and sails one hundred and fifty leagues further, to about Portsmouth, in New Hampshire, or the southern part of Maine, 69 ; finds the natives fierce and discourteous, *ib.* ; sails along the coast for fifty leagues, and discovers thirty-two islands, supposed to be Penobscot Bay, 71 ; sails north-east for one hundred and fifty leagues, and approaches Newfoundland, at which point he determines to return to France, *ib.*; time and manner of his death not known, 93 ; Mr. Biddle's hypothesis concerning it, *ib.*

Vespucci (Amerigo) made the first settlement in Brazil in 1503, 9

Virginia, the first British penal settlement, 10

W.

Ward (Luke), works, lxiii, 6

Willoughby (Sir Hugh), works, lx, 6

Worthington (William), account of, 26

X.

Xavier (François), works, lix ; birth, etc., 6

Z.

Zahrtman (C. C.), remarks on the alleged voyages of N. and A. Zeno, xciii.

Zeni, *family of,* genealogy, 72
Zeno (Antonio), joins his brother Nicolò in Frisland, 76 ; his letter, giving an account of the discovery of Estotiland, 81 ; sails, with Zichmni, for Estotiland, discovers Icaria and Engroveland, 85
Zeno (Nicolò) sails from Venice in the year 1380, 73 ; cast away, in a storm, upon the Island of Frisland, *ib.* ; attacked by the natives, but protected by Zichmni, duke of Sorani, 74 ; Zichmni sends him on board his fleet, and takes him into his service, 75 ; made captain of Zichmni's navy, and attacks Estlande, 76 ; left in command of the Island of Bres, 77 ; sails to Engroveland, where he finds a monastery of Friars Preachers, 77 ; death, 81
Zeno (Nicolo and Antonio), observations on their voyages, xcii
Zichmni, saves Nicolò Zeno from the natives of Frisland, 74 ; conquers Frisland, 75 ; attacks Iceland, and Talas, Broas, Iscant, Trans, Minant, Dambere, and Bres, 77 ; expedition towards Estotiland, and discovers Icaria and Engroveland, in which latter place he builds a city, 85

For EU product safety concerns, contact us at Calle de José Abascal, 56–1°, 28003 Madrid, Spain or eugpsr@cambridge.org.

www.ingramcontent.com/pod-product-compliance
Ingram Content Group UK Ltd.
Pitfield, Milton Keynes, MK11 3LW, UK
UKHW041951230426

12048UKWH00008B/274